THE MANY DEATHS
OF TOM THOMSON

Gregory Klages

THE MANY DEATHS OF TOM THOMSON

Separating Fact from Fiction

DUNDURN
TORONTO

Editor: Michael Melgaard
Design: BJ Weckerle
Cover design: Laura Boyle
Cover image credit: Archives of Ontario, William Colgate Collection, F1066-6. Photographer unknown.
Printer: Webcom

Library and Archives Canada Cataloguing in Publication

Klages, Gregory, author
        The many deaths of Tom Thomson : separating fact from fiction / Gregory Klages.

Includes bibliographical references and index.
Issued in print and electronic formats.
ISBN 978-1-4597-3196-7 (paperback).~ISBN 978-1-4597-3197-4 (pdf).~
ISBN 978-1-4597-3198-1 (epub)

        1. Thomson, Tom, 1877-1917~Death and burial. 2. Thomson, Tom, 1877-1917. 3. Painters~Canada~Biography. I. Title.

ND249.T5K53 2016   759.11   C2015-908787-2
                                                 C2015-908788-0

1 2 3 4 5   20 19 18 17 16

	ONTARIO ARTS COUNCIL
Conseil des Arts du Canada Canada Council for the Arts	CONSEIL DES ARTS DE L'ONTARIO
	an Ontario government agency
	un organisme du gouvernement de l'Ontario

We acknowledge the support of the **Canada Council for the Arts** and the **Ontario Arts Council** for our publishing program. We also acknowledge the financial support of the **Government of Canada** through the **Canada Book Fund** and **Livres Canada Books**, and the **Government of Ontario** through the **Ontario Book Publishing Tax Credit** and the **Ontario Media Development Corporation**.

Care has been taken to trace the ownership of copyright material used in this book. The author and the publisher welcome any information enabling them to rectify any references or credits in subsequent editions.

— *J. Kirk Howard, President*

The publisher is not responsible for websites or their content unless they are owned by the publisher.

Printed and bound in Canada.

VISIT US AT
Dundurn.com | @dundurnpress | Facebook.com/dundurnpress | Pinterest.com/dundurnpress

Dundurn
3 Church Street, Suite 500
Toronto, Ontario, Canada
M5E 1M2

In memory,

J. Carman Klages

1936–2014

Contents

A Note on the Text

Many of the primary sources consulted for this book do not consistently apply English spelling, grammar, or capitalization. Original usage and formatting has been retained as frequently as sense allowed. In order to help distinguish these idiosyncrasies from transcription errors, they are indicated with a [sic] mark. Where texts have been altered, the changed text is indicated by its insertion in square brackets.

The author takes responsibility for any typographical errors within this text.

Portions of many (though not all) of the documents discussed in this book have been transcribed and can be consulted digitally (in English or French) on the *Death on a Painted Lake: The Tom Thomson Tragedy* website, part of the Great Unsolved Mysteries in Canadian History project.

The MacCallum and Thomson collections, along with smaller deposits in other publicly accessible archives (such as the archives of Trent University in Peterborough, Ontario, which hold the diary of Mark Robinson, the park ranger who led the search for Thomson), allow reasonably clear sense to be made regarding what was happening at Canoe Lake in the spring and summer of 1917.

For more information on specific sources, please see A Note on the Sources and Selected Bibliography at the end of this work.

Introduction

THE MISUNDERSTOOD DEATH OF TOM THOMSON

Except to a very limited number of friends, Tom Thomson is a
remote and mystical figure that broke into the art firmament with
a sudden and dazzling brilliancy, and then disappeared as suddenly
into the unknown. During the last decade his career has been
wrapped in mists of mystery and half truths somewhat obscuring a
clear vision of the man and his work.

— A.H. ROBSON, *TOM THOMSON*, 1937

——— ——

BY ALMOST ANY MEASURE, Tom Thomson can be regarded as a Canadian national icon. His name is synonymous with artistic skill, love of the wilderness, and national pride. His paintings have become a standard reference point; canvases such as *The West Wind* and *The Jack Pine* — whether seen as originals or reproductions, in coffee-table books or calendars, on T-shirts or postcards or coffee mugs — are among the most easily and widely recognized Canadian artworks.

Along with his paintings, Thomson's fame rests upon his reputation as a "model Canadian." He is memorialized as a skilled yet modest artist, quiet but confident, capable in rough outdoor skills such as fishing and canoeing yet possessing the sensitivity of an artist. He is recalled as a man who gave up days working in a Toronto office to follow his passion for the lonely, lovely lakes of Algonquin Park.

Thomson exhibited his first painting in 1913 and died four years later. By the mid-1920s, he was being hailed as one of Canada's most visionary artists. In the 1940s, novelist Hugh MacLennan included Thomson in his list of the top ten Canadians, beside towering personalities such as explorer Samuel de Champlain; Canada's first prime minister, Sir John A. Macdonald; and Sir Frederick Banting, the discoverer of insulin.

Today Thomson is most often mentioned in association with Canada's Group of Seven, despite having died three years before its formation. As the Group's artistic reputation grew during the 1920s, key members recognized his role in their artistic development. Their public statements of respect served to cement his reputation to theirs, elevating Thomson to a place equivalent to being an eighth, deceased member of the Group. In some of the early international exhibitions featuring their work, Thomson's pieces were given a very prominent position.

While he was alive, Thomson's art was not exhibited outside Canada. The most he was paid for a painting was five hundred dollars. Almost one hundred years later, Thomson's artworks have been the subject of high-profile international exhibitions in London and Moscow, and have sold for over one million dollars at auction.

Tom Thomson and his artwork have worked their way into every nook and cranny of Canadians' cultural sensibilities, from the highest of cultural institutions to the most low-brow of kitsch. He has been the subject of plays, rock songs, books of poetry, films, and parlour games.

That a landscape painter has achieved such a level of fame is rather amazing given that he only painted seriously for about five years. It might also come as a surprise that, during that brief period, his paintings were not generally seen as the product of unique genius and insight. He first took up work in the arts as a designer, and his early efforts at painting were considered dull. Even his circle of friends and supporters saw that his painting might benefit significantly with help from more experienced, formally trained artists.

Assistance from his friends did not necessarily lead to widespread commercial and critical success. The works created by Thomson and his peers received many colourful, less-than-friendly assessments. In 1916, Toronto critic Hector Charlesworth suggested their paintings were closer to "gobs of porridge" than works of art, and their "purposeless medley of crude colours" evoked comparisons to the contents of a "drunkard's stomach."

Most of Thomson's works were small, quickly realized impressions of landscapes made in the open air as experiments with capturing light and form. It should come as little surprise, then, that during his life Thomson did not sell many of his works. He would accept a few dollars for his small, rough paintings. Reports suggest that he was often willing to give these works away as gifts or to pay debts.

Tom Thomson was never able to live off the income from his art. By 1917, he had apprenticed as a machinist, attended business school, and worked as a designer, a fire ranger, and a guide for fishing parties. He was certainly not recognized as one of Canada's leading artists, even though the Ontario government and the National Gallery had each acquired one of his larger works painted on canvas.

Then, on July 8, 1917, Thomson mysteriously disappeared while out on a routine canoe excursion in Ontario's Algonquin Park. His empty vessel was discovered within hours of his departure, but no sign of his fate could be found. Eight days later, his decomposing body rose to the surface of the same lake on which he had disappeared. His fate was quickly labelled a tragic accident, although quiet whispers around the lake offered other opinions. Rumours that Thomson had committed suicide or that he had been murdered began to be voiced even before Thomson's remains were buried.

Any current narrative of Tom Thomson's death is far more than a simple retelling of a commonly agreed-upon set of facts. It brings together almost a century of first-hand recollections, research, storytelling, interpretation, and speculation. It is also the end product of difficult decision-making by investigators. Stories about Thomson's death have evolved since 1917 — the pool of available historical documents has grown, the "facts" offered in some first-hand accounts changed each time the witnesses told their stories, elements of speculation have been repeated until they have become widely accepted as truths. Making sense of the stories concerned with Thomson's death requires careful analysis, as well as a certain degree of guesswork.

Despite clear interest in Thomson's life (and death) and undisputed respect for his work, assessment of how he died has been dealt with primarily as a hobby by persons who showed little concern for rigorous research and analysis. Many of these authors have engaged in elaborate speculation involving Thomson's demise. Speculation is, naturally, part of the work of anyone dealing with the past. Over time, however, the theories offered by these researchers have spiralled further and further away from what documents produced at the time of Thomson's death indicate. These sometimes wild stories — often involving suggestions of conspiracies and cover-ups — have gradually displaced the simpler facts found in the historical evidence.

Over the course of a century, and particularly over the last few decades, facts, errors, and myths regarding Thomson's life and death have become jumbled into provocative, thoroughly entertaining, but untrustworthy stories. New sources becoming available, and growing interest in Thomson's life, have made this an ideal time to seriously re-evaluate what we know about Thomson's last days. Much as we might occasionally seek to restore and refurbish Thomson's paintings after years of exposure to public attention, after one hundred years it is time to wash away the sediment of gossip and speculation that has come to obscure our view of how Tom Thomson met his sad and tragic end.

The Many Deaths of Tom Thomson highlights the most frequently told stories about Thomson and his death, and traces the origins of the misinformation in them. It also seeks to establish what can be authoritatively said about Thomson's tragic passing.

To clarify what can reasonably be proposed about Thomson's death, the multitude of speculative claims must be tested against available historical records, something that has so far been done in an inconsistent and selective fashion at best. Such a corrective enterprise has been made easier within the last twenty years, as a significant supply of previously hard-to-access documents has been made available to the public.

The evidence provided by those who claim special, first-hand knowledge of the events surrounding Thomson's death must also be carefully considered. In the Thomson case, "witness" testimony certainly merits skepticism. More than one of the "witnesses" offered testimony that changed over time and that conflicts with the historical record. Some testimony suggests witnesses began to insert details into their own story that they lifted from other accounts.

As surprising as it might seem, the research for this book was not undertaken to establish a singular, definitive, "final" answer of how Tom Thomson died. Its primary goal was to clarify *what did not occur* by separating out the abundant and persistent myths from facts. This process of sifting and weighing, however, revealed that much of the evidence that popular theories were built upon was deeply flawed. Careful assessment revealed that the available evidence supports only one plausible explanation for Thomson's demise. It will remain for you, the reader, to decide how well the explanation provided improves upon previous interpretations of the historical record.

PART ONE

THE LIFE OF
TOM THOMSON

1

TOM THOMSON'S LIFE

We are all working away but the best I can do
does not do the place much justice in the way of beauty.
— TOM THOMSON, LETTER TO DR. JAMES MACCALLUM, OCTOBER 1914

IN THE FACE OF awestruck admiration for his paintings and curious gossip about his death, it is easy to lose sight of the fact that Thomson was a fairly common, middle-aged man of his era. While his name is now invoked with reverential tones, no one who knew him expected him to become a national hero whose work would be celebrated a century after his death. For much of his life he was not even a particularly well-known painter.

The facts of Tom Thomson's life tell a simple story. He was a beloved son and brother, a valued friend, and an artistic peer who helped to inspire his friends to pursue their cherished dreams. His death was a terrible blow to many who knew him, during a time when tragic losses of young men's lives were all too common.

Tom Thomson was born on August 5, 1877, in Claremont, Ontario, a small community northeast of the provincial capital, Toronto. Within a few months of his birth, his family moved several hundred kilometres northwest to Leith. Leith was another small town, situated walking distance from the shore of southwest Georgian Bay. The Great Lakes port town of Owen Sound (with a population of about four thousand people) was also within walking distance.

The region offered all of the distractions and entertainment a young boy could desire. Fields and forests abounded, and the bay offered pursuits such as boating, fishing, and swimming.

In Leith, the Thomson family grew to ten children — six boys and four girls — nine of whom would reach adulthood. Tom was third among the Thomson sons, and the sixth child of the large family.

As a boy Tom suffered an illness and was kept out of school for a year so that he might be better able to restore himself through fresh air and exercise. This period is likely when he gained a true appreciation for the outdoors.

By all accounts, his teenage years were uneventful. He left secondary school at the then-late age of seventeen. This might be interpreted as Tom having found something interesting and useful in academics.

During the late 1890s, Tom inherited two thousand dollars from his paternal grandfather's estate. Instead of indulging in extravagances, Tom appears to have saved his money. He began apprenticing as a machinist with an Owen Sound firm. The job lasted less than a year, reportedly due to a personality conflict between Tom and his foreman.

Two of his older brothers had enrolled in the Canada Business College in Chatham, Ontario. After quitting the foundry, Tom followed in their footsteps. The program does not appear to have captured his imagination. His dissatisfaction may have had something to do with the school rather than the curriculum, however.

George, Tom's older brother, had completed his business studies in Chatham and had better luck in applying the skills he had learned. He moved to Seattle, Washington, and opened a business college there with a cousin. Tom followed George to Seattle in 1901 and enrolled in his college.

He left the school after six months, lured away by employment with Maring and Ladd, a photoengraving firm operated by another graduate of the Canada Business College. Tom liked the job, and his efforts showed promise. His work was impressive enough that in 1903 a rival Seattle firm poached Tom away from Maring and Ladd by offering higher pay. Surprisingly, Tom continued to live with the Maring family despite working for a rival firm.

In 1904 or 1905, Tom returned to Ontario. It has been suggested that Tom left Seattle after making a marriage proposal that was responded to with laughter. However, this tale has never been proven.

When Thomson came to Toronto, it was a city in the midst of significant change and growth. A fire had swept away much of the city's business district only months before his arrival, so construction was booming. Some of the buildings still regarded as lynchpins of today's city — such as the central rail hub, Union Station — were going up. With a population of over two hundred thousand, it was the largest city Tom had ever visited. The urban world was alive with action and noise.

Within the city's growing economy, Tom discovered that his skills as a photoengraver, lettrist, and designer were in demand. He quickly found employment as an illustrator with the Legg Brothers photoengraving firm.

Over the course of the next few years, he would work for three firms, letting his nose and his friendship with other designers lead him where they might. By the early 1910s, he had settled in at Grip Limited. A.H. Robson, who would write a pamphlet about Thomson in the 1930s, was the art director at the firm. Grip also employed several of Tom's close friends, such as J.E.H. MacDonald (who quit the firm in November 1911), William Broadhead, Franklin Carmichael, Arthur Lismer, and Fred Varley.

While he was still with Legg Brothers, Thomson took art classes. The earliest oil painting identified as Thomson's dates from 1907 and was produced for evaluation by his teacher, painter William Cruikshank, a member of the Royal Canadian Academy of Arts.

During his time at Grip, Thomson and some of his artist friends made excursions out of the city, combining fishing and artmaking on visits to locations such as the Humber River, the Scarborough Bluffs, and Lake Scugog.

In May 1912, on the recommendation of Grip co-worker Tom McLean, Thomson and another artist friend, Ben Jackson, set out to visit Algonquin Park. The park was not yet twenty years old. As a relatively easy-to-access portion of the vast northern territories recently added to the province of Ontario, it promised spectacular sights and unique experiences. The men took the train north from Toronto, disembarking at Canoe Lake station in the midst of the park.

Mark Robinson was the park ranger responsible for monitoring visitors arriving and departing through the Canoe Lake train depot. On May 18, 1912, he noted in his daily diary that the "T. Thompson [sic] Party" had arrived on the evening train.

Thomson's first visit to the region must have been an enjoyable one. In late July 1912, Thomson and another co-worker, William Broadhead, set off on a two-month-long canoe trip that would take them from Biscotasing, a Hudson's Bay Company post near Sudbury, to the Mississagi Forest Reserve, and then via the Mississauga River out to Bruce Mines on the eastern Georgian Bay shore.

On their way back to Toronto, the men stopped off in Owen Sound, likely to visit Thomson's family. Here, they were interviewed for an article that would appear in the *Owen Sound Sun*. The tone of the newspaper's coverage reveals how the region was perceived by those living in "old" Ontario, and intimates at what sort of skills were believed necessary to survive in such an environment.

The article notes that the "young men" appeared "bronzed and weather beaten from exposure to sun and wind" on their trip through the "wilds of New Ontario."

At the outset of their adventure, they loaded up packs containing a variety of essentials, from tents to dried food, photographic equipment, and, of course, art supplies. Fully stocked, each pack totaled about two hundred pounds. Clearly, the article implies, those who travelled in the area must be hardy.

Reinforcing this perspective, as well as insinuating the difference between Canadian men and their English counterparts, the article records Broadhead's story about a group of "English aristocrats" who departed from Biscotasing, "taking with them camp beds, chairs, carpet slippers, table napkins and other civilized luxuries." Although Thomson and Broadhead did not know how the group fared, the article's author suggests readers "can easily imagine."

The region offered challenges, even for the hardy. The men admitted to having "dumped" their canoe once, due to a cloudburst. Noting that the men were "expert swimmers," the article adds that they did not lose any of their essentials in the mishap.

The land the men travelled through offered plenty of riches; sights that denizens of southern, settled regions might regard as exceptional. The men reported close encounters with moose, bears, wolves, and deer. Along with its scenic beauty, the article suggests the allure of the region might also stem from other considerations, that the area was rich with multiple kinds of assets waiting to be tapped: "rich in mineral wealth," "rich because of its forests," "rich because of its immense waterfalls and consequently water-power," and "rich because of the abundance of fish and game."

Having spent the better part of a summer travelling through New Ontario, Thomson learned that the less-settled areas recently added to the province offered excellent subjects for landscape painting. Not only did the region provide compelling visuals, it also offered a pleasing environment for extended sojourns away from the pressures and distractions of city life. Upon returning from the wilderness, he also discovered that his experiences were greeted with curiousity and respect. These trips made an impression upon Tom Thomson that would clearly shape the remainder of his days.

On one or both of these voyages, Thomson not only took photographs, but also dabbled at using oils to paint the landscape *en plein air* — out in the open as he was looking at the scene. This was really the first time that Tom Thomson had focused on attempting to capture the landscape in oil paint. He had experience as a designer and lettrist; he could engrave photos and plan out print advertisements and business cards, but he had not, until then, spent much time painting the landscape for its own sake.

Although his painting did not reveal it — yet — sometime and somewhere while canoeing and painting in New Ontario, Thomson had found his muse.

Returning from the north, Thomson's life changed in two ways. With many of his friends, including A.H. Robson, he left Grip Limited and moved to another firm, Rous & Mann. He also met Dr. James MacCallum, an ophthalmologist, who had grown up in Collingwood, Ontario, a lakeside community east of Owen Sound not far from where Thomson's family lived.

MacCallum had a strong interest in the arts, having become a member of Toronto's Arts and Letters Club only a few months before. MacCallum had been told about Thomson's trip north and was eager to see his paintings. He would come to play a critical role in Thomson's development as an artist.

The works that Thomson had produced during the summer of 1912 showed enough promise that his friends, and likely MacCallum, encouraged him to develop some into larger, more formal works on stretched canvas, a method seen as more appropriate for gallery exhibition. The following spring, Thomson submitted one of these works, *Northern Lake*, to be considered for inclusion in the Ontario Society of Artists' (OSA) annual exhibition. It was accepted. As it was his first work displayed in an art exhibition, he must have been overjoyed when he received news that the Ontario government had bought the work for the sum of $250. This price was equivalent to about two months of Thomson's wages.

Thomson returned to Algonquin Park for much of the summer and fall of 1913. Returning to the city in November, he met another figure who would play an important role in his life, painter A.Y. Jackson. Jackson had been convinced by MacCallum to relocate from Montreal to Toronto rather than move to the United States. MacCallum had won Jackson over to this idea by offering to purchase enough of Jackson's paintings over the next year to give him a guaranteed living income.

Upon seeing the sketches Thomson produced that summer, Jackson and MacCallum encouraged Thomson to commit himself to painting full-time. To clinch the idea, MacCallum offered Thomson the same deal he had just made with Jackson. After some consideration, Thomson accepted. In January 1914, Jackson and Thomson moved into a shared studio in the Severn Street building that Dr. MacCallum and another painter, Lawren Harris, had just custom built for use by artists.

Thomson exhibited two works in the spring 1914 OSA show. One was purchased by the National Gallery for five hundred dollars. He left for Algonquin Park again soon thereafter, accompanied by his former Grip peer, Arthur Lismer. Doctor MacCallum invited Thomson to visit his cottage on Georgian Bay on this trip, and Thomson decamped there in late May. However, he found the social environment not to his liking, and ventured out alone on another lengthy canoe trip. By August 10, he was back in Algonquin Park, according to the daily diary of park ranger Henry A. (Bud) Callighen.

Thomson's activities in the fall of 1914 suggest that he led an active social life. In September he was joined by A.Y. Jackson, who had just returned from a trip west to paint the Rocky Mountains. In October, Fred Varley and his wife, as well as Arthur Lismer and his wife and daughter, all visited Thomson in the park.

In October 1914, Thomson wrote a letter to Dr. MacCallum that was dominated by financial concerns. He tells the doctor to ask a potential customer for ten or fifteen dollars for a sketch, a price that Thomson "should be greatly pleased [with]" if it is agreed to. If the client found the price too high, however, Thomson admits that the doctor can "let it go for what they will give." He also advises that "the same applys [sic] to all the others," excepting one that Tom expressed a desire to develop into a more formal work.

In the same letter, Thomson describes how he had considered applying for a job as a park ranger, but discovered that the process was complicated and slow. Knowing "that I might not get on for months," he had decided to return to Toronto to find work in "some engraving shop for a few months." Thomson closes his letter by asking if the doctor could telephone Tom's bank and find out his balance. He suspected that "I have probably used most of it up by this time."

Thomson returned to the city in mid-November 1914, but was back at the park within a few months. A ranger's diary places him there in mid-March 1915, and records him working as a guide for a party from Pittsburgh in late April.

Also in late April, Tom informed Dr. MacCallum that he had made about twenty-five sketches that spring. He was somewhat blasé about the quality of his work during this time, stating, "Some of them might do for canvases but will not pick out any until something better turns up."

Thomson had planned on earning some extra money by guiding in the summer of 1915, but with the number of tourists lower than usual, competition for guiding jobs was high. Thomson told J.E.H. Macdonald that by late July he had had only two or three weeks of guide work. He reported that he had made "quite a few sketches," although "lately [had] not been doing much." The dearth of jobs and perhaps a creative dry spell led Thomson to consider some sort of change. He speculated that he might take a "long hike" further north or "take in the Harvest Excursion and work at the wheat for a month or two." Whether he decided to pursue either of these options, he expected to return to Algonquin in late September.

However, September found Thomson still in the park, despite poor weather. He noted to MacCallum, "We have had an awful lot of rain this summer and it has been to some extent disagreeable in the tent, even with a new one." The inclement weather perhaps also affected Thomson's mood, making him lonely. He suggested to MacCallum that visitors would be appreciated, for "I should like awfully well to have some company."

Learning from the unfortunate progress of 1915, Thomson applied for work as an Algonquin Park fire ranger for the 1916 season. He was accepted, and although he discovered that the job alleviated his loneliness and money concerns, it made the job of painting more difficult. Not only were most of the people he encountered confused about why someone would want to paint, the extra bulk of a painting kit was an unhelpful burden when fire ranging. By early October, Thomson summarized his feelings about the job in a letter to Dr. MacCallum, stating bluntly, "We are not fired yet but I am hoping to be put off right away."

Despite an unproductive summer, Thomson returned to Toronto invigorated to paint. His skills were improving and his ideas about how and what to paint were evolving. Over the winter between 1916 and 1917 Thomson produced some of his most noteworthy large works on canvas. Some, such as the *The West Wind* and *The Jack Pine*, have become national icons. Others, such as the possibly unfinished *The Drive*, show Thomson experimenting with imagery and application of paint.

After two less-than-satisfying summers, Thomson craved painting in the park free of the encumbrances of duties. His enthusiasm to capture the snow led him to take the train straight to the park in the spring of 1917, foregoing a visit to his family in Owen Sound. Letters written at the time show Thomson anticipated camping out on the land as he had done previous summers. This practice suited his temperament and budget. He expected to guide fishing parties again, and was idly mulling a trip to the west. He had left several large works in late stages of completion back at the shack in Toronto, but his thinking was moving in new directions, and his primary concern was to test out his ideas by returning to making small, experimental works. If he could connect with his muse, if he could push himself forward, he might be on the verge of a new way of representing the landscape.

2

TOM THOMSON'S ART

He forced us to see the essential violence
of the Canadian landscape.
– HUGH MACLENNAN, *NEW LIBERTY*, 1949

——— ——

BETWEEN 1913 AND 1917, the period when Thomson was active as a land-scape painter, glimmers of artistic experiment were showing in major European and North American centres. The invention of photography and the motion picture led to deep questioning among artists regarding how to represent their world. The horrors of the First World War compelled a change in style, palette, and imagery.

The war in Europe also led many to reassess long-standing beliefs about what civilization meant, and Canada's relationship to European ideas and practices. For a single man in his fourth decade of life – a man who knew many others of his age were making sacrifices to go fight – Thomson must have been pulled in competing, irreconcilable directions. However hard these tensions might have been to endure, they seem to have helped Thomson develop his artistic sensibilities at a speed that left many of his peers flabbergasted.

It is difficult for us today to imagine the artistic world of Toronto during Thomson's time. Photography was still a revolutionary technology. Most painting tended toward realistic representation. European artists were just beginning to experiment with radical new styles. In 1911, Picasso created his *Still Life with Chair Caning*, which incorporated a "shattered," multiple perspective view of a still life with a piece of actual chair caning as part of the work. About the same time, Marcel Duchamp undertook a similar approach to representation of the body, painting his now legendary work, *Nude Descending a Staircase, No. 2*. In 1913, an American collector organized a New York exhibition of some of the most modern, avant-garde French works. The Armory Show, as the project came to be called, shook expectations about what artworks should look like, and what artists should be aspiring to achieve.

The art developing in Europe was a far cry from what Canadians could see in the country's few commercial galleries, and certainly had little in common with what recognized art institutions offered on their walls. While Europeans were beginning to experiment with styles such as cubism and dynamism, born of the urban, industrial age, for Canadians the artistic standard of the pre–First World War years was much closer to the work that had been the fashion in Paris or London several decades earlier. Patrons expected sedate, unchallenging images, particularly when it came to landscape painting. Popular landmarks, historical scenes, and pastoral views were all acceptable, as long as the artist respected certain formal expectations. "Good art" in early twentieth-century Canada was expected to use colours pleasing to the eye in representing scenes worthy of consideration, using clear technical prowess and refinement.

Having taken design classes at business school, Thomson showed an aptitude for rendering and visual composition. Working in advertising and illustration, he took great pride in his skill at lettering, creating several works combining lengthy quotations of text with decorative and pictorial elements. He also dabbled in less "functional" works, such as caricatures and drawings of architectural features.

It can't be stated authoritatively when Tom Thomson first tried to add oil paints to his repertoire. He did not use them with any consistency before he began making trips to New Ontario. Having brought painting supplies with him on his first trips north (assuming he did not borrow his travelling buddy's kit), it would seem that Thomson came to the idea of experimenting with oil during the spring of 1912.

Thomson's oil paintings of 1912 and 1913 are tentative works. Most are made on small pieces of board, perfect for carrying in a knapsack. These works are simple sketches, usually horizontally oriented works that depend heavily on greys and browns, punctuated occasionally by inclusion of pale yellow accents. They are memorable for their lack of features, often showing shorelines viewed across wide expanses of water, with flat, overcast skies.

Despite the somewhat awkward realization of Thomson's work, a number of his co-workers and critical friends began to see real potential in his paintings. Along with his sharp eye and deft hand, his interest in painting the "unsettled" areas north of Lake Simcoe helped to suggest a new direction for Canadian artists seeking to make a unique future for painting in the country.

About the same time that Thomson was discovering the charms of New Ontario, some of his artistic peers were coming to the belief that Canadians should shake off the shackles of European art and develop their own artistic canon. Both A.Y. Jackson and Lawren Harris had trained in Europe and were struggling with this very idea, but were not sure exactly how to bring it to fruition.

Jackson was certainly hoping to gather fellow painters who wanted to portray Canada in a way that aggressively challenged the accepted styles established by Europeans. These styles were far too concerned with presenting believably representative images, a style that had come to dominate audience expectations. As he wrote to Lawren Harris in March 1913, "Make something perfectly natural, fool people if possible, paint a stable and glue bits of straw on the front so you can't tell just when the painted article ends and the real stuff begins." Jackson sought to overthrow this kind of representational vapidity. Though evocative of the kinds of complaints that led Picasso to create *Still Life with Chair Caning* (a work which Jackson was very unlikely to be aware of), he was not alone even within Canada.

In the 1913 *Year Book of Canadian Art*, critic Fergus Kyle suggested that a place to begin building a Canadian art scene would be to see Canadian places portrayed in art, or for anything painted by Canadians to be recognized as something more than derivative of superior European practitioners. As he describes it, "It would be good to see a bit of this fair land well expressed in pigments by an outsider — say, a member of the Glasgow School; it would be good to see a bit of anything at all well expressed by a man whom we know working in Canada." Kyle notes that works included in the Ontario Society of Artists' exhibitions showed promise, and was gladdened that young Canadians who had been educated in Europe were recognizing different methods might be required "in attacking the subjects that face them when the sketch-box is opened at home."

In the same book, painter Wyly Grier addressed a similar need for a new Canadian artistic sensibility. He suggested that the realities of life in Canada limited most artists to their own creative work during evenings and weekends, a condition that hampered significant personal progress and experimentation. What would be required to build a "national art," in Grier's opinion, was fearlessness. The metaphors he draws upon suggest what kind of person would be required to take up the cause of progress:

> I believe that our art will never hold a commanding position, to use a soldier's phrase, until we are stirred by big emotions born of our landscape; braced to big, courageous efforts by our climate; and held to patient and persistent endeavour by that great pioneer spirit which animated the explorers and soldiers of early Canada. The thing needs courage.

Although he was not widely known in Toronto art circles at the time, Thomson's work suggested that he was someone with qualities these cultural revolutionaries were seeking. The single work that Thomson had submitted to the OSA's 1913 spring exhibition, *Northern Lake*, received positive mention in two reviews. Kyle offered that the work was "remarkable for its fidelity to the northern shore." Another reviewer, Margaret Fairbairn, suggests that Thomson's painting, and those of several others, were "astonishingly truthful." According to Fairbairn, by departing from the "dignity" and "serenity" of works produced by their more established predecessors, Thomson and some of his peers produce work that is "virile," with "fearless brushing, strange, crude color — all a reflection or echo of the spirit of the times."

The trip that Thomson and his Rous & Mann co-workers took to Algonquin Park in October 1914 changed the future of Canadian art and placed Thomson firmly in its centre. The artists were universally struck by their surroundings. Future Group of Seven member Fred Varley suggested that he had been prepared to give up painting until he made the visit. As he told Dr. MacCallum, "I had given painting the go-by — but I'm going full tilt into it now."

Varley and another future member of the Group of Seven, Arthur Lismer, found the landscape challenged their skills. Also writing to MacCallum, Lismer confessed, "I am finding it far from easy to express the riot of full colour & still keep the landscape in a high key."

A.Y. Jackson offered similar analysis, pointing out the differences he found between painting the Rocky Mountains and Algonquin Park: "The country up here is much more intimate than the mountains, and color close up is brighter than color a long way off."

MacCallum had asked for reports on Thomson's progress, and all three artists were positive about it in their letters. They suggested his work was quickly moving away from his previous style: that his use of colour was becoming bolder and his application more experimental.

His painting style was changing. He showed increasing interest in use of crude, blocky rendering of shapes that more than one of his peers described as "cubistical." Influenced by Jackson, his colour palette became brighter. His representation also became more complicated, moving toward the decorative. Complementing his interest in far shores, he began to include counterpoints of close objects, such as windswept, gnarled trees. He struggled happily with the challenge of capturing the appearance of rough water and racing clouds, the ephemeral effect of light on fall leaves and decaying bark.

Reviewing the 1916 OSA exhibition, Margaret Fairbairn commented that the two Thomson works included in the show were promising, although they were both disconcerting in their realization. She offered, "Mr. Tom Thomson's *The Birches* and *The Hardwoods* show a fondness for intense yellows and orange and strong blue, altogether a fearless use of violent color which can scarcely be called pleasing, and yet which scoops an exaggeration of a truthful feeling that time will temper." These were the last works that Thomson would submit to an OSA exhibition; the summer of 1917 would be his last alive.

Thomson's tragic death provided motivation for his artistic friends. His advocacy had made them aware of challenging Canadian venues in which to paint that existed only a few hours' train ride outside of Toronto. His enthusiasm for Algonquin Park helped to bring them to a region that they quickly came to see as embodying the Canadian spirit, where the natural world collided with human needs in an epic struggle, and where the winner did not yet feel like a foregone conclusion. Thomson's willingness to engage completely with what proved to be a fatal land gave his peers impetus to take his life and work up as something symbolic. The dead Thomson became the living artists' muse.

Two years after Thomson's death, Harold Mortimer-Lamb wrote in *The Studio* magazine that Thomson had left behind many charming and powerful works. However, his real legacy, in Mortimer-Lamb's view, was that his works "express a typically Canadian spirit, in a degree never before so concentrated and consistently maintained." Mortimer-Lamb suggested that Thomson's skills developed so quickly that they almost appeared to have been brought about by "spontaneous generation." Given that Thomson had little art training, it was especially miraculous that works produced during his short life as a painter "not only represent a high-water mark of landscape-painting in Canada, but would compel homage in any company anywhere." In fact, Mortimer-Lamb felt that Thomson's status as amateur might actually have served as an advantage. "No conventional training in the schools could have stood him in such good stead as the preparation circumstances afforded him."

Even in death, Thomson's accomplishments were viewed through a lens of masculine accomplishment. Mortimer-Lamb offered of Thomson's non-aesthetic skills: "He went to Nature and communed with her in all her moods. He was the most constant of lovers, and with increasing intimacy came profound knowledge."

Attempting to fit Thomson's work among those that his peers created after his death, Mortimer-Lamb quoted A.Y. Jackson at length. The attributes that Jackson noted a new cadre of artists were aspiring to fit almost exactly with the attributes that reviewers had found so challenging in Thomson's work. "There was," Mortimer-Lamb quotes Jackson,

> no attempt or intention to found a school or secede from the art bodies. There was, moreover, nothing revolutionary about our ideas. We felt that there was a rich field for landscape motives in the North Country if we frankly abandoned any attempt after literal painting, and treating our subjects with the freedom of the decorative designer, just as the Swedes had done living in a land with a topography and climate very similar to our own.... We tried to emphasize colour, line, and pattern even if need be at the sacrifice of atmospheric qualities. It seemed the only way to make a right use of the wealth of motives the country offered.

There was no doubt among his peers that Thomson's work deserved a place among those that they would later produce. When a number of them came together as The Group of Seven in 1920, they credited Thomson as one of their inspirations. They elected to include some of Thomson's works, such as his large *The West Wind*, in an exhibition touring through the United States.

At the time, Group of Seven member J.E.H. Macdonald, acting as one of the caretakers of Thomson's artistic legacy, wrote T.J. (Tom) Harkness, the executor of Thomson's estate. A Sarnia Art Gallery committee was interested in buying one of the paintings. His comments suggest how strategically Thomson's works were being made available:

> We have heard that they are being strongly influenced to spend <u>all the money</u> on <u>two</u> very commonplace pictures by two of the older Canadian artists, & it is to prevent this waste of money, & to attempt to give a better <u>Canadian</u> character to their collection that we would like them to have this picture of Tom's. The picture is well suited to a public collection, being too large for a private house, & this seems to be a good opportunity to place it well.

Macdonald's hope was satisfied; the gallery would acquire the Thomson work.

In 1924, Thomson's importance among the new generation of Canadian artists was again indicated when a substantial number of his works were included in an exhibition of Canadian paintings presented at the Wembley Palace of Arts in London, England. Here, again, Thomson's works received positive press. Rupert Lee noted, "One finds many reasons for considering Tom Thomson's work as the type of this new spirit which has come into Canadian art." For Lee, Thomson's skill was his single-minded approach to representation as decoration. "His creed is a simple one. He makes of his picture a decoration, and its main beauty lies in the delicate adjustment of its component silhouettes." In some ways picking up elements of the "cubistical tendencies" observed by some of Thomson's peers, Lee suggested that Thomson's use of space and form reflected his passion for decoration over representation:

> Instead of an insistence on weights and volumes we have an arrangement of shapes. There is a recession of planes, but more from a sense that the silhouettes lie one behind the other, and the sensation of perspective is intellectual rather than physical.

The Wembley exhibition moved to Paris's Jeu de Paume and received similarly positive reviews there. The National Gallery's Eric Brown noted that after high-profile exhibitions in the United States, London, and Paris, "Canadian art is on the foreign maps."

One difficulty confronting the Parisians, according to Brown, was their "ignorance of Canada as a country, which seemed far more complete than anything encountered in London." As a form of national diplomacy, "the exhibition conveyed the Canadian idea and country more vividly than has probably ever been done since Jacques Cartier attempted to describe the St. Lawrence."

Some of the paintings particularly made a strong impression on the Parisians. Brown stated: "The Thomson group became one of the most popular spots in the galleries and every epithet implying interest, originality, nationality, individuality, not to mention *épatant*, was rife."

The characteristic of Canadian landscape painting that most struck Parisian reviewers is one that was arguably exemplified by the work of painters such as Thomson. Brown noted this impact: "One critic expressed ... that any landscape ever painted in France made you feel the presence of man, but that in the Canadian landscapes you feel his absence."

In 1936, Thomson's friend, A.H. Robson, who had also been his supervisor at the Rous & Mann and Grip design firms, wrote a pamphlet memorializing Thomson. Robson noted that the paintings Thomson had produced during a very brief period were nonetheless "sufficient to proclaim him, beyond question, one of the most significant painters in the art history of the Dominion." This is all the more impressive as only thirteen works of Thomson's were held in public collections.

Even at this early date, Robson felt it had become necessary to inter-ject some facts into discussion of Thomson's art. Robson observed, "Except to a very limited number of friends, Tom Thomson is a remote and mystical figure that broke into the art firmament with a sudden and dazzling brilliancy, and then disappeared as suddenly into the unknown. During the last decade his career has been wrapped in mists of mystery and half truths somewhat obscuring a clear vision of the man and his work."

For Robson, Thomson's achievement was largely in his original approach to a land that few artists had ever considered. Thomson, Robson believed, "did not travel the well-trodden highways of derivative painting but made trails of his own where no man had stepped before." He suggested Thomson "was the first painter really to interpret the north in its various subtleties of mood and feeling, free from influences of European traditions and formulas."

Robson believed Thomson's originality was in large part based on some-thing that no foreigner could have: a close familiarity with the Canadian landscape. He stated that Thomson's "personal knowledge of the country and his inherent honesty dictated its own technical methods of expres-sion." By immersing himself in the land he was trying to represent, "the feeling of personal kinship which [Thomson] ... gained [camping in the woods] resulted in numerous sketches of widely varying moods of the north not usually observed by the more casual visitor."

On the basis of these two points, Robson offers that Thomson's "tragic and untimely death on Canoe Lake robbed our Dominion of a great interpreter of the Canadian wilderness."

By the late 1930s, references to Tom Thomson tended to rest at this confluence of ideas about Canadian identity, masculine integrity, the violent aspects of nature, and loss.

His work only gained in resonance after the world had been convulsed by a second global conflict. In a 1947 speech by Roy Atherton, the United States' ambassador to Canada, Tom Thomson was raised as the embodiment of an ideal Canadian, someone who modelled the qualities of freedom and integrity. Making reference to the critical 1917 Canadian efforts to take Vimy Ridge from the German enemy, Atherton observed:

> Thomson, painting all that spring of 1917 in Algonquin Park, painting feverishly as though he knew the light would fade soon for him, Thomson was saying for the first time and for all time what those other Canadians, so far away, were dying for.

In 1949, renowned Canadian novelist Hugh MacLennan took up a similar theme when he named Tom Thomson as one of the ten greatest Canadians. Writing in *New Liberty* magazine, MacLennan suggested that one of Thomson's significant contributions to Canada was that "he forced us to see the essential violence of the Canadian landscape." In MacLennan's estimation, Thomson and the painters he influenced visually communicated to a generation who might easily forget what their pioneer forebears had accomplished: "They told us what a lonely country Canada really is. They made clear the significance of farms being cleared out of the bush and great cities rising against such a background." This aspect of Thomson's work could not make the same impression on a foreigner as it would a Canadian. It was the first truly Canadian art. "The art of Tom Thomson was not international and it had no direct bearing on the great European tradition. It was native and extremely simple and fresh...."

Tom Thomson's manner and place of passing had become folded into a particular way of making sense of his life and artwork. After his death, he came to represent a kind of brave honesty, integrity, and simple clarity that contrasts strongly with the hopelessness, frustration, and self-doubt that followed the First World War. Thomson's love of nature served as a shining counterpoint to all-too-obvious risks of industrialization and urbanization that had emerged during the war. In an era that raised questions about manly and national duty, Thomson's decision to stay in Canada, to immerse himself in the Canadian "spirit" in a way that did not involve killing other men on European battlefields, spoke to a kind of positive patriotism in which war-tired Canadians could take consolation.

Thomson's tragic death also spoke to the sacrifices that commitment to integrity might require. If Thomson had avoided the war effort while lounging in the tea rooms of Toronto and malingering in his studio while soldiers marched down Yonge Street to Union Station, he might never have been regarded as a national hero. That he died in a canoe, on a lake in Algonquin Park, struggling to in some way capture the excitement and challenge of the "rich" new landscape entering Canadian consciousness allowed him to be placed in a pantheon of Canadian heroes: explorers, discoverers, soldiers, defenders, and with the addition of Thomson, artists.

3

TOM THOMSON'S LAST SUMMER

Talented and with many friends
and no enemies, a mystery.
— ENTRY FOR TOM THOMSON IN OWEN SOUND KNOX UNITED CHURCH BURIAL REGISTER, 1917

AS CANADIANS GAINED appreciation for Thomson's painting, interest in the artist's life grew. His death in Algonquin Park, the place that served as the inspiration for so much of his art, offered sadly ironic grist for story-telling and speculation. With each telling and retelling, the available facts became seamlessly interwoven with gossip and speculation. Over time, Thomson's story took on mythic characteristics, coming to depend on an uneven balance of memory, creative interpretation, and evidence. As it is told today, the imagined story of Thomson's death generally accords with the following tale.

By March 1917, Tom Thomson's thoughts were turning northward. Spurred by the steady lengthening of the days and melting snows, he began fanta-sizing about the northern forests and lakes of New Ontario that he knew so well, the quiet and peaceful spaces far from the busy streets of Toronto.

Time in Algonquin Park would represent a welcome escape for Thomson. News from Europe indicated Canadian soldiers were engaged in a difficult struggle. Lists of men martyred for God and King were a daily inclusion in the newspapers. Some have suggested that Thomson had unsuccessfully volunteered to join the army. The accounts are fuzzy about when he might have volunteered and why he was turned down. The reports also disagree on whether he had volunteered to fight in Europe or in the Boer War, which took place over a decade earlier.

If Thomson had been turned down to fight in Europe, every notice, every story about the war likely grated on his conscience. Instead of fighting, perhaps he sought consolation by challenging his manliness through living in the park among the lumbermen and explorers and wild animals, without the creature comforts of civilized life. In the park, he could live for months without the dirty looks of the wives and loved ones left behind by men who had volunteered to go fight, or concern for money or social etiquette. Alone with his paints and his canoe, he could simply bask in the glory of nature and forget the war, the city, and his own doubts and fears.

On his way to the park, Thomson passed through the village of Huntsville, where he visited his friends, the Trainor family. Hugh Trainor was a lumber foreman who worked in the park region, who also leased a cottage on Canoe Lake. Some have claimed that the oldest Trainor daughter, Winnifred (commonly referred to as Winnie), was Thomson's lover. Her family often spent time at their cottage on Canoe Lake. She and Tom had become close during his time in the park, and it is often speculated that she harboured the wish that Tom would propose marriage.

In late March or early April, Thomson made his way to Mowat. The Canoe Lake hamlet consisted of a permanent population of about twenty people. It was a station stop on the train line running through the southern portion of the park, from Scotia in the west to Golden Lake in the east. Thomson took up residence at Mowat Lodge, which was far more affordable than the tourist-oriented Algonquin Hotel further to the east. He intended to rent a room until the ice came off the lake, after which he could camp in the park.

The lodge was operated by Annie and Shannon Fraser. Thomson had frequented their establishment many times over the previous three or four years, and often lent a hand with small tasks around the place. Even though his work as a painter might have been seen as bohemian, he was in many respects regarded more as a member of the Canoe Lake community than a "tourist" from the south. Given the amount of time Thomson lived and worked in the park, many of the people who lived around Canoe Lake — from park ranger Mark Robinson to guides and visiting cottagers — regarded Thomson as a friend.

Popular accounts offer that Thomson quickly settled down to work, establishing a busy painting routine. Over the preceding winter, he had been considering a plan. He would create a painting a day, trying to record the scenery and weather in the park, and how it changed from day to day as winter gave way to spring.

Thomson's working method when painting in nature was to make small, rough works on boards about the size of a regular sheet of paper. He referred to these pieces as "sketches." Some of the sketches he would scrap, while others would be sent by rail to Toronto. If he regarded a sketch as intriguing or provocative, Thomson would return to it over the winter, working it up into a larger work painted on to canvas.

By Thomson's own account, he was having a productive spring. He informed his patron, Dr. MacCallum, that he was making paintings, although he regarded many of them to be below his own standard for quality. He planned to keep at it, regardless.

At the end of April, Thomson was down to fifty dollars in his bank account. He applied for a licence to guide fishing parties around the park. During the spring, he led a few groups, but weather, blackflies, and the war conspired to limit the number of opportunities. In May, before the blackflies reached their worst, Dr. MacCallum spent a few days at Canoe Lake with Thomson, viewing his spring sketches while enjoying some time fishing.

Thomson was certainly more enthusiastic about his painting than taking on guiding work. His sketching ideas had helped him gather a certain degree of creative momentum.

Several people who were around Canoe Lake that summer have stated that as Thomson's records of the change from winter to spring accumulated, he become increasingly proud of his accomplishment. He may have asked Mark Robinson if it would be all right to set up his sketches in his ranger hut at nearby Joe Lake to dry, which would also serve as an informal exhibition, with Thomson showing his friends and neighbours his success.

When he had done this at Mowat Lodge in the past he had allowed some of his closest friends to claim a favourite painting for their own.

By early July, Thomson knew that a few more fishing parties were scheduled for the remainder of the summer. Inspired by the paintings his friend Arthur Lismer had produced while travelling to the Rocky Mountains a few years earlier, Thomson planned to head west to paint the mountains himself, or to find work helping with the fall harvest. He certainly intended to keep up with painting as his guiding work permitted.

On July 7, Thomson indicated to Dr. MacCallum that in the next day or two he would send along the sketches he had made over the preceding three months. MacCallum would never receive the package.

That night, many accounts suggest Thomson sat around the fire with some of his Canoe Lake pals. As the men drank bootleg liquor, their talk became more animated. Thomson may have asked Shannon Fraser to pay off a significant debt that had been outstanding for two years. Or talk might have also turned to the April successes of Canadian soldiers in liberating Vimy Ridge, or Owen Sound flying ace Billy Bishop's exploits, which led to arguments, particularly with the German-American cottager Martin Blecher Jr. Either way, threats were levelled and a fight broke out, with Tom taking on either Blecher or Fraser. Whichever was his adversary, the night ended with bitter feelings all around.

The next morning, Fraser and Thomson fished just below the Joe Lake Dam. There was an elusive fish hiding in the waters there that Fraser, Thomson, and Mark Robinson had been vying to successfully land. Unsuccessful despite his best efforts, Thomson decided to go on another fishing excursion that was sure to produce some amusement, if nothing else. He hoped to catch a large trout and leave it on Mark Robinson's doorstep to give the impression that he had finally brought in their fish. According to Fraser, Thomson pushed his canoe out from the dock at Mowat Lodge a little after noon.

In mid-afternoon, Martin Blecher and his sister were crossing the lake in the Blechers' small motor-driven boat. They sighted a canoe floating upside down in the lake. Thinking it was simply a boat that they had heard had broken loose from its mooring at the Algonquin Hotel, they left it be.

The next day, Thomson had still not returned from his fishing trip. Fraser raised the alarm with Mark Robinson. Both men expected that Thomson had simply chosen to take a little more time fishing than he had originally planned, and would return shortly. In case Thomson had run into any trouble, such as twisting his ankle while dismounting his canoe, Robinson organized a few men to search the shorelines.

Over the next few days, as anxiety about Thomson's whereabouts grew, the search expanded in intensity and area. A ranger was sent into Huntsville to inquire whether Thomson had gone to town. Robinson and his young son walked some of the portages and trails. Tom's brother George was notified. George made a trip by rail from the Thomson family home near Owen Sound (where he was holidaying) to Canoe Lake. All these efforts were to no avail. Not a sign of Tom was found.

On July 16, eight days after Tom Thomson had disappeared, a visiting cottager, Dr. Goldwin Howland, discovered Thomson's body floating in Canoe Lake, within a half kilometre of where his journey began. The body was taken to the shore and the doctor examined the corpse, accompanied by Mark Robinson. He concluded the cause of death was accidental drowning, noting a bruise on the body's forehead and blood issuing from its ear. As the corpse had likely been in the water for over a week, and with nowhere to keep the body, the decision was made to bury Thomson's remains in the village cemetery as quickly as possible. Thomson's body was buried the day after its discovery in a ceremony attended only by his local friends and neighbours.

A few hours after Thomson's burial, the coroner arrived from North Bay. Intending to investigate the cause of death, the coroner was confronted with a situation in which he could not inspect the corpse in question. Instead, he opted to investigate the death by gathering some of the people from around the lake and interviewing them together that night in the Blechers' cabin. On the basis of evidence gathered during these interviews, and without seeing the body, the coroner supported the examining doctor's conclusion of accidental drowning.

On July 18, within twenty-four hours of the coroner departing Canoe Lake and less than thirty-six hours after Thomson's body was buried, an undertaker arrived at Canoe Lake station with instructions to prepare

Thomson's body for transportation to the family plot in Leith, Ontario. Shannon Fraser drove the undertaker — with the coffin he had brought — to the cemetery.

Later accounts report that the undertaker, working quickly by lantern light, exhumed Thomson's body and transferred it into a new coffin by midnight. Apparently, Fraser helped the man load the coffin onto the wagon and hauled it back to the train station to be shipped out on the morning train.

The morning after Thomson's body had been exhumed, Mark Robinson was rather surprised when he encountered the undertaker on the station platform. No one had notified him — the resident park authority — of the visitor's arrival, nor sought approval to exhume the body. Robinson brought the issue to the attention of park superintendent William Bartlett. Bartlett saw that there was no sense insisting that proper bureaucratic procedures be followed in this case — in light of the tragedy, it seemed only humane to let Thomson's remains be taken home. Although Robinson was not pleased, he opted to let the issue rest. Little good would come of quibbling with the undertaker over park regulations. Later that day, he did visit the cemetery to ensure that the site was properly returned to its previous state. On arriving, he noted that the hole left behind by the undertaker when he removed Thomson's coffin seemed unusually shallow.

Robinson was suspicious. Too many things surrounding Thomson's accident, death, and exhumation didn't make sense. How could a skilled canoeist like Thomson accidently drown in a lake he knew well? What did that bruise on Thomson's temple mean, and why was his ear bleeding? How could the undertaker dig up a coffin so quickly by himself and leave such a little hole? Something was not right. What happened to Thomson, and to his corpse, would vex Robinson for the rest of his life.

That night, Thomson's body arrived in Owen Sound by train, accompanied by George Thomson. His coffin rested at the family home, and on Saturday was moved to the church for a funeral service and reburial in the Leith Cemetery, a few kilometres outside of town.

A doctor opened Tom's funeral service with a prayer; Reverend Pilkey of the United Church officiated. Among those travelling to Leith for the burial were Tom's father, his brother George and his wife, his sister Margaret (Peg), his brother-in-law Tom Harkness, and the Harknesses' daughter, Jessie.

Reverend Pilkey made the following entry in the Owen Sound Knox United Church Burial Register:

Thomson, Thomas (artist).
Accidental drowning.
Canoe Lake, Algonquin Park
July 8th, 1917.
Age – 39 years, born Aug. 1877.
Buried at Leith, Ont – July 21st, 1917.
"Talented and with many friends and no enemies, a mystery."

4

MOURNING TOM THOMSON

*Poor boy, he worked so hard, denied himself so much
and now to think he is gone.*

— MARGARET (PEG) THOMSON, LETTER TO DR. JAMES MACCALLUM, AUGUST 2, 1917

OVER THE WEEKS immediately following Tom Thomson's death, his family and friends struggled to make sense of the tragedy. They wrote letters of condolence and of inquiry, attempting to resolve the complicated circumstances of Tom's death and haphazard burial. Many of these documents — which remained in the possession of the Thomson family — only became publicly available during the 1990s. They provide unique and timely accounts of what occurred at Canoe Lake in July 1917 and during the weeks after, as well as give critical insight into the minds of many of Thomson's friends and relatives. Among these early discussions we can find indications of emerging theories, tensions, and conflicts among those associated with Thomson.

Within days of Tom's burial in Leith Cemetery, his sister Margaret (who lived in Owen Sound) wrote his sister Minnie, relating how the family had learned of Thomson's death and sharing how their parents had been coping with the tragedy.

Margaret suggests that after they learned Tom was missing, the family held out hope that he had merely suffered an accident. Tom's brother George had immediately left for Canoe Lake. The family held out hope for Tom's safe return, even after George returned from Canoe Lake with little new information. Margaret wrote, "George came back from the Park Saturday night and Monday we got a message saying that 'Found Tom this morning.' We thought by the message he was possibly alive and nearly everyone thought so."

Their hopes were soon dashed, however. "Our terrible suspense was ended on Tuesday afternoon," Margaret lamented, "when we got the definite word that Tom was really gone." She described the confusion and stress the family had suffered due to a bad telegraph connection which stymied getting messages between Owen Sound and Canoe Lake. "They sent us a message that the body was awaiting burial and it was delayed a day or more," she explained. The undertaker at the scene had decided that Tom should be buried in Mowat, as he said "it would be impossible to ship the body." In Margaret's estimation, however, "he didn't know his business at all and made a regular mess of things."

Margaret expressed appreciation for the help provided by Winnifred Trainor, whom she had not met or spoken to until after Tom's death. In her letter, Margaret describes how she was called to the phone at midnight to speak to Trainor (she does not specify which day this occured). Trainor told her that she was "a friend of Tom's." Trainor informed Margaret that Tom's remains had been buried, and "wanted to know if we wanted anything done." The family informed Trainor that they wanted Tom brought home, and "she did everything in her power and stayed up all night to help us." At three o'clock the following morning, Trainor called George to update him on what she had accomplished. On the basis of the details, it is safe to surmise that the telephone conversation would have happened during the night between Tuesday, July 17, and Wednesday, July 18.

The afternoon after receiving the call, Margaret narrates, George returned to Canoe Lake and "brought Tom's body on the Friday night train to Owen Sound." She states that the "body was left at the undertaker's Friday night and the funeral service was Saturday morning." She discusses how her mother wanted to remember Tom, and offers that upon the return of his remains, "none of us wanted to see him even if the body had been fit to see." She adds that the family had been comforted by the efforts of friends to ease their sorrow. "There are some beautiful flowers sent," she notes, "some from Mr. and Mrs. Fraser of Canoe Lake." While this observation might not have seemed significant at the time, later developments make it worthy of note.

Margaret's letters provide a unique perspective on the news that was reaching Owen Sound, and important insight into how family members interpreted the information they received. Margaret's letters also allow us to better understand what actions the family was taking in response to news being received from Canoe Lake.

Two receipts submitted to the estate for reimbursement provide verification for some of the things Margaret mentioned in her letter. On July 21, George submitted the following costs to the executor of Tom's estate, his brother-in-law Tom Harkness, who was married to Elizabeth Thomson:

> $54.80 for train travel
> $8.15 for rail shipment of Tom's corpse
> $4.40 for expenses related to Churchill, the undertaker who exhumed Thomson's body
> $1.80 for cigars for the Rangers who searched for Tom
> $1.50 for express shipping of Tom's "sketches, etc."
> $0.60 for phone call from Toronto

On July 25, Trainor provided a Bell Canada receipt for six phone calls she had made on July 18, the day Thomson had been buried at Canoe Lake: two to Owen Sound ($1.10 and $2.50) and four to Kearney (totalling $1.40), which is where R.H. Flavelle, a furniture dealer and one of the original undertakers who had treated Tom's remains, lived.

On July 23, Harkness wrote Flavelle regarding the bill for services rendered in preparing Tom's body for burial. The arrangements for the first burial at Canoe Lake had been made by Shannon Fraser, without consultation of the family; this was to cause some confusion. Flavelle had submitted costs totalling $107.25, a large part of which was $75 for a casket and rough box, and $20 for embalming. Harkness clearly expressed his anger at the amount Flavelle was charging, stating, "I think your account is exorbitant and ... I will not pay it in full." Instead, Harkness informed

Flavelle that he would deduct $15 from the cost of the casket, and $10 from the embalming fees. "If you are not satisfied," Harkness instructs, "I will pay amount of account less $25.00 into court and you may proceed to collect the balance."

The conclusion that Flavelle's fees were excessive, Harkness explains, was based on having submitted "your account to competent undertakers." Based on the information he obtained, Harkness was "allowing just double for embalming that is charged in this part." He also noted how Flavelle's fees compared to those of F.W. Churchill, the undertaker who had prepared Thomson's body for return to Owen Sound: "The man we got to furnish [the] metallic lined casket to bring the body home only charged $75.00 for his work and the casket and we paid his fare to Canoe Lake."

Flavelle promptly responded that "it is an utter impossibility to alter prices." He diplomatically outlined the unique challenges that Canoe Lake had posed for preparing Thomson's corpse for burial:

> This was no ordinary case. We had to go 1½ miles through the woods after leaving train, then another mile by water, taking casket with us. We then took body to an island where we embalmed it and brought it back to Mowat Lodge Cemetery where we buried it.

With regard to the casket, he noted that "the buyer asked for the best I had, choosing the $75 one rather than $50 or $60."

Flavelle also noted that Fraser engaged the services of the embalmer, and attempted to explain the higher-than-usual embalming fees:

> I am well aware that $10 is the usual charge for any ordinary case in town or near vicinity, but this was no ordinary case, requiring double quantity of fluid otherwise necessary, besides the Embalmer's Railroad expenses (for 53 miles and return) meals and lodging from 3.45 p.m. to 8.45 p.m. the next night.

Perhaps most revealing are Flavelle's closing comments, where he states, "If you refuse to pay bill as rendered I will collect from buyer saving you some unnecessary trouble." This is eventually what Flavelle did, sending his bill to Fraser on August 2, 1917.

For his part, Fraser was also seeking coverage of some expenses. On July 24, he wrote Dr. MacCallum, shedding some light on Tom's last activities:

> Poor Tom is gone he was in fine shape when he left me on Sunday 8 of July Sunday morning he says to me i will go up with you and help me [lift] over a boat [over] the Joe Lake dam so we went up and it was raining hard and he was wet [through] when we got down to the dock he said i will go down to the dock he said i will go down to west lake and get some of those big trought [sic] and i will be back eather to night [sic] or tomorrow morning he said good by [sic] and i never seen him again.

Speculating on what might have happened to Thomson, Fraser suggested that

> he must of taking [sic] a cramp or got out on shore and slip [off] a log or something the Paddles was tied up in the canoe and canoe turned over when we found him he was in a bad state so we burried [sic] him ... his brother came up and took him a way [sic] with him he was dug up and put in a sealed coffen [sic].

Concerning Thomson's effects, Fraser outlined that "his brother sent his pictures to you and he took the other [stuff] home with him I have the canoes here but they haven['t] said what they will be worth." Finally, Fraser noted that "[I wouldn't] charge any thing for my trouble but I had 3 men out looking for him." At $2.50 per day, Fraser reports costs of $7.50 for Dickson, $5.00 for Rowe, and $5.00 for Fire Ranger McDonald. While it is likely that Fraser hoped MacCallum would pay these expenses, he doesn't make a direct request for funds.

On August 6, almost two weeks later, Fraser wrote Tom Harkness to notify him that Flavelle had sent him the bill for the burial expenses. Fraser sent the bill along, suggesting, "I was just going to pay it," without explaining why he did not. He also added his perception of how much Flavelle was charging for his work: "he had pretty hard work up here with [Tom's] body so I thought [his costs] would of [sic] been more." Under the conditions, Fraser was suggesting that Flavelle's charges were entirely reasonable. As he noted, "the [body] was in a offel [sic] state so we had to hurry and it rained all day all the other man had to do was change boxes so sute yours self [sic] about the bill."

As he had when writing Dr. MacCallum, Fraser raised the topic of payment for the searchers. In this letter, however, his report of the rates paid the searchers differed from those he had reported to MacCallum. Writing Harkness, Fraser states that he gave George Rowe $5.00 and Larry Dickson $3.50. He didn't raise the issue of any payment for McDonald. Likely as a way of supporting his intimation that the estate should compensate him for these costs, Fraser notes that "Mr. [R]owe and Dickson found him." Fraser also brought up two canoes Tom Thomson had left behind, of which he said, "I seen [sic] the Rangers and they said the canoes was worth $10.00 dollars a peace [sic] they leak pretty bad they are Pretty old canoes and full of holes so they said that was all they are worth."

Fraser's concern for money might suggest that he had come to fear that the estate might not cover the costs he had independently approved, such as the choice of casket or hiring of searchers. Attempting to justify his decisions, he noted the difficult situation and appealed to pity, offering, "We got so excited we diden [sic] know what to do so we did the best we could do." Whatever the reason for his concerns, Fraser's anxiety that his actions were coming under criticism is clearly shown.

In the midst of claims being made for compensation from the estate, two of Tom's sisters travelled to Toronto to sort through his belongings. They also visited an exhibition of his works being shown at the Canadian National Exhibition. Upon returning to Owen Sound, Margaret Thomson again set pen to paper, writing Dr. MacCallum to express her grief:

> Our hearts are still almost broken and I don't know whether
> our sorrow will ever wear away or not. His death was the first
> break in our large grown up family. Tom seemed to have a place

in each of our hearts, that could not be filled by any one else. He was so good and so kind and he seemed almost perfect in every way. He was so much alone that we seemed to think more about him than any of the others of the family. Poor boy, he worked so hard, denied himself so much and now to think he is gone.

She lamented not having written Tom during the summer, as she expected "many a time he must have been lonely when out in the wilds." Regretting not sending him some "homemade cooking," she lamented, "It seems I have been denied this pleasure."

Turning to the business of her brother's art, Margaret expressed her family's support for holding a memorial exhibition of Tom's paintings. She added, "You will know better than we what to do. We wouldn't like to see any of his work sold at a sacrifice and we trust everything will turn out rightly." She also shared that the family would appreciate construction of a memorial cairn that had been proposed by some of Tom's Toronto friends.

On August 11, Winnifred Trainor responded to a letter from T.J. Harkness. Although Harkness's letter has not surfaced, we can extrapolate what he was inquiring about from Trainor's response. Trainor had travelled to Canoe Lake after Thomson's body was discovered, and in her letter she provides insight into the events around Thomson's first burial. She blamed Fraser's ill-considered actions for the ensuing sad comedy of errors:

> You know the contents of the first telegram thoughtlessly composed — and you know the tangle now that has to be unravelled — owing to the thoughtlessness of not having a sealed casket — which anyone knows is needed in a case of that kind and also required by law. If you knew Mr. Fraser I think you would use your own judgement. This is strictly confidential as the Frasers are alright in their way. We are friends with the Frasers, as we have a swell House at Canoe Lake, where each summer it has been our custom to Holiday there. But I could explain better if you knew them.

About 6:00 p.m., as she was waiting to leave Canoe Lake after the funeral service, she became aware of a "telegram of instructions which was found waiting at the train." Upset that the Thomson family wishes had not been respected, Trainor describes her efforts to address the situation:

> I'm sorry I did not go up the day before — I suggested things
> at Canoe Lake, but was refused. If I see you I can tell you all....
> After I got ans[wer] to what was going on at Canoe Lake — I
> did all in my power to get things righted. I was told there it
> could not be done, but I thought I'd have a try and I knew that
> time was precious.

Catching the train heading west out of Canoe Lake, Trainor had time to consider her options. She decided that as soon as she was able, she would attempt to notify the Thomson family as well as contact the undertaker in Kearney and in her own town of Huntsville:

> When I got to Scotia [Junction] arriving at 7:30 p.m. the wires
> were down between [Huntsville] and Scotia. So then I looked
> up the G[rand] T[runk] R[ailway] agent & sent out message
> after message to H[unts]ville all free of charge, & perfectly
> lovely about it all. I had to wait there till nearly 3 a.m.

This explanation of her activities on the early morning of July 18 helps to put in context the bill for telephone calls that Trainor submitted to the estate.

Trainor was clearly dissatisfied with Fraser's handling of communication and decision-making regarding Tom's burial. She was likely mortified that Tom's family's desires had not been acted upon from the outset. Along with the explanations she provided to Harkness, she conducted some helpful research. She reported:

> I called to see the undertaker Mr. Churchill and he wished
> is [sic] name not to be used. So I know these remarks will be
> treated strictly confidential ... I asked him plain questions and

got straight replys [*sic*]. He is a very consientious [*sic*] man. I can't write all to-night but he said the bill was steep. Flavelle is only a furniture dealer and undertaker not an embalmer so took an embalmer along from Sprucedale near Parry Sound. So that was double expense instead of acting a man and pass [*sic*] the order on. That is from the money side. Even if had no heart ... Mr. Churchill said to act as per your letter. They include here everything with the price of the casket. The one from Kearney was not any better & Rough box was not painted & I don't think it had handles on. Mr. Churchill always pays his own keep when out. He says it is not right as he would have to pay for it while home. A copper lining costs more than the casket itself. So you see he is billing a good [amount?].

All of this information could not mask that Trainor was still grieving Tom's death. Echoing the kinds of sentiments expressed by Thomson's sister, Trainor noted that she had sent a letter to Tom "five weeks today," and received a final one from him that must have been written very soon before his death. She sadly added, "Our letters crossed & to-night a sad note to his brother-in-law. It seems to me almost unbeleivable [*sic*]. And I'm so sorry and words are so thin."

Dr. MacCallum's response to Thomson's death was quite different than Trainor's. At the beginning of September, his letters were almost completely focused on the business side of Thomson's estate, particularly focusing on the sale of Tom's remaining paintings. In a letter that was likely written to George Thomson, MacCallum inquired whether a leather trunk that he expected to be found somewhere among Tom's belongings had been located. He also detailed a trip he and Tom Harkness had made to a Toronto bank to collect what remained in Tom Thomson's account.

He was rather pleased with his ability to grease the wheels of petty bureaucracy, for as he boasted, the bank staff "were bound to make us get out letters of administration. When Harkness demurred they wanted me to take them out, but by saying I would go to the General Manager

— a relative of mine — they agreed to a bond which both Harkness and I signed, so that is finished."

MacCallum's primary concern, however, was with how to dispose of Thomson's paintings. Of course, he wanted some of Tom's paintings for himself. "I want to buy some of these last sketches of Tom's especially the little ones — you set the price and I will pay it," he stated.

He was also clearly trying to create a market for these works, yet did not want to commit to any sales or prices until he had approval from the family. His letter noted:

> I broached the idea to the Curator [of the National Gallery] that they should buy 40 or 50 of the sketches and keep them as an Encyclopedia of the North Country. He seemed to be impressed with the idea but said his trustees had to go cautiously during war time — I see by the papers that their appropriation for buying pictures was cut off.... He thought he ought to have some at least tentative amount which could be discussed between him and me before anything official presentation [sic] to his board. There of course he had me, because I hesitated to name any price.

MacCallum certainly had what seemed a multitude of buyers for Thomson's sketches.

> Cummings wants to be allowed to meet any offer made for that moonlight picture in his studio.... The Insurance agent returned the sketch ... a patient said I will give you $25.00 for that now, so we will not lose on it — What am I to do in such an event [?] — I hate to let money get away for this war is going to make money very tight here — yet I cannot say yes until I have your consent — This man has money and I can probably talk $30.00 or more out of him if you say so.

MacCallum was not only concerned with getting the best prices possible for Thomson's works. He also seemed to be considering how to build longer-term, critical interest in Thomson's works, whether as brilliant art on its own, or as "a record of the North." In this regard, the price for which he was willing to sell Thomson's works seemed to conflict to some degree with what Thomson himself had been willing to charge for them. MacCallum tried to outline a particularly challenging purchase offer:

> I have traced up some sketches to a magazine editor — he was given 7 or 8 to choose from — he told Tom he could not pay more than ten dollars a piece and was to take 4 — now he wants to give me a cheque for $40.00 and return the balance — His story is corroborated by Williamson who was present during the transaction — One good thing is that in my judgement he had rotten taste in selecting them. Another factor is that we shall want to make use of his magazine — What do you advise [sic].

MacCallum — perhaps as an investor, perhaps as a friend — was trying to generate money for the Thomson estate, as well as find the most productive sales for Thomson's works. While he was happy to merely unload some works, there were certainly others that he sought to keep control of, or to direct to particular types of collectors and art institutions.

By early September, Shannon Fraser provided Tom Harkness with "the bills I paid [sic] george rowe and lowery [sic] Dickson." He mentioned that Flavelle was still pursuing him for money, but thought that Harkness was going to pay the undertaker. He also sent along five dollars "to make up the balance for the canoes," suggesting that he was simply deducting from the purchase money the amount he had paid to the guides who searched for Thomson. He noted that he would send Thomson's blanket to Harkness "right away."

The same day that Fraser was writing Harkness, Trainor was writing a letter of her own. In her missive, she suggested that as she had already sent the "original receipts" (presumably for the phone calls she made on

July 18) it was "hard to write this same receipt." It is not clear if the difficulty stems from some kind of concerns about legality, or the emotional challenge of revisiting the events. She did add, however, that "[i]t seems like two years instead of just 2 months to-day since Tom was drowned."

In a September letter to Dr. MacCallum, Tom's sister Margaret reflected on her visit to Toronto, where she had had a chance to meet with Trainor. She reported that Trainor gave the impression of having Tom's best interests at heart, as "she told me she had known Tom for four years and spoke as though she thought a great deal of him." On this understanding, Margaret spent much time trying to learn Trainor's perspective on what had happened at Canoe Lake. In particular, she raised concerns regarding the trustworthiness of the Frasers, as she "hadn't much faith in them after reading a letter Mr. Fraser sent to my brother-in-law." Inquiring with Trainor about a 250 dollar loan Tom had made to the Frasers to buy canoes, Margaret was told that Tom had reported in the spring that he had been repaid, although in small amounts.

Like Margaret, Trainor did not have much respect for the Frasers. Trainor's assessment of Shannon Fraser was "the meanest man she ever saw and that her Father detested him." Similarly, Trainor informed Margaret that

> Tom didn't like Mr. Fraser, as he hadn't a good principle. She said that he was intending to leave there in a week or so, and that he didn't want them to know where he was going, as they were so curious about everything. She said that he had warned her not to put anything in her letters that she wouldn't care to have them read, as they always seemed to know his business. He said he didn't know whether they opened his letters in the office or whether they read them after he had opened them, as he used to leave them in his overcoat pocket.

Trainor also told Margaret that Shannon had acted peculiarly with the instructions about how to handle Thomson's remains. Reporting what she learned from Trainor later, Margaret stated, "The telegram which my brother [George] sent with the directions telling what to do with the body,

Mr. Fraser received and didn't let on to anyone. She said she couldn't understand why he wanted to keep that to himself."

The negative perceptions of Shannon Fraser's worth reported by Trainor were certainly instrumental in shaping Margaret's thinking about how her brother might have died. She confessed, "Sometimes I wonder if the man did do anything to harm Tom. I suppose it is wicked to think such a thing, but if anyone did harm him, it was for the little money they could pocket."

Only two months after Tom Thomson's corpse had been discovered, the Thomson family's patience with Shannon Fraser was at its limit. In mid-September 1917, Tom Harkness asked Fraser some pointed, if not openly hostile, questions:

> In your letter to me Aug. 7th you claimed to have paid Mr. Rowe $5.00 and Dickson $3.50 for finding Tom[']s body. Tonight you send receipt from Rowe for $5.00 and from Dickson $10.00. Then Dr. MacCallum told you to send the account for finding Tom to him which you did and he paid you. We do not understand this. Why should you send any account to anyone out of the family and why did you not let me know that you collected from Dr. MacCallum [sic].

While the discrepancies in charges related to searching for Tom were troubling, they took on an even worse hue when considered along with unresolved questions about debts that Fraser might owe the estate. Harkness notes that "you told Geo. Thomson that you owed Tom a small amount but you have not given me any information about it." Harkness also gave no indication of Trainor's claim that Fraser had repaid Tom for financing a purchase of canoes. Instead, he challenged Fraser, asking bluntly, "Did you pay Tom for the canoes he bought for you and when [sic]."

As his letter progressed, Harkness's temper increased. His manner moves from businesslike objectivity to aggressive accusation. Certainly, his frustrations in dealing with Fraser were becoming more explicit. He wrote:

Surely Tom had some personal property. Had he no truck or grip or clothes except what you showed Geo Thomson and how do you account for Tom only having .60 cts when found [sic]. I know what he drew from the bank when he was away, and he was guiding a few weeks and no doubt was paid for it and where do you suppose his money went to [sic]. I tell you frankly Mr. Fraser I am suspicious that you are not dealing square and I hope you will be able to give a satisfactory explanation of everything.

Harkness does not indicate what he will do if Fraser is not able to provide a satisfying response to all of his questions.

The same day Harkness was writing Fraser, Trainor was writing another letter to Harkness. She informed him of much of the same information she had discussed with Margaret, providing more details than Margaret communicated to MacCallum. Trainor noted that "Tom said this spring while at our house that he had loaned Fraser $250.00 for canoes, but that he had got it all back but in little bits though." Despite the repayment of the debt, Trainor felt that the Frasers had treated Tom poorly. "I do not think Frasers deserve one thing. Tom no doubt was paying his board well, supplying fish work & etc.... Tom ploughed and planted their garden & ploughed Larry Dixon's [sic] garden too." Meanwhile, the Frasers "were charging him a $ a day for his board when he could have got it anywhere for $4 [a week?]. You see the Frasers were money grabbing as usual but it will all come back to them."

Trying to establish just how greedy Fraser was, Trainor opined, "It was awful of Shannon Fraser to charge cartage on the casket. When Tom the day he was drowned helped to cadge a boat for Shannon to rent." Concerning any property of Tom's that might remain at Mowat Lodge, Trainor stated bluntly that if the family did not vigourously pursue its return, "Shan will sell the things & keep the money." Once again, as she had in her previous letter to Harkness, she suggested that the Frasers' greed would generate its proper response, reassuring him, "Never mind they'll get it yet."

As she had with Margaret Thomson, Trainor noted others' opinions to back up her own negative assesment of Shannon. She wrote that "Mark

Robinson the Ranger hates him." Even Tom, she stated, had had his differences with the Frasers, leaving the lodge in 1915 because he was "dissatisfied." According to Trainor, however, Tom might have had difficulty with a number of people around Canoe Lake. "Tom did not care for Martin Blecher."

Along with her apparent dislike for several of the most visible Canoe Lake residents, Trainor closes her letter by revealing that she continues to think of the dead man. "I suppose Tom would be greened if he knew all now." However Tom might have perceived the situation, it certainly seems that many of Tom's friends and family were upset.

The confusion surrounding the estate and Fraser's obligations to it was still unresolved by November, four months after Thomson's death. Shannon had not sent Tom's remaining personal effects to Harkness, nor had he explained his inconsistent claims regarding money he paid out to the searchers.

Money issues aside, Harkness was even more chagrined with rumours coming out of Canoe Lake about Tom's death. One of Tom's friends, J.W. Beatty, who led the work to build a memorial cairn at Canoe Lake, had heard from Fraser that Tom had likely committed suicide. Confounded, Harkness blurts with exasperation to Dr. MacCallum, "I cannot for the life of me understand how he claiming to be a friend of Tom's can so easily swallow all Fraser bunk." As Harkness describes, "I've thought the thing over from every viewpoint and the more I think of it the more fully I am convinced that Tom had no hand in taking his life." In his assessment, "Tom was one who had a high moral sense of duty to his fellow man and [Beatty] must know perfectly that he had nothing to run away from." Sure as he was of Tom's character, the rumours said more about the people feeding them than they did about Tom. As Harkness notes, "It makes me sore to think Fraser who claimed to be such a friend of Tom's would make all those suggestions."

Something about the rumours of Tom committing suicide fed doubts in Harkness's mind, however. Could the doctor and coroner have been mistaken in their assessment? Perhaps hoping to better understand the rumours that were circulating, Harkness told MacCallum that he intended to contact the coroner who had ruled on Tom's death to ask him about "letters said to be produced at the enquiry," almost certainly by Fraser.

For his part, Fraser was likely beginning to feel hemmed in by the number of people seeking information about his treatment of Tom's estate. On November 11, he told Dr. MacCallum that he had bought Tom's two canoes at Canoe Lake, and that the Thomson family had told him to subtract payment for the men who searched for Tom out of the price of the canoes. As the family was providing this money, Fraser was returning $14.30 that MacCallum had paid him for this purpose, after subtracting $3.20 for the cement and carrying charges related to building a memorial cairn at Canoe Lake. There were no labour charges, Fraser adds, as all of the men contributing work "were only to [sic] glad to do so."

MacCallum forwarded Fraser's letter to Harkness, pointing out the difference between the amount Fraser had requested from Harkness to compensate the searchers and the amount he had returned to MacCallum. Recognizing that some of Tom's effects were still unaccounted for, MacCallum adds that Beatty would contact Fraser for more information.

In December, Tom's brother George became aware of rumours that had been circulating in Canoe Lake. His response was similar to Harkness's. On December 23, George wrote MacCallum to thank him for his efforts in mounting an exhibition of fifty of Tom's paintings at Toronto's Arts and Letters Club. George's discussion of his brother's art is a brief segue into what seems his real intent in writing MacCallum. He related that a few weeks earlier he had heard that the coroner's conclusion was that Tom's death was a suicide. The evidence which swayed the coroner's decision was apparently provided by Shannon and Annie Fraser. If there was any suspicion of suicide, George stated, "[t]here was no intimation of this to me while I was at Canoe Lake." His perspective was that there "is an infinitely greater probability that [Tom] met his death through accident or foul play ... the latter I should deem more probable than suicide."

The idea of his brother committing suicide was "absolutely unthinkable," according to George, and he proceeded to outline the reasons for his thinking. He noted that "in Tom's case a very material recognition of his ability and a future bright with promise" seemed to indicate optimism rather than woe. Aside from the prospects of Tom's art career affecting his outlook, George's letter indicates speculation circulating that Tom had committed suicide over a love interest, namely Winnie Trainor. This was as equally implausible to George as the idea that Tom had killed himself in frustration over his painting. He believed that Tom's "relations with the Trainor girl [wouldn't] have much bearing upon the case." George's assessment was that Trainor would have likely had a limited influence on Tom's thinking. He noted with a hint of superiority that he had spent a few hours in her company, and that "even in that short time I formed a pretty fairly accurate estimate of her worth and attractions."

Given the absence of evidence to support the gossip that Tom had committed suicide, George was left trying to understand why Fraser would circulate such an idea. The only reason George could offer was that Fraser had possibly read a newspaper article mentioning Tom might have been the victim of foul play. Fearing that he would be a suspect, George believed that Fraser might be "twisting little incidents innocent enough ... into some kind of evidence supporting suicide." This he might be doing to "throw off any suspicion of foul play against himself." In conclusion, George suggests to MacCallum, "I wouldn't put any faith whatever in his word."

Becoming more incensed as he considered the suicide gossip, George wrote Fraser two days after writing MacCallum. Adding to the information he had told MacCallum, George stated that the coroner's finding of suicide was based "on evidence soley [sic] [given] by you and Mrs Fraser." In light of the Frasers' claims of friendship with Tom, George insisted, it was especially surprising that they would "turn round and seek to place upon his name a stain which will be difficult if not impossible to wipe out. His most virulent enemy could not have conceived a scheme to do him a more lasting injury."

Unfortunately, there was little that George could do other than to call Fraser to account for his actions. He did indicate that he was aware of Fraser's dubious, overlapping requests for compensation from Tom Harkness and Dr. MacCallum, implying that Fraser's reputation was already sullied. Noting that Fraser's legal obligations to the estate were not yet satisfied, George reminded Fraser that all of Tom's belongings should be sent to Harkness, the administrator of Tom's estate. Adding embarassment, George also reminded Fraser that he had not yet provided Harkness with information regarding how much was in Tom's account at Mowat Lodge when he died, money which was owed to the estate.

George's letter certainly compelled a response. On December 29, Shannon produced two letters: one to George Thomson and one to Dr. MacCallum. Differences between the two letters suggest that they were actually written by two different people, although both are signed in Shannon's name. Comparison with the grammar, spelling, and vocabulary of other letters signed by Shannon suggests that he wrote the letter to MacCallum, while someone else — likely Annie — wrote George in her husband's name.

The letter directed to George expresses the Frasers' "great shock" at his claims, informing him that "as sincere friends of Tom's, it hurt us not a little that you, his brother, should accuse us of desecrating his memory." The letter's author states clearly that "at no time was there a suggestion of suicide advanced by any of those giving evidence [to the coroner] & the verdict as given was 'death due to drowning.'" The author says that the Frasers are "grieved indeed that you should be labouring under such misapprehensions." As the coroner did not reach a conclusion of suicide, rendering George's anger unjustified, the letter's author advises that "you might at least do us the justice of verifying such reports before wantonly accusing us, his friends, of insincerity."

Aside from attempting to set the record straight regarding what was presented at the inquest, the letter also tries to close the outstanding issue of any debts between the Frasers and the estate. The author notes that Dr. MacCallum's cheque had been returned and that the outstanding debts were covered by the sale of Tom's canoes to the Frasers. Beyond covering the debts, there was four dollars remaining for Thomson's estate, which was enclosed with the letter. Additionally, with regard to the "few remaining personal effects," they would be forwarded to Mr. Harkness. By way of explanation, the letter adds that they were "held subject to your wishes."

The closing paragraph of the letter betrays a different perspective on what the Frasers might have been thinking almost six months after Tom died. The author suggests to George that "all the debt of kindness was not confined to any one side," and that "if you would look back over the events that took place following his death, you couldn't help but admit that we gave much of our time & money to make things comfortable for all concerned. Yourself included." The Frasers' claim to have been acting with genuine care for Tom would seem to be supported by the fact that they had sent flowers to the family for the Owen Sound funeral, as noted in Margaret Thomson's correspondence with her sister Minnie.

The letter to Dr. MacCallum, which was surely written by Shannon himself, struck a similar tone. While the claims are consistent with those made in the letter to George Thomson, the letter does contain a few additional tidbits of information. Fraser laments, "I am just in receipt of a letter from Geo Thomson accusing me & Mrs Fraser of telling the corner [sic] that poor Tom committed suicide." He explains that his wife was not at the inquest and never spoke to the coroner. He adds, "No one ever mentioned such a thing as suicide at the inquest," and that "I thought so much of Tom & would be the very last to even mention such a thing." Fraser does indicate that others doubted the coroner's conclusion, noting, "Several people have said to me it was no accident & I always assured them it was an accident." In his defence, he suggests that MacCallum can "ask Mr McDonald or Mr Beatty if we didn't do all we could to say Tom's death was an accident."

Shannon's letter to MacCallum calls into question George's judgment and behaviour, particularly in light of the Frasers' work. While stating how he is "feeling very badly" about George's claims, Fraser suggests that "Geo Thomson ought to be the last one to say anything as he came up here & did not do anything to find Tom's body did not even get men to grapple went back home & left everything for me to do." This, he proposes, led people around Canoe Lake to gossip. "The people were talking about him wondering if he had no money," Fraser confides.

In mid-February of 1918, Tom's sister Elizabeth (Tom Harkness's wife) wrote MacCallum to update him on developments. The Frasers had finally sent Harkness a package of Tom's property that remained at Canoe Lake, including hats, a "worn out" suit, Hudson's Bay blankets, a single pair of underwear, four pairs of socks, pails, plates, cups, and two pipes. A pair of snowshoes remained unaccounted for, however.

Despite having this issue more or less resolved, dealing with the Frasers had left as low an impression on Elizabeth as it had on her husband. She provides a brief assessment of Fraser's vexing behaviour. She notes that when "George was at Canoe Lake the first time, Fraser showed him your telegram offering to pay expenses." George, however, could not accept such kindness, and instructed Fraser that all bills should be submitted to them. Nonetheless, Elizabeth points out, Fraser sent a bill to MacCallum.

She also mentions that when George was on "his first visit to Canoe Lake," the Frasers had shown him Tom's account with them, including the things he had purchased for his fateful canoe trip. Based on the Frasers' report that Tom had left with goods such as cold meat, raw potatoes, and pancake flour, the family felt assured that "he had met in with a party" and would likely return fine. Based on later information, it would seem, the family learned that Tom did not have these goods with him, leading to confusion. As Elizabeth confides, "Why Fraser put up the bread & butter yarn puzzles me." Fraser's miscommunication and excuses led her to conclude that "his whole story from beginning to end is a muddle of contradictions."

What eluded her was why Fraser was behaving this way. "He is," she observed, "certainly ignorant and without principle." She, too, had heard that Fraser was gossiping about the possibility that Tom had committed suicide. "I feel such a horror of him to think he deliberately undermined all Tom's lovely character at a blow when he was not here to defend himself," she wrote. Although she had wanted to go to Canoe Lake to confront the rumours, the "family did not want me to go alone so things were just allowed to drift."

The decision to let things "drift" seems to be how issues between Tom Thomson's estate and the Frasers were left. Since the 1990s, the Thomson family has not deposited any further letters exchanged between the family and the Frasers with any archives. The Frasers never spoke out publicly about their involvement in the affair.

At some time during the fall of 1917, the family's perspective on Winnie Trainor changed. Margaret pressed Trainor for information at their only face-to-face meeting, and although Trainor was instrumental in helping the family manage the initial exhumation arrangements, rather quickly ended communication with her. George suggested he had taken away a dim impression of Winnie after spending only a few hours with her. Thomson family members would later report that based on her letters, they had come to understand Trainor did not have a full and confident grasp of her mental faculties. This suggestion provides an intriguing rationale for why the Thomson family might have sought to distance Trainor.

Elements that later gained traction in speculation about Thomson's death can be found in the claims and counterclaims offered during the fall of 1917. As the immediate concerns regarding Tom Thomson's estate were resolved, speculation regarding the case would become increasingly shaped by the hostility and suspicion that remained between the Frasers and Thomson's family, friends, and Dr. MacCallum. Suggestions that Thomson's death was anything but accidental would certainly increase. That Fraser might have had a much more active role in Thomson's death would come to dominate storytelling, and over the decades his suspicious dealings with the estate and Thomson's friends and family would come to be seen as signs of guilt. Exactly what Fraser might have been guilty of, however, would become only more confused.

Clearly, during the fall of 1917, some clarity was emerging about Tom Thomson's last days. Attempts to resolve Tom's estate raised as many questions as they answered, however. Over time, claims and counterclaims, gossip and speculation served to further complicate what understanding had emerged in the months following Tom's death. What had been established as fact was suggested to be dubious, and new, alternative "facts" began to be introduced. This problem was to become more vexing as time passed and new correspondents entered the discussion.

PART TWO

THE MANY MYTHS OF THOMSON'S DEATH

5

SIGNS OF FOUL PLAY

I thought I would jot down a few of my remembrances because
legend fills a vacuum and masquerades as truth.
— R.P. LITTLE, "SOME RECOLLECTIONS OF TOM THOMSON ... ", *CULTURE*, 1955

SOON AFTER TOM THOMSON's death, a number of his friends and supporters offered fond remembrances of the man, along with lamentations for the loss to Canadian art. Thomson was still not a widely known or respected artist outside of a closed circle of people, primarily living in Toronto, who followed contemporary painting. As discussed in chapter 2, Thomson would rise to wider attention with the successes of the Group of Seven painters, who came together in 1920 to exhibit what they promoted as a new, distinct Canadian vision. These artists would point to Thomson as a "lost brother," an inspiration for their painting style as well as the imagery they drew upon. With the Group's ascent to international attention, along with their credit paid to Thomson's work, his reputation as an important Canadian artist likewise grew.

Although a number of art journals had included lengthy articles about Thomson soon after his passing, a decade after his death the details of his biography were not widely known. Blodwen Davies was a Toronto author and journalist who had an interest in the Group of Seven's work. The positive reception of Thomson's and the Group's work in Europe during the late 1920s inspired her imagination. Sometime during late 1920s, she conceived of writing the life story of Tom Thomson.

In 1930, Toronto's Ryerson Press published Davies's biography of Thomson, entitled *Paddle and Palette: The Story of Tom Thomson*. The book was the first published biography of the artist. It drew attention to Thomson's lack of formal art training and his love of the natural world, and explored his painting style.

In *Paddle and Palette*, Davies devotes a mere three brief paragraphs to Thomson's death:

> At noon on July 8th [Thomson] set out across Canoe Lake with his supplies for another jaunt into the wilderness. By three o'clock that afternoon his empty canoe was seen floating on the Lake.
>
> It was several days later before his body was found. During that time his friends could not believe that Thomson was dead. They hoped and believed that he was lost in the woods.
>
> He was buried first of all near the spot where he was found, but shortly afterwards his body was removed to Leith where it lies in the graveyard of the little old Presbyterian church which he had attended as a boy.

Davies's brief comments certainly don't give the impression that any controversy surrounded Thomson's demise. However, as work on the book progressed, Davies became aware that some of the stories about Thomson's life — and regarding his death — were not universally accepted. After the first book was published, she continued to correspond with Thomson's friends and family, eventually learning things that compelled her to write a second, "corrected" volume focusing on Thomson's death. The second book, *A Study of Tom Thomson*, came out five years later in a self-published, short-run edition.

One of the people that Davies contacted was Mark Robinson. Robinson had met Thomson in 1912, while working as an Algonquin Park ranger. He would have regular contact with Thomson until 1915, when he left the area to serve with the Canadian Army in Europe. He returned to work as a ranger during spring 1917, and would lead the search for Thomson. Davies did not likely expect Robinson to provide many new insights into Thomson's art. She was in for a surprise, though. Robinson would, over the course of several letters, offer lengthy reflections on Thomson's creative process. He would also, over the course of decades, become one of the leading proponents of the theory that Tom Thomson had died by foul play.

Robinson responded to Davies's query in March 1930, stating that he and "Thomas Thompson [*sic*]" were friends. His letter includes a number of stories intended to give insights into Thomson's personality. Robinson opens his letter by stating that "Tom was a study at all times." He explains:

> One day he was Jovial and Jolly ready for a frolic of any kind so long as it was clean and honest in its purpose. At times he appeared quite melancholy and defeated in manner. At such times he would suddenly as it were awaken and be almost angry in appearance and action.

Despite Thomson's moodiness, Robinson spoke highly of him. He informed Davies that Thomson "loved to camp and guide and many a sick friend Tom paddled around fishing and growing strong and back to health again and would take no remuneration of any kind." Additionally, he noted that "Tom was an excellent woodsman, canoeman, swimmer and guide."

Thomson's good sense of humour was one of the things that Robinson recalled. He wrote that in the summer of 1917, some of the locals had been trying to catch a particularly large, elusive trout that lived below the Joe Lake Dam. On the morning he died, Thomson had decided to play a little trick on Robinson. Having failed to catch the trout that morning, Thomson's plan was to catch a similar fish in order to deceive Robinson that he had bested him in their little competition. Robinson doesn't mention speaking to Thomson that day, however, so it is unclear how he knew about Thomson's intentions.

Suspecting that Davies was interested in Thomson's painting, Robinson relates several stories attesting to Thomson's desire to faithfully reproduce the specific colours and textures of the park's scenery:

> One day we were looking at a white Birch tree and I said Tom it would be rather hard to get all those old snarles [sic] in with the Brush. Not at all he answered, and a few days later he showed me a canvas, almost perfect in copy of the Living tree. On another occasion we were looking at an old Pine stump that was partially covered with moss and the grey colour of the wood was of many shades of grey. [H]e looked at it and said there [sic] one of the hardest things to paint in the woods, see those different shades of grey. [An] artist must get them in perfect or the sketch is a fraud on the Public there aren't more than two or three in every hundred who will notice it but it's not true to nature and imperfect notes destroy the soul of music so does imperfect colour destroy the soul of the canvas. I mention these facts just to show the Honest purpose of Tom's views on the different things in life.

Robinson also suggests that Thomson's desire to truthfully capture the park environment led him to an unusual experiment in the spring of 1917. As he described it to Davies:

> The spring before his untimely death he painted a canvas a day showing the various stages of the advancing spring and summer. He was very fond of this work and one day dashing into my cabin he said may I have my records on those walls for the summer. I assured him that he could but death stepped in and they were never hung. I saw a great number of these canvasses they were good. I think Tom's Brothers and sisters got most of them.

Robinson repeatedly refers to the works Thomson produced, even those made *en plein air* at Canoe Lake (which are quite likely the only works of Thomson's that he would ever see), as canvases. Although this might merely reflect the loose use of technical terminology by someone unschooled in art (Thomson only ever painted in the park on small, easily portable boards), it does indicate that a degree of discrimination is required in interpreting Robinson's testimony.

Along with stories about Thomson's life, Robinson provides a detailed narrative of the events surrounding Thomson's death. Outside what he had recorded in his daily diary during July 1917, this is the first written account provided by Robinson. The degree of detail he provided Davies merits lengthy quotation:

[Thomson] went to Mowat Lodge or the Trainor cottage got a few supplies and left to get the big fish at one of the little Lakes.

J. Shannon Fraser ... was at the lake as Tom left and was the last man (as far as the Public know) to see Tom alive he left at about 12:50 pm and at the inquest it came out that Martin and Bessie Blecher American German tourists with cottage at Canoe Lake ... found Tom's canoe floating not 3/4 of a mile from where he started out from the Trainor cottage at about 3 p.m. an east wind was blowing and this canoe could not have been there under ordinary conditions. [T]hey did not report finding the canoe until the following morning when the canoe was brought in from behind Little Wapomeo Island. Then J. S. Fraser reported the matter to me and at once I passed the report on to Supt. Geo W. Bartlett who like myself refused to believe Tom was in the lake but might be lost in the woods with a broken leg he ordered a search to be made and I kept it up until his body was found by Geo Rowe Guide of Canoe Lake PO Ont and Dr. Howland of Toronto in Canoe Lake not far from a rocky point on the west shore of Canoe Lake and about equal distance between the two Wapomeo Islands.

I assisted Roy Dixon undertaker of Sprucedale Ontario to take the body from the water in the presence of Dr. Howland there were no marks on the body except a slight bruise over the left eye his fishing line was wound several times around his left ankle and broken off there was no sign of the rod his provisions and kit bag were in the front end of the Canoe when found. [T]he lake was not rough. We burried [sic] his remains in the little cemetary [sic] at Canoe Lake, Martin Blecher Sr. reading the Anglican funeral service at the grave. Later his remains were taken up and went to Owen Sound for burial. Dr. Ranney of North Bay conducted what inquest was held. Tom was said to have been drowned. It may be quite true but the mystery remains.

Robinson does not make clear what, exactly, the mystery he refers to might be. Logic would seem to suggest he was questioning the verdict of accidental death by drowning. He does indicate that he believes that a number of people who were around Canoe Lake in the summer of 1917 might have known more about Thomson's death than they reported. Robinson kindly suggests "a few friends" that Davies might find useful to contact for her book. Among them he includes Shannon Fraser, but warns Davies, "If Fraser will tell the truth much could be got from him but weigh well his remarks." He also suggests that Davies could "interview Martin and Bessie Blecher but again be carefull [sic] They possibly know more about Tom's sad end than any other person [sic]."

Robinson's letter certainly piqued Davies's curiousity. His revelations regarding the Blechers and the intimation that Thomson might not have died from accidental causes propelled her to more doggedly pursue information. She sent Robinson a list of precise and focused questions about Thomson, focusing on the search for his body:

Q: *Did the Bletchers [sic] aid in the search for Thomson?*
A: They did on the lake. They did not search in the woods as far as I know.

Q: *Did they make any attempt to direct the search?*
A: No, they were very quiet in every way.

Q: *Do you remember where Thomson went to try to enlist?*
A: Toronto and Kearney.

Q: *Do you remember what the defect was that prevented his enlistment?*
A: I do not but expect it was his feet.

Q: *Was there anything wrong with his heart?*
A: There may have been but I scarcely think so as he could throw up his canoe and go uphill over portages without any trouble.

Q: *How deep was the water in which Thomson was found?*
A: About 30 feet.

Q: *How far was it from shore?*
A: 125 yards.

Q: *Was his fishing rod and line found?*
A: No.

Q: *Do you think it was his own line which was wound around his ankle?*
A: It might have been his own line but not his regular fishing line.

Q: *Did you see a mark on his forehead and if so what was it like?*
A: A slight bruise over the left eye brow [sic].

Q: *Were his paddles found?*
A: One was found tied in his canoe for portaging.

Q: *Was his knife or anything else missing from his person?*
A: Not as far as I know.

Robinson's testimony provides some useful insights into what he recalled happening at Canoe Lake almost thirteen years earlier. He gives no sense of suspicious behaviour on the part of anyone, including the Blechers, despite his suggestion that they they might know more about Thomson's death. He also provides few indications that Thomson had encountered foul play, noting only a "slight bruise" on Thomson's forehead. He notes that Thomson's knife was not missing. The only elements of Robinson's description that seems to record anything out of the ordinary are that Thomson's canoe held only one paddle "tied in," and that fishing line that was not his own was tied around this ankle.

Robinson also related a piece of gossip in addition to answering Davies's list of questions. A friend had told him that Winnifred Trainor claimed to have been engaged to Thomson. "Perhaps so," he offered, "but I did not see anything to indicate more than ordinary friendship."

On May 31, 1931, the *Toronto Star* included information regarding Davies's plans to write a second biography of Thomson. By spring 1931, Davies had corresponded with four of Tom's siblings (two brothers and two sisters), several of Tom's childhood friends, several of his artist peers, and two of his friends from Algonquin Park. The article notes that Davies was hoping to hear from people who knew Thomson during his boyhood and early adult life. The article led a number of Thomson's acquaintances to contact her.

Among comments supplied by these people, two contradictory perceptions of Tom Thomson emerge. Some suggested that he was always happy and friendly, while others remembered him as moody, often finding him quiet, if not morose. Several suggested that Tom had trouble developing a vision for his life, and noted that he struggled to find a path to productive work. A family friend from Tom's school years, who had occasionally gotten drunk with Thomson as an adult, suggested Tom was disappointed with his lot in life and doubted his abilities as an artist. This same man suggested that Thomson seriously considered returning to work in the trades. These depressed feelings would sometimes, the friend claimed, be exacerbated by alcohol consumption.

Two of Tom's siblings suggested that he had a genuine love of fine things — clothes, food, music — while others suggested that he was very happy with the simple trappings of his life in the park, and generous with what money he had, when he had any to spare.

The accounts provided by family and friends are contradictory on several points that have become critical in speculation regarding Tom Thomson's fate.

Two of Thomson's sisters claimed that he had attempted to enlist in the military several times, always unsuccessfully. A man Thomson had served with as an Algonquin Park fire ranger during the summer of 1916 attested, however, that Thomson was critical of Canada's involvement in the war, and stated confidently that Thomson had not tried to enlist.

Davies also received similarly contradictory accounts of Thomson's outdoor skills, such as canoeing and swimming. Several reports of Thomson's boating accidents and risk taking were submitted. Others swore that since he had grown up within walking distance of Georgian Bay, Thomson had been a skilled swimmer since boyhood.

What emerges from these accounts is a richly textured view into a man's life, but the accounts are difficult to reconcile with each other. Was Thomson a sad, self-conscious alcoholic? A happy-go-lucky outdoorsman? Could he have, like most of us, exhibited many different personality traits over the years?

In June 1931, Tom's brother George provided Davies with some very intriguing information. He stated that he had a copy of the coroner's findings from the July 1917 inquest, written in Dr. A.E. Ranney's own hand. George may not have been aware that the coroner did not conduct an autopsy, and that the notes about the body had been provided by Dr. Howland. Regardless, the statement — as transcribed by George Thomson — relates that Mark Robinson identified the corpse as that of Tom Thomson, and describes the clothes found on the corpse. Perhaps the most critical aspect of the affidavit as transcribed by George Thomson reads:

> Head shows marked swelling of face, decomposition has set in, air issuing from mouth. Head has a bruise over left temple as if produced by falling on rock. Examination of body shows no bruises, body greatly swollen, blisters on limbs, putrefaction setting in on surface. There are no signs of any external force having caused death and there is no doubt but that death occurred from drowning.

Based on this information, George tells Davies that he favours the theory that Tom had a fatal accident, although he admits the possibility of foul play. He closes his letter by telling Davies that the Thomson family "would very much deplore any discussion of the matter before the public," as it would likely serve to diminish Tom's reputation.

Only a month earlier, Davies had received a letter from Dr. Ranney, the coroner who conducted the inquest into Tom Thomson's death. Responding to a query from Davies, Ranney checked his notes to refresh his memory (as the events in question dated back fourteen years, the doctor reminded her). Ranney related how Dr. Howland had examined the body (Howland's notes were critical to Ranney, as Thomson's corpse was buried before Ranney arrived in Canoe Lake). Ranney's notes describe a bruise on the body's right temple, caused "no doubt" by the body striking a rock when drowning. Howland's conclusion was drowning, and this view was supported by testimony from six other witnesses at the inquest.

Along with the testimony that Davies was collecting by mail during 1930 and 1931, she also visited Canoe Lake. Her findings compelled her to make an intriguing request of the provincial government.

In July 1931, either Davies or her paramour, Dr. Frederick Banting, spoke to Ontario's attorney general regarding Thomson's death. The issue of opening Thomson's Canoe Lake burial site was broached. Following the conversation, Davies produced an eleven-page summary of what she had learned to lend credibility to her request. This document, it is important to note, was only rediscovered by this author in 2008. It thus merits particular attention. It provides a useful view into what Davies had discovered over the preceding year and sheds light on how her findings emboldened her to seek such radical intervention.

In her submission, Davies recounted some of the stories already described, such as Thomson "painting a record of the weather, one sketch a day, from the middle of April to the middle of June." She also mentions that he approached Mark Robinson near the end of June 1917 to see if he would allow Thomson to hang "ninty-odd [sic] sketches" in the ranger's hut.

Davies described Thomson's last morning as one of relaxed idyll. She stated that "he rose rather late and breakfasted with Mrs. Fraser at Mowatt

[sic] Lodge. He was in good spirits and came in 'freshly shaved, hair brushed and shining.' He sat long at the table, eating and talking in a leisurely way. Then lit a cigarette and wandered out." Thomson and Shannon walked over to Joe Lake portage to try and catch the elusive trout that some of the men had been trying to catch. Unsuccessful, Thomson arrived at his notion to catch a substitute in a prank he would play on Mark Robinson. Returning to Mowat Lodge, Davies reports, Thomson fetched his canoe. She notes:

> He had no bread. Fraser went up to the Lodge got him a loaf and Thomson stowed it away, with a can of corn syrup, under the bow of the canoe. He took no provisions in addition as he did not intend to stay any longer than it took to get the fish....
>
> Thomson left Mowat Lodge dock about twenty-five minutes to one o'clock on Sunday. He paddled down the lake and outside Little Wapomeo Island. There was an unoccupied cottage on the Island. He then passed out of sight into the stretch of water between Little Wapomeo and Big Wapomeo Islands. There his canoe was found and there, nine days later, his body was found. His watch had stopped shortly after one o'clock. It was not ten minutes paddle from Mowatt [sic] Lodge dock to the place where his body was found.

After Thomson's departure, Davies continues, nothing seemed amiss until the following morning,

> when Martin Blecher reported that he had seen a canoe floating between the Islands on Sunday afternoon at three o'clock. He did not report it, he said, as he thought it was a canoe belonging to Colson at the Algonquin Hotel, Joe Lake, which had drifted away from Joe Lake Portage where Colson kept some of his canoes. However, it was Thomson's canoe, which was familiar to all at Canoe Lake. It was painted a peculiar shade of green. Friends of Thomson's immediately recognized the canoe as his. A search was instituted, but none of

Thomson's friends believed Thomson to be drowned. He was a powerful swimmer from boyhood. He had been travelling in a light east wind in a light rain. Mark Robinson tramped the woods for seven days whistling and calling, thinking Thomson had landed on shore and had fallend [sic] and injured himself. The Blecher family alone of all Thomson's acquaintaces [sic] searched the lake from Mowatt [sic] Lodge to Tea Lake Dam, although Thomson's canoe had been found between the Islands near home.

Davies also notes that "bread and can of syrup were found in the canoe." On Monday, July 16, Davies relates, "Dr. Golden [sic] Howland, of Toronto" discovered Thomson's body. Howland was staying at the Little Wapomeo cottage owned by Taylor Statten. Thomson's body had become "entangled" with the doctor's fishing line. He informed the authorities, and the body was towed to Big Wapomeo Island and "anchored there." The coroner in North Bay, Dr. Ranney, was notified, but did not arrive that day.

In the absence of the coroner, Davies explains, Mark Robinson made the decision to remove Thomson's body from the lake the following day. Dr. Howland then conducted an examination. Davies faithfully transcribes the version of Howland's affidavit that she received from the Crown attorney in North Bay.

Returning to her story, Davies reports that an undertaker from Kearney had arrived at Canoe Lake on the Monday night. The next day, he embalmed the body, then it was moved to the mainland and buried "in a sandy spot on the edge of a small hill."

The coroner arrived on the Tuesday night, 9:12 p.m. train. He was likely surprised to discover that the body he was to examine had already been buried, as "he said he had wired his intention to arrive Tuesday. Those in charge of the case at Canoe Lake were unable to find any trace of such a message being filed." The coroner held the inquest in the Blecher home "instead of in the hotel nearby." The Blechers, Davies notes, "were not popular with the community, [and] served beer and cigars to those who attended." Davies does not record who attended the inquest, but relates that Mark Robinson elected to paddle across the lake to fetch George Rowe when he discovered that Rowe had not been summoned to the meeting.

Davies, referring to the meeting as "the trial," states, "nothing came out ... of the quarrels between Martin Blecher [Jr. and Thomson]." The quarrels, she reports, "are said to have been violent." Apparently, Thomson had written Arthur Lismer about the fights, but the letters had "not been preserved." Although she does not state what the quarrels might have concerned, she claims that "Thomson was unhappy about the war." She states that Thomson's friends, such as Dr. MacCallum, had been placing "a great deal of pressure on him, some in order to induce him to enlist, others to prevent him from doing so." Martin Blecher Jr., Davies claims, had escaped the draft, going so far as to evade an agent of the U.S. War Department who came to Canoe Lake searching for him.

It was Blecher who was "believed responsible for spreading a report of suicide," Davies offers. "He repeated this statement as late as August of 1931," she relates, when he "told Dr. Harry Ebbs that Thomson's legs were bound together with a piece of rubber. This statement was untrue. He also stated that the body was cramped and rigid. This was also untrue."

Summarizing what she believed the evidence to be, Davies concludes that the inquest failed to explain what she took as "obvious": that "Thomson was struck over the head with a weapon which inflicted a bruise four inches long on his temple and which caused bleeding from the ear. The bruise could only have been caused while Thomson lived." Additionally, the inquest did not establish how Thomson's body could have remained submerged for so long, when "the waters of Canoe Lake are mild enough for swimming by a children's camp all July and August." The body, she notes, "was bloated to twice its natural size." Her explanation is that the body might have come up earlier and "was sunk a second time." Supporting this idea, she mentions that "there was a fishing line tied around one ankle."

Although Davies does not indicate from whom she gathered this information, it can be assumed that her primary source regarding Thomson's corpse and the conduct of the inquest was Mark Robinson.

Compounding her concerns about an inadequate inquest, Davies explains that the Thomson family had commissioned an undertaker to go to Canoe Lake "with a metal casket to exhume the body and carry it to Owen Sound." The undertaker arrived some time between 9:15 p.m. and midnight. Shannon Fraser drove the man and his casket to the cemetery, and arranged a signal that the undertaker could use to indicate when he wanted Fraser to return for him. According to Davies, Fraser "recalls that he was not long back at the hotel before he saw the signal and at once returned to take up the casket again."

The late hour of the undertaker's arrival might explain why park ranger Mark Robinson was not immediately notified. According to Davies, Robinson did not become aware of the undertaker's visit until rising "at dawn" and, on visiting the grave, "discovered that the man's job was done," and that Thomson's corpse was "sealed in the metal casket." However, Davies states, Robinson "does not believe that the body was ever disturbed." The only rationale she provides to support this perception is that "the flowers that had been laid on the grave at the funeral were not moved." Apparently, Robinson's conclusions were shared widely, as "none of those concerned in the episode believe that Thomson was ever disturbed."

Working toward her request for the attorney general, Davies states that the "burying place at Canoe Lake is not a consecrated cemetery. There have been four or five buried there; there is only one small enclosure with a couple of grave[s] in it. Thomson's grave was outside the enclosure." Given the status of his burial place, one argument against an exhumation was removed.

Opening the Canoe Lake burial site, Davies reasons, "would lay at rest the rumors which are persistent in the north ... that he still lives there." Even the Thomson family, Davies suggests, who had been hesitant to disturb Tom's mother by pursuing action earlier, "now regret his removal to Leith and would be glad to know he had not been disturbed."

She argues that opening the burial site, and re-examining Thomson's remains if they were found, might also prove a boon to the Thomson family as well as many of Tom's friends. "Any action which would prove that Thomson died as the result of foul play would remove the stigma of suicide from his name," Davies notes. Offering a simple but persuasive logic, she suggests:

> Those who know Thomson could not believe that it was suicide … if he had been in a mood to take his own life, he would have gone off on a trip into the wilderness and been heard of no more. It is utterly at variance with Thomson's character to suppose, that even in a fit of depression, he would have tried to commit suicide ten minutes from his own camp.

Davies did not have to wait long for a response. Less than a month after submitting her request, Deputy Attorney General E. Bayly suggested that "[a]s all this happened over fourteen … years ago … exhuming the body would not disclose anything definite."

Bayly may have misunderstood Davies's argument, or chosen to reinterpret it. He argues that exhumation of a corpse after more than a decade would not offer any new information. Davies was not asking for the body to be exhumed, however; she wanted the original burial site to be reopened in order to confirm if Thomson's corpse had been moved. If a body was discovered there, some kind of investigation might be merited. What Bayly's response implies is that regardless of where Thomson's body might be, Davies had not indicated enough solid evidence existed to reconsider the coroner's findings or to initiate a police investigation of Thomson's death.

Although her effort to interest the government had not been successful, Davies's concerns did resonate with Eric Brown, director of the National Gallery of Canada. In September 1931 he offered his support for her efforts to reopen the burial site. He also provided some advice about the best avenues of approach to the government. His suggestion was to make a "personal and authoritative approach to the attorney general and afterwards perhaps to the C[anadian] M[ounted] P[olice]." This method would possibly "get something going without publicity."

By the time Davies received Brown's advice, of course, she had already been informed that the attorney general's office was not eager to act on her concerns. Brown's position, that "the importance to Canadian art of clearing up the whole situation is extreme," might have served to buoy her desire to pursue the case, regardless of the government's response. She continued to collect information related to the artist's life and death.

Three years later, Davies was still investigating the matter. In April 1934, George Thomson provided Davies answers to several questions. She had mentioned Mark Robinson's claim that Tom had offered him the now-famous *The West Wind* canvas. George dismissed the idea. First, he clarified that to his knowledge, his brother had never painted on canvas at Canoe Lake. Second, he offered that "to me it is too unlikely a thing to happen that Robinson should have been offered so huge a picture. A small picture or sketch perhaps, but not so large a painting."

Addressing the issue of where Tom's goods had been found, George stated, "Tom was at Mowat Lodge when he was drowned. His sketches and other possessions were there." This was also where Tom had collected provisions for his final canoe trip, George reminded Davies.

Finally, George included a short statement that he had Tom's "watch and it stopped at 12:14." He did not, unfortunately, indicate whether this was a response to a particular question posed by Davies, or if it was information he was volunteering because he thought might it be of interest to her. In 1931, Davies submitted to the attorney general that Thomson's watch had stopped "shortly after one o'clock." Davies may have been trying to confirm this information.

Having spent five years investigating, Davies had come to the conclusion that much of the story of Tom Thomson's death had not been told, leading her to self-publish *A Study of Tom Thomson*.

Many of the stories that Davies told about Thomson in 1935 were similar to those included her 1930 book. The major difference was the addition of new elements to the story of Thomson's death.

Her discussion of Thomson's activities on the morning of July 8, 1917, covered much the same territory as that discussed in *Paddle and Palette*. In *A Study of Tom Thomson*, Davies described how Thomson rowed his canoe up to the dock at Mowat Lodge and fetched a loaf of bread from Shannon Fraser. Setting the scene, Davies continued, "The morning had turned grey. There was a light east wind blowing, with a drizzle of rain. Thomson bid the crowd that had gathered on the dock a gay farewell and in a very engaging mood set out on his mission to carry out a practical joke on a fellow fisherman."

This brief excerpt includes two important differences from Davies's 1930 account of Thomson's departure. In her 1935 text, she described the weather on the morning of Thomson's disappearance. More important, in the second book she indicated that multiple people (whether at the dock or in the immediate vicinity) witnessed Thomson's departure. Her description of the last sighting of Thomson also indicates her impression that he was in a positive, optimistic mood the day that he disappeared.

In A *Study of Tom Thomson*, Davies also provided much more information regarding Thomson's route across the lake than had been recorded from any witness:

> A short distance down the lake [from Mowat Lodge] and separated from the mainland by only a narrow channel, is Little Wapomeo Island, the property of Taylor Statten, who had a cottage on it. At the time the cottage was empty. The channel between the island and the mainland was choked with drowned timber, so Thomson paddled around to the east of Little Wap, then passed out of sight of Mowatt [sic] Lodge and the cottages round about it. He swung in across the channel between Little Wap and its sister island, Big Wapomeo, apparently with the intention of hugging the main shore until he came to the portaging place by which he would cross over into one of the little lakes where the big trout were to be found.

Unfortunately, Davies does not indicate whose testimony her 1935 account of Thomson's departure or the route he took across the lake was based upon. The information does not appear in any of her correspondence that is held by Library and Archives Canada.

In 1930, Davies's narrative moved from Thomson's disappearance directly to his burial; there was no indication of how Thomson had died. In 1935, however, she rhetorically reconstructed Thomson's murder:

Who met Tom Thomson on that stretch of grey lake, screened from all eyes, that July noon? Who was it struck him a blow across the right temple — and was it done with the thin edge of a paddle blade? — that sent the blood spurting from his ear? Who watched him crumple up and topple over the side of the canoe and sink slowly out of sight without a struggle?

Of course, Davies presents her queries as if these events are agreed-upon facts: that Thomson *did* meet someone on the lake, that he *was* struck, that blood spurted from his ear, and that his body sank without struggle.

Davies's storytelling strategy proves problematic again when she turns to narrating the discovery of Thomson's corpse. She describes how Dr. Howland took his daughter out troll fishing on Canoe Lake on the morning of Monday, July 16. About 9:00 a.m., Davies states, the child "felt something heavy on the end of her line." The doctor took the line from the child, and as he saw a body emerging from the depths, opted to let it sink back down before notifying guides George Rowe and Larry Dickson, who would later secure the body.

In relating this information, Davies didn't state whether she was recounting evidence or exercising creative licence. Her correspondence from the period does not provide any indication of a source for this detailed information.

That it took eight days for Thomson's body to be discovered, and apparently only by chance, reinforced Davies's suspicions. She asked her readers: "Did Thomson's body take eight days to rise in a shallow lake in the middle of July?" The answer was, of course, that this did not make sense. If the body did not respond to nature how we would expect it to, then clearly some critical element was missing from our knowledge, she implies.

For a description of Thomson's corpse, she turned to the affidavit from Dr. Howland that the Nipissing District Crown attorney's office had supplied her with in 1931. She stated that Howland's document noted Thomson's body had a four-inch bruise on its right temple, air issuing from its mouth, and bleeding from the right ear. Aside from the bruise, the body had "no other sign of external marks visible."

Davies suggested that the decision about Thomson's cause of death was clearly flawed. She noted, "Seven witnesses testified to what they knew of the case and death was declared to be due to 'accidental drowning.' No one remarked that only a living body could be bruised or could bleed, or that Thomson's lungs were filled with air, not with water."

Despite shocking suggestions that a horrible lapse in judgment and prosecution of the law had taken place in the case of Thomson's death, *A Study of Tom Thomson* received very little attention. Davies had published a biography of Thomson with an established commercial publisher only five years previously. Publishers were not likely interested in a second biography of Thomson so soon after a first, particularly when the only difference was that it contained unsubstantiated claims about Thomson having been murdered. Davies opted to self-publish her work in a volume of 450 copies. As promotion of the work was difficult and costly, it generated paltry sales. It certainly had little influence on thinking about Tom Thomson or his death for many years.

Thomson's death was, nonetheless, a topic that amateur investigators would regularly return to over the following decades.

During the 1940s, prolific historian and secondary school teacher Edwin Guillet turned his attention to the Thomson case. As part of a series of essays about important Canadian legal cases, Guillet prepared an assessment of what he believed to be the most plausible cause of death for Tom Thomson. While Guillet only produced five typewritten copies of his essay, his work helps to reveal how thinking about Thomson's death evolved over the years after the publication of Davies's second book.

Similar to Davies, Guillet doubted the conclusion reached at the inquest. He observed that as Thomson had the reputation of being "the best canoeist, fisherman, and guide in the district, [Thomson] would hardly seem to be a fit subject for accidental drowning — even if all the signs did not suggest a very different conclusion." If this result was incorrect, Guillet offered, the condition of Thomson's corpse "suggests two causes of death ... [t]he first is foul play, and the second suicide during temporary mental derangement."

Murder certainly seemed a more likely explanation than suicide, according to Guillet. Although he noted that Thomson was "moody and morose at times," this was "usually when he was in the city, not in the wilds." Suicide might be explained as a case of "[s]udden derangement ... but it seems unlikely."

To support his interpretation of foul play, Guillet turns to the bruise on Thomson's temple, which seemed to have produced the bleeding from Thomson's ear. Given the fact that "blood does not flow from a dead body," Guillet offered that "the blow and the bleeding occurred before death."

The belief Thomson had been murdered was held by some of Thomson's friends, Guillet claims. Some people had even tried to answer the question of whether Thomson had "any enemies with an overpowering motive to kill him." Guillet recounts how Sir Frederick Banting — who had provided some assistance to Blodwen Davies's research regarding Thomson — visited Algonquin Park to investigate the case, but discovered "little more than an old forest ranger's statement that Thomson was murdered; and when asked to give details the old man did not choose to do so." Guillet also noted that Thomson's supervisor at Grip, A.H. Robson, had apparently heard gossip that "Thomson and a guide or forest ranger were in love with the same girl, possibly a half-breed; and that through jealousy Thomson was murdered by his rival."

Finally, Guillet cast doubt on how the inquest into Thomson's death had been conducted. Noting the lack of water in Thomson's lungs, and the bruise and the bleeding found on Thomson's corpse, he reasoned that "the state of decomposition of the body led the inquest to be concluded in much too hurried a fashion."

Nonetheless, Guillet offered a rather disappointing opinion:

> Barring some belated confession of complicity in the tragedy, or some other evidence that has been well hidden for twenty-seven years, it is certainly far too late to re-open the inquest upon the tragic death of Tom Thomson, "the poetic painter."

Guillet's unsatisfying resolution contains an uncomfortable truth. Even by the 1940s, finding a clear answer to the question of how Tom Thomson had died would be nearly impossible. The difficulties inherent in answering the question, however, would serve to make Thomson's death an increasingly compelling topic for speculation, conjecture, and gossip.

As 1943 marked the fiftieth anniversary of Algonquin Park's creation, park authorities commissioned a history of the initiative. Written by Audrey Saunders, *Algonquin Story* was published in 1947. An indication of Tom Thomson's value to the park can be gathered from the fact that Saunders devoted two chapters (about 10 percent of her two-hundred-page book) to discussing Thomson's work there, and to considering the circumstances of his death.

Likely intending to establish the trustworthiness of her stories about Thomson, she notes that much of her narrative derives from testimony she gathered from those who were living at Canoe Lake during the summer of 1917. Ironically, she notes that at least one important witness — Mark Robinson — is known for his embellished tales about Thomson. Perhaps Saunders believed that the facts of the story were so well known that no amount of storytelling could cloud the truth. As she suggested when turning to the events of July 1917, "Tom Thomson's actions on the morning of the day of his death are fairly well defined." She reveals how flawed her statement is, however, by providing a narrative that diverges significantly from any previously written.

Saunders suggested a new chronology for Thomson's final morning. She shared that Mark Robinson recalled seeing Tom and Shannon Fraser pass his cabin "early in the day," and that Fraser had later told him that he and Tom were discussing the trout the men had been trying to catch.

After Shannon returned to Mowat Lodge, Saunders stated, Thomson visited Mrs. Colson at the Algonquin Hotel, where he had a cup of tea. Colson did not notice anything unusual about Tom that morning, Saunders noted, suggesting that "[h]e seemed his normal self, and chatted in a friendly fashion."

Sometime later, Thomson must have returned to Canoe Lake. About 1:00 p.m., Saunders reported, "the guests at the Lodge" saw Thomson leaving "his dock" in his canoe with fishing tackle and "some food supplies in the bow of his canoe."

On July 10, Tom's canoe was discovered "floating empty behind Little Wapomeo Island." Saunders indicates that because the canoe was found "floating in an upright position," the rangers did not believe Thomson would have drowned. As well, "the paddles were lashed into place as if for portaging, and some of the food was still in the bow."

On Monday, July 16, Thomson's body was discovered when Dr. Howland sighted an object "come up to the surface of the water." He had been sitting on his cabin porch at Little Wapomeo Island, and called to two passing guides, George Rowe and Larry Dickson, to alter the path of their canoe to investigate it. Finding Thomson's corpse, the men towed it "over to Big Wapomeo Island." One of them left to notify park authorities while the other remained to watch over the body.

Upon receiving notification of the discovery, Park Superintendent Bartlett ordered Mark Robinson to the island, where he was instructed to remain until the coroner arrived from North Bay. As this was expected to take more than a day, "Mark took along supplies sufficient for his sojourn on the island." Robinson and one of the guides kept watch over the body that night. This information is also noteworthy, in that no previous accounts had suggested Robinson maintained an overnight vigil with the body.

On July 17, according to Saunders, the coroner arrived, and Dr. Howland was "called in to assist in making the examination of the body." Similar to Davies's recounting of the state of the body, Saunders noted there was no water in Thomson's lungs, and he had a "dark bruise on [his] temple." The cause of death was determined to be "accidental drowning." Saunders speculated that Thomson might have "died from heart failure, or he could have fallen and struck his head on a rock when he landed his canoe." She makes no mention of foul play.

As for questions regarding when Thomson's corpse was finally laid to rest, Saunders stated that "many of Tom's old friends have always felt that he would have preferred to remain buried in his beloved Algonquin Park," but in her assessment, "there is really no reason to doubt that [the] change in burial place was made."

Saunders's account incorporated several new elements into a narrative of Thomson's last day and death. If believed, her mention of Robinson watching over the corpse would suggest that even Robinson's diary might be missing important information. Her claims regarding the condition of the canoe are also intriguing. No previously published accounts had mentioned that the canoe was upright. Upon whose information this claim is based Saunders does not state. The novelty of some her claims suggests that skepticism regarding Saunders's account is wise.

After Saunders's version of the story, little was written about Thomson's last days for almost a decade. In 1955, a man who had been living in Canoe Lake during the summer when Thomson went missing, Dr. R.P. Little, offered his recollections of Thomson and the tragic events of July 1917 in an essay published in *Culture* magazine.

Little offered that he found Thomson to be shy but generous. He guessed that Thomson was likely short on cash and was happy to use his paintings to pay debts, or do odd jobs to earn a bit of money. For instance, Thomson provided the Frasers several days' work planting a vegetable garden, and did the same for the Trainors.

As for Thomson's feelings about the war, Little reports that Bud Callighen, a park ranger, had told him that Thomson wanted to enlist, and sought to contribute to the war effort. "Certain persons" who were more interested in his developing his artistic career had dissuaded him, however.

Little suggested that Thomson "seemed in excellent spirits" during the spring of 1917. In May, Little claims, Thomson held an exhibition in the dining room of Mowat Lodge of all the works he had produced that spring. He offered some of these to his friends.

Little was not at Canoe Lake during the time of Thomson's disappearance or the discovery of his body. When he returned from a camping trip in late July, he learned that Thomson had drowned. Nonetheless, in his essay he provides an account of what he had learned about the fateful events after the fact. Some elements of his report differ enough from previous accounts to merit discussion.

Little suggested that "Mr. Fraser last saw [Thomson] as he was letting out his copper fishing line while paddling through the narrows to the right of the twin islands." No previous account had provided such detail about what Thomson was doing after he left the dock. Certainly none mentions that he was actually fishing on Canoe Lake before he disappeared.

Little's account also provided an entirely new story regarding the Blechers' actions upon sighting Thomson's canoe. He reported that Martin Blecher Jr. and his sister "towed Tom's canoe back to Mowat Lodge and put it in their boat house." Two days following Thomson's departure, according to Little, "Charlie Scrim discovered Tom's canoe in Mr. Blecher's boat house." All previous accounts had attested that Thomson's canoe was found floating on the lake.

Little also offered new observations about the canoe and its contents. He stated that the following was found in the canoe:

> Tom's lunch (consisting of bread, butter, and jam), some supplies, and cooking utensils, which Tom always carried, while the paddles were placed as if for portaging but this could have been done by Martin Blecher to hold them in place. The copper trolling line was missing.

A search for Thomson was undertaken to no avail. Some must have feared that Thomson had drowned, though, Little suggested that "dynamite was exploded in the lake without result." For those unfamiliar with the practice, the intention was to use the the shock of the explosion to bring objects submerged in the water to the surface.

Little described how Thomson's body was spotted by Dr. Howland and retrieved by guides Dickson and Rowe. Upon examination of the remains, it was discovered that Tom's "copper line was broken but some strands were wrapped about one of Tom's ankles." While Robinson had mentioned this discovery in a letter to Davies in 1931, she did not include it in her 1935 book. Little's is the first published account that mentions fishing line around Thomson's ankle.

Little also notes that an inquest was held, and the "body was put in a steel casket and buried in the graveyard at Canoe Lake." There were only two markers at the cemetery, and the one dating from the 1890s "marks the grave of the first white man buried there."

Little's observations about the burials of Thomson and others in Mowat Cemetery are significant. His assertion that the body was buried in a steel casket does not accord with the invoice provided by the undertaker to the Thomson estate in 1917. As well, Little's intimation that Mowat Cemetery was established in a place that had been previously used for burials by Aboriginals is plausible. Whether Little intended to suggest that other burials, likely of Aboriginals, had occurred there is not clear, however.

As entertaining as Little's story might be, it does suggest that the facts surrounding Thomson's death were becoming more and more muddled.

During the early 1950s, an audio recording was made of park ranger Mark Robinson recounting the events around Tom Thomson's death. At this time, he had the opportunity to set the record straight. However, his testimony was wildly inconsistent with versions of the story he had offered in 1917 as well as during the 1930s.

While Robinson's later account would not become widely known for several decades, it has become the version of Robinson's testimony — if not the story of Thomson's death — most often turned to by those suggesting Thomson did not die by accident.

The exact date of Robinson's testimony is hard to ascertain. The Algonquin Park Museum and Archives (APMA) holds three recordings of Robinson discussing Thomson's death. One is dated to 1955, another to 1956. A third audio file consists of both recordings — the one dated to 1955 and the one dated to 1956 — with about ten minutes of silence between them, as if the files might document a single event. Robinson died in December 1955, so the 1956 dating can be dismissed. For the sake of convenience, I will hereafter simply refer to these works as Robinson's "1950s recording."

The APMA's file describes the recordings as "an interview by Taylor Statten." Statten was a lawyer and criminologist who held the lease for the cottage on Little Wapomeo Island where Dr. Howland had been staying in 1917. Statten was also instrumental in developing several summer camps at Canoe Lake. At the conclusion of one of the audio recordings held by the archives, however, audience applause can clearly be heard. Robinson frequently sounds as if he is reading from prepared notes. The location of and purpose for Robinson's presentation is unclear, as the introduction of the presentation where such information might be stated was not preserved.

Robinson's comments in this recording suggest that he sought to correct what he believed were errors in Audrey Saunders's telling of Thomson's story. In offering his corrections, he provided some new stories of his own. The false precision of much of Robinson's 1950s testimony is misleading, particularly to those who don't take the time to compare his claims to those he had offered in the 1930s. The differences are critical, however, and should serve to throw the entirety of his testimony into doubt.

Robinson consistently expressed a clear admiration for Thomson during the talk. He suggested that Thomson was quietly heroic, noting how Thomson and Charlie Scrim had once rescued two canoes full of people in danger of drowning, but had not taken any credit for the feat. He also suggested that Thomson "wasn't a man that would drink." Although he might "take a couple of drinks ... and stop, and when he did stop nobody could coax him to take any more."

This claim stands in stark contrast to the information provided by some of Thomson's friends during the 1930s. That Robinson would feel a need to comment on Thomson's alcohol consumption does suggest that the issue was emerging as one of concern.

Robinson repeated his claim that Thomson had tried to enlist in the military. He also added that Thomson tried to enlist in Toronto and "some outside point in the country." Turned away each time, Robinson reported, Thomson returned to Algonquin Park in 1915 and comforted himself with the idea that he could "fill a place here at home of a man who's gone to the army." This claim suggests that Thomson had tried to enlist during the first year of the war and given up trying to enlist by 1915, before Robinson had himself left to fight in Europe.

During the 1930s, Robinson had recounted to Blodwen Davies how Thomson wanted to hold an "exhibition" in Robinson's ranger cabin of "ninety-odd" works he had painted during the spring of 1917. Robinson was vague on details regarding the project, however. With a clarity that seems questionable after the span of more than thirty years, Robinson described how Thomson came to his house and said, "I have something unique in art that no other artist has ever attempted." Robinson continued, "I can hear him, 'I have a record of the weather for sixty-two days, rain or shine, or snow, dark or bright, I have a record of the day in a sketch. I'd like ... to hang them around the walls of your cabin here.' ... I think that was about four or five days before he disappeared...."

That Robinson had not chosen to share these details with Davies in 1930 is rather surprising. His story about Thomson wanting to exhibit his works in the ranger's cabin would seem to challenge previous tales relating that Thomson had already exhibited his spring 1917 works at Mowat Lodge in May and given many away. For these stories to coexist, Thomson would have had to have been producing multiple sketches every day, and been sure to keep one from every day. Additionally, if Thomson had already arranged to exhibit the works at Mowat Lodge, why would he seek to "exhibit" the works again in a more private venue, such as the cabin that served as Robinson's home in the park?

The most intriguing component of Robinson's tale was his description of Thomson's final hours. The story he told revolves around elements that he had not included in any previous accounts. As Robinson was in the midst of preparing lunch, he stated, he sighted Tom Thomson "going up with Mrs. Colson and up to ... and Mr. Colson, up to their hotel." He continued, "After a while I saw Shannon Fraser ... come walking up past the station and turn and go up past the ... up along the other side of the river from my cabin and Tom came down almost at the same time from the Colsons'. He seemed to be carrying, I thought, a fishing rod or something.... I was standing watching them." Curious about Fraser and Thomson's intentions, Robinson stated, "I took my glasses out to see if Tom was going to have a try for the trout.... I ran down the shore, up my ... up the path up my side and I sat down looking down on the two fellas down below me." Failing to catch the fish, Thomson conceives of the idea of catching an alternate as a way to prank Robinson. Of course, Robinson was privy to this conversation: "I sat right above them looking at them. Well, Tom hadn't seen me, I sat still and as he, as he went up onto the bank and turned, Tom looked back and I waved to him. 'Howdy,' he says. That's the last time Tom Thomson spoke to me." If Robinson had indeed observed all of these events, it is very suspicious that he had not mentioned them in the accounts he had told over the preceding thirty-five years.

Reporting what he had heard at the inquest, Robinson indicated that according to "several people" who "were stopping at Mowat Lodge," Tom Thomson left about 1:30 p.m. This claim offers a far less menacing tone than Robinson offered in 1930, when he suggested that Fraser was the last man to see Thomson alive.

Continuing with his narrative, Robinson stated that on the morning of July 10, Charlie Scrim reported to him that Thomson's canoe had been discovered floating upside down between Big Wapomeo Island and the mainland. Robinson suspected something was amiss immediately. Noting that there was only ninety minutes between Thomson's departure and the sighting of his empty canoe, and that Thomson had travelled "hardly half a mile," Robinson concluded that "[t]here was something fishy."

This is certainly a case of Robinson's memory playing tricks on him. If indeed he believed something was "fishy," he certainly hadn't recorded this sentiment in his daily diary in 1917, when he noted that after locating the canoe and interviewing the Blechers he expected Thomson would soon return.

With regard to the condition Thomson's canoe was in upon discovery, Robinson sought to correct Saunders's account. The canoe, he assured his listeners, had been found upside down in the water. Additionally, upon inspecting the contents of the canoe, Robinson discovered that "the paddles were tied in for carrying ... his paddle that he used in paddling was not there." The only thing that remained in the canoe aside from the paddles was the food that Fraser had packed in a rubber sheet, Robinson claimed.

Robinson's brief comment regarding the paddles deserves note. He seems to be suggesting, unlike in any previous account offered by himself or others, that Thomson might have had three paddles with him on his last voyage: a "paddling" paddle and two others that would presumably be kept tied in the canoe to help with portaging.

Although he was not present for the discovery of Thomson's body, in his 1950s account Robinson nonetheless described what had occurred. He explained how Howland had seen something bob to the surface of the lake and directed guides Dickson and Rowe to investigate. After they identified the object as Thomson's body, Robinson reported that Howland instructed them to "tie it to a tree there out in the water." Hugh Trainor and George Rowe put a blanket over the body in the water while Charlie Scrim reported the find to Robinson.

Duly reporting the discovery to Park Superintendent Bartlett, Robinson was told, "You'll have to handle it for the government." Robinson commented, "I didn't have the chance to handle it myself; if I had there'd been more done about it." He does not explain what he means by this comment, but considered alongside other comments by Robinson, he seems to be suggesting that his dissent about the inquest was quashed by Bartlett.

In his 1917 diary, Robinson had noted that there was some "adverse comment regarding the taking of testimony" at the inquest. In the 1950s recording, he stated that the coroner reached a verdict of "accidental drowning" quickly, "almost before we had time." He also noted that "[o]ne of the old guides started to remonstrate a little but, 'the case is closed,' was the coroner's response." With this decision, Robinson appears to have felt his responsibility to the government had been satisfied, as he noted no other attempts to ensure additional evidence was considered.

In the 1950s, Robinson added an entirely new narrative element into the story of what had occurred between Thomson's disappearance and the discovery of his corpse. Robinson noted that he was instructed — presumably by Bartlett — to "go to the little house up here and see what was around there." The "little house" Robinson is referring to is likely the former mess hall used for employees of a lumber company, sometimes also referred to as the "manse." Earlier in the recording, he suggested that this was where Thomson was living at the time he disappeared. Robinson visited the building with Hugh Trainor. They found, according to Robinson, approximately forty sketches and several letters, mostly written from Winnie Trainor to Tom Thomson. Robinson read them and returned them to Mr. Trainor. While this is an interesting claim, the idea that Thomson was living in the cottage flies in the face of evidence from July 1917, where even Thomson notes that he is living at Mowat Lodge. While it is possible that Thomson was storing items in the cottage, the discovery of forty sketches also calls into question Robinson's claim that Thomson had asked only days earlier to display more than sixty sketches in his cottage.

Robinson's 1950s account rather surprisingly offers the most detailed description of Thomson's corpse that Robinson ever provided. He stated that

> it was badly swollen and around the left ankle there was a fishing line wrapped sixteen or seventeen times.... This was wrapped on as carefully, right around and around and around and around and [the undertaker] Roy Dickson [sic] asked me if I had a sharp knife ... and he said, will you just remove those strings, and I did, and I counted them, that's why I know that there was sixteen or seventeen. I have it down in my diary and notebook just exactly how many there were.

He also reported that "across the left temple here there was a mark, it looked as if he had been struck ... struck with the edge of a paddle."

Once again, Robinson's perspective appears to have evolved considerably over the course of almost forty years. He had never previously mentioned the number of times the wire was wound around Thomson's ankle. Contrary to his claim, of course, he had not written down how many times the wire was looped around Thomson's ankle. In fact, his diary entry regarding Thomson's corpse did not include mention of any wire or fishing line being found on Thomson's corpse at all.

Along with providing new "facts," Robinson's account contains several remarkable feats of memory. He recalled that the two undertakers were the ones who had decided on burying Thomson's remains at Mowat Cemetery. He reported that guides George Rowe and Larry Dickson had dug Thomson's grave at approximately six feet four inches deep. He also recalled that Dr. Ranney had arrived at Mowat Lodge around 10:30 p.m. Robinson described how he had visited the cemetery after Thomson's body was exhumed and discovered a hole in the gravesite that was about twenty inches across and about the same deep. All of these would be impressive if recalled days after the events in question; that they are mentioned for the first time more than thirty-five years after makes them suspect at the very least.

After three decades and likely countless times retelling his memories related to Thomson and Thomson's death, Robinson's opinion by 1955 is clear. He had come to believe that Thomson was a murder victim, a position he clearly states at the close of the recording. The person he considered the prime suspect was Martin Blecher Jr.

As a sign of Blecher's poor integrity, Robinson reports that Blecher was a deserter from military service, adding that a U.S. Army representative had visited Canoe Lake with the intention of seizing Blecher and returning him stateside. This claim was not consistent with statements a representative of the U.S. military had sent to Blodwen Davies during the 1930s. The army found that Blecher's failure to report for duty in August 1918 was due to circumstances beyond his control. In the highly unlikely chance that a military representative had visited Canoe Lake, the military's records suggest that Blecher was not guilty of wilfully breaking any regulations.

Between the 1930s and 1950s, a key person in the evolving story of Tom Thomson's death was park ranger Mark Robinson. The accounts that he provided to Blodwen Davies propelled her belief that Thomson had been murdered. His account of the 1950s indicated that he was more confident in this conclusion than he had been during the 1930s.

While many commentators had recognized Thomson's art as meriting discussion, few suggested that his death was worth much consideration. The few researchers who did turn their attention to the issue related narratives that spiralled further and further from the historical record. As memories faded, gossip and speculation proliferated. These accounts were included in publications that were more readily available than the historical evidence, and made for far more titilating stories.

Before long, however, talk about Thomson's death would be spurred to a new, hyperbolic pitch. The discovery of a body in Algonquin Park would raise the prospect that perhaps all of the questions regarding how Tom Thomson had died might be answered.

6

A BODY DISCOVERED

[M]ake no bones about it; they wanted [Thomson's]
original grave opened.
— DR. NOBLE SHARPE. DIRECTOR. ONTARIO PROVINCIAL POLICE CRIME LAB. 1967

——— ——

IN EARLY SEPTEMBER 1956, four men vacationing at Canoe Lake succumbed to curiousity regarding Tom Thomson's final resting place. Believing that Thomson's body might never have been removed from Mowat Cemetery, the men took it upon themselves to excavate where they thought Thomson's body had been buried. Since there was no marker indicating where there was not supposed to be any body, the men worked from intuition and anecdotes, eventually making a shocking discovery. What they found in Mowat Cemetery that wet, cold September afternoon greatly changed how Tom Thomson's death has been talked about ever since.

During late September 1956, William Little, superintendent of Brampton, Ontario's provincial reformatory (no relation to Dr. R.P. Little, who had written about Thomson a year earlier), and Jack Eastaugh, of Etobicoke, visited Canoe Lake. Both men had been counsellors at the lake's Camp Ahmek many years earlier, and as adults acquired leases for Canoe Lake cottages.

Both men were aware that Tom Thomson had died on the lake. They also knew there was some doubt about the truth of the stories regarding Thomson's accidental death and exhumation from the park. Little "had been told 25 years ago by a forest ranger who investigated Thomson's death that the body was in its original grave." This ranger, Mark Robinson, told Little that "the undertaker hired to transfer the body took an empty coffin to the new grave." The tale must have made an impression on Little, who wondered about it for decades.

After talking with two other friends staying at the lake, Frank Braught and Leonard "Gibby" Gibson, the men decided to find out if Thomson was still buried at Mowat Cemetery. Robinson had told Little that Thomson's grave would be found on a hilltop close to the lake, near a tall, old birch tree, and would be close to two marked graves. After several failed pits were dug, the men discovered bones. They took some of the remains and sought out advice from a doctor who was vacationing on the lake. He identified the bones as human. The doctor notified the Ontario Provincial Police (OPP). On October 5, the police sent out representatives to assess the findings and proceeded to complete excavation of the remains, taking them to Toronto for further analysis.

In 1970, William Little would provide an account of the dig in his book, *The Tom Thomson Mystery*. This book is the source that most researchers have depended on; however, it is not the only version of events that exists. Some alternative accounts recorded at the time suggest that Little's book is not entirely accurate.

On Saturday, October 6, Frank Braught, one of the four men who had made the discovery, spoke with friends at Canoe Lake. The conversation was recorded, likely by Taylor Statten (the same man who had recorded Mark Robinson speaking about Tom Thomson's death, and who leased the Little Wapomeo Island cottage at the time of Thomson's death). Braught described in detail how the idea of investigating Thomson's original burial site came about, as well as the process the men, and later provincial officials, used to exhume the remains that were found. Unlike Little's version of events, Braught's account was never published and is rarely considered in writing about Thomson's death. It is, however, one of the accounts that significantly challenges how Little sought to have his and his friends' activities understood.

Braught stated that on the night of Friday, September 29, William Little and Jack Eastaugh visited the Camp Ahmek staff dining area. When conversation turned to Tom Thomson, Little and Eastaugh repeated rumours they had heard that Thomson's body was never removed from its original grave. Someone shared that Fraser thought the undertaker was not in the cemetery long enough to dig up and move the body into the new coffin. Eastaugh mentioned that Shannon Fraser had picked up the coffin and undertaker at the grave the morning after he arrived. Apparently, some of the train men who handled cargo found the coffin lighter than expected.

Based on these intriguing stories, the men hatched their plan to resolve where Tom Thomson was buried. Together, they considered the potential legal problem of disturbing a grave, but Eastaugh reasoned that what they proposed to do was not illegal, as the available evidence indicated that there was no longer a body there, and thus no grave would be disturbed.

The three men arranged for Leonard Gibson to drive them to Mowat Cemetery, on the other side of the lake, in his Jeep the next morning. The next day, the men breakfasted and arrived at the cemetery around 10:00 a.m. Making a rough visual assessment, they guessed a plot would fall just outside the cemetary fence, and so began to dig there. By the time they had dug down five feet, they discovered the clay was so solid that it could not have been disturbed. They filled the hole and moved a short distance. The next hole produced a similar result. They settled on a third spot, a three- to four-foot-long, trough-shaped depression, with a ten-foot high balsam growing in the middle.

After the men moved some soil, Gibby was tasked with pulling the tree out with his Jeep. Upon digging, the men quickly discovered the mixing of dark and light layers of sand, which suggested the soil in this spot had been disturbed at some point. When the hole was about four feet deep, Gibby plunged in headfirst, "using his hands to dig like a badger," Braught related. Eastaugh held Gibby's feet so that he would not have to hold himself up. The group were all surprised when Gibby handed some wood out of the hole. Their excitement built when he offered up what were clearly bones. Gibby came up to confer with the others, and likely wanting to get closer to the source of excitement, Braught went down into the hole. He described how he pushed his arm into the hole Gibby had uncovered, reporting that it was quite easy to do so. Braught retrieved some bones as well.

The men had encountered a situation that was unexpected, although not-so-secretly hoped for. Unsure how to proceed now that they were definitely dealing with remains, the men used some boards to cover the hole and attempted to disguise the scene. They asked Dr. Harry Ebbs, another leaseholder on the lake, to come to the site with them in the afternoon. Ebbs suggested the bones were human, and that he would take them to Toronto to try to get some more perspective on the type of person to whom they might have belonged. On October 1, Braught claimed, Ebbs reported the men's discovery to the park superintendent as well as the provincial deputy minister of forests and lands. The men were told that officials would be coming to the site to investigate.

Once remains were discovered, the rationalization the men had used to convince themselves to initiate digging didn't seem nearly as comforting. The men grew anxious about their legal position. As Braught described it:

> We realized that we were in a serious position because in the first place we went there with the idea that no one could arrest us for disturbing a grave without an official authority to do it, if anyone was there.... But as I said, we were told that the body had been removed, therefore we were simply investigating the situation to find out if it had been or not.

The paradox in this logic is obvious. They would be fine, as long they did not find any remains. If they didn't expect to find remains, however, there seems to be little motivation to search for them. The men don't seem to have considered what their next step might be if they did, indeed, find Tom Thomson's remains. Thinking that they had done just that, they began to fear the consequences.

On Friday, October 5, OPP corporal A.M. Rodger and OPP Crime Lab director Dr. Noble Sharpe arrived at Canoe Lake to investigate. They spent several hours at Mowat Cemetery working with Dr. Ebbs, Gibson, and Braught.

The search began with clearing the soil off the burial site. Braught noted that the investigators had brought a sieve with them to sift soil from the grave for any small items, such as buttons or rings, which could help identify the body.

After removing the covering soil, the first thing Corporal Rodger brought out was the skull. Ebbs and Sharpe began their work. Laying the skull in a "clean place on the leaves" they proceeded to use sticks to clean dirt off the left side of the skull, the side which the coffin had come to rest upon. One tooth was missing, but the most intriguing discovery was a hole in the left temple bone, about three-quarters of an inch in diameter. The hole had no fracturing around it, which led the men to suspect it might have been produced by a gunshot. As there was no corresponding exit hole on the right side of the skull, Dr. Sharpe suggested the skull should be left as it was until an X-ray could be used to determine if a bullet might be found within.

Braught surmised that the sandiness of the soil limited water working its way into the coffin, which helped preserve its contents. Within the grave, Braught stated that the men found the remains of a canvas shoe, coffin "upholstery," lead coffin mountings, and two plates. One was engraved "Rest in Peace." The other was blank. Braught related that before the men knew the second plate was blank, Corporal Rodger gave them all a shock when he yelled out something like, "Look, it says Tom Thomson!"

On the recording, Braught added that Dr. Ebbs had noted some of the teeth in the skull were close together in a distinctive formation. Braught's friends suggested that someone who knew Thomson well might be able to remember if his teeth had that formation. The first person mentioned was Winnie Trainor, but the group exclaimed, half joking, "Nobody wants to meet her!" As proof of what kind of person she was, someone stated that she was going to take an axe and chop down the "totem pole" that had been carved in Thomson's memory and raised on Canoe Lake's Hayhurst Point during the summer of 1930. They discussed their belief that she and Thomson were romantically involved. Braught added that "she's got a lot of his sketches."

At the time Braught's comments were recorded, only a week after the dig, no one knew what the police investigators and experts might conclude. It was suggested to Braught that the attorney general would require the Thomson grave in Leith to be exhumed. If this was done, Braught feared that people in Owen Sound would be very upset, as the community had been fundraising to build a memorial gallery dedicated to Thomson's work. Part of their fundraising pitch, he noted, was that they were close to where Thomson had been raised and was buried.

Along with Braught's often overlooked account, a second piece of testimony offers unique insights into the 1956 exhumation. On October 9, 1956, Corporal Rodger filed a two-page report concerning his involvement in the exhumation that had taken place at Canoe Lake only a few days earlier.

Much of Rodger's version of the story is consistent with Braught's. His description of what was discovered differs in some key ways, however.

According to the report, on October 5, Rodger and Sharpe excavated at the site, discovering remains of a wooden casket at the four-foot level. The casket had been lined with some kind of fabric and had a metal nameplate and ornaments. It had been buried inside another box, suggesting it was not the typical rough box "commonly used" for burials "in the isolated areas." Rodger stated that an almost-full skeleton was recovered, and noted that the toe bones of the right foot were within the remains of what was likely a woollen sock. Otherwise, he suggested, the body appeared to have been buried unclothed. Although the soil was screened for evidence, nothing of further interest was discovered. The remains were boxed and taken to Toronto by Dr. Sharpe for further analysis.

Over a week passed before the first newspaper stories about the gruesome Canoe Lake discovery appeared. On October 10, 1956, the *Globe and Mail* reported that the four men involved in the find suspected the remains were those of well-known Canadian artist Tom Thomson. The men, the report states, "were not convinced that the artist died accidentally." They instead favoured the idea that Thomson had been murdered. The *Globe* suggested that the men's theory was not widely supported.

Other people around Canoe Lake thought the remains might "be that of an unidentified lumberjack" who worked in the area when the Gilmour lumber firm operated there. A local resident, Jean Chittenden, told the *Globe* reporter that she had heard there were "several unmarked graves" aside from the two burials indicated by stone markers.

As the story about the remains discovered close to Mowat Cemetery broke and speculation began to circulate that the remains might be those of Tom Thomson, popular interest in the story increased and coverage widened. Two days after the *Globe* story ran, other newspapers included accounts from two of the three undertakers who had dealt with Thomson's remains.

The *Toronto Star* published a letter from M.R. Dixon, one of the two undertakers who had first handled Thomson's corpse (the other being R.H. Flavelle). The idea that Thomson was murdered seemed utterly ridiculous to him. Dixon suggested that he had "a very distinct recollection of all the official proceedings at that time." He described how Algonquin Park headquarters had summoned him to "remove the body from the water and prepare it for shipment." Upon arriving in the park, Mark Robinson told him that no certificate of death had been produced. Without this official document, Dixon was unable to work on the body. Likely called into action by Mark Robinson, Park Superintendent Bartlett produced a certificate of "death by accidental drowning," claiming that his position made him "ex-officio a coroner."

With the documentation in hand, the undertaker and his associate began their work. Dixon explains that "there was certainly no blood on the face or any indication of foul play, just the usual postmortem staining that is on the body of any person that is in the water of a small lake for 10 days in the heat of the summer."

A Canadian Press representative sought out the perspective of F.W. Churchill, the undertaker who had exhumed Thomson's corpse from its Algonquin Park grave and prepared it for shipment to Owen Sound. The account Churchill provided is rife with factual errors. These might be attributed to his advanced age and the fuzziness of memory that comes with decades passing (he was in his seventies, and the events in question had occurred almost forty years before). Regardless of questionable recall,

Churchill did offer an intriguing new suggestion of how he had come to be asked to exhume Thomson's remains. Churchill asserted that

> Mr. Thomson's relatives and friends were not happy with the burial spot, Miss Blodwen Davies, a friend, wanted him buried at Leith. She phoned the undertaker at Kearney, who had been in charge of the funeral near Canoed [sic] Lake, but he refused to exhume the body. Then she phoned me in Huntsville. I was not anxious to do the job, but she begged me and finally I said yes.

Churchill assures the newspaper that he had transferred Thomson's "badly decomposed but still recognizable" remains into a metal box that he could seal, and returned the empty coffin and its surrounding "rough box" to the grave, which he then refilled. He also notes that one of Thomson's brothers accompanied the coffin on the train to Owen Sound.

Churchill's obvious mistake is mentioning Thomson biographer Blodwen Davies, who was, at the time of the events at Canoe Lake, a young woman living in Fort William (now Thunder Bay). However, could the woman who contacted Churchill have been Winnifred Trainor? Churchill's testimony fits closely with the account Trainor provided the Thomson family, as well as the phone bill she provided the estate regarding costs related to Thomson's death.

Given her long-standing interest in Thomson's life (and death), and the fact that Churchill referred to her by name, Davies quickly responded to Churchill's claims. She denied having contacted Churchill and stated definitively that she had never met Tom Thomson. She also said that she did not visit Canoe Lake until 1930. It was during this time that she concluded Thomson had met with "foul play, but not premeditated," and decided that his body remained in Algonquin Park. Given the "incriminating nature" of her findings, and that she believed she could identify the responsible person, "I was not able to publicize anything," Davies claimed.

Taylor Statten read some of the media coverage of Churchill's claims, and recorded a response on October 17, 1956. He prefaces the recording by noting that he was not in Canoe Lake at the time of Tom Thomson's death. However, he relates what he claims Shannon Fraser told him about the 1917 exhumation.

According to Statten, Fraser took the undertaker to the cemetery to drop off the coffin. As darkness started to fall, Fraser suggested the undertaker come down to the lodge for something to eat. He could spend the night there and get to his work in the morning. The undertaker declined, telling Fraser that he would get to work. He asked Fraser to return the next morning and pick him up, when he'd have the coffin ready to go to the train station. Fraser did as requested, but concluded that there was not a body in the coffin. That Fraser picked the undertaker up the morning after dropping him off is the same claim that Frank Braught had made a few days earlier, when Statten recorded his comments.

During his reflection, Statten notes that Ed Colson, proprietor of the Algonquin Hotel, had also confided that he was sure there was no body in the coffin. Similarly, Mark Robinson, after looking at the original gravesite the day after the exhumation, concluded that the body had not been removed.

On October 18, 1956, Ontario attorney general Kelso Roberts announced that the remains found at Canoe Lake were not those of Tom Thomson. He stated specialists had determined that the skeleton was that of a male "Indian or half-breed," about twenty years old. He also noted that investigation into the nature of the hole in the deceased person's skull would continue.

Given the date of Roberts's announcement, it is rather surprising that the preliminary case report by Dr. Noble Sharpe was not submitted until October 30. Sharpe's three concise, typewritten pages are rich with information. Sharpe does not reiterate the material contained within Corporal Rodger's report, but clearly had it in hand as he suggests that it offers an accurate account of events. He also adds observations made at the exhumation site.

Although the four men who discovered the remains concluded that the body had been buried within a coffin because they found wood before bones, Sharpe suggested that this might not be the case. The body might have settled into the rotting coffin materials if the lid rotted before the sides. Sharpe suggested that the type of coffin — lined with cloth, with metal ornaments, and with a fine-enough finish to merit being placed within a rough box — "appears to be too expensive for an Indian or casual worker such as a lumberjack."

Sharpe noted that the remains were found in light, sandy, well-drained soil. Withered hazelnuts were found with the bones, which Sharpe attributed to water seepage, or possibly rodent activity. Sifting of the soil found within the burial plot produced no buttons or rings, suggesting the body was not clothed, and had perhaps been wrapped in a shroud that had rotted.

With regard to the remains, Sharpe concluded from the loss of calcium in the bones that the body had been buried between twenty and forty years. He also suggested that within that time period, he would expect to find some remnants of flesh if the body had been embalmed. Finding none, Sharpe concluded that no embalming appeared to have taken place.

Sharpe and Dr. J.C.B. Grant, of the University of Toronto Anthropology Department, analyzed the skeleton. Both concluded that the bones were definitely those of a muscular male in his mid- to late twenties, between five foot six and five foot ten inches tall. Dr. Grant's assessment was that the man's facial features were "strongly mongoloid," and his teeth had a "shovel" shape characteristic of "North American Indian" heritage.

Sharpe observed that the skull found at the site had a hole in the left temple (parietal) region nearly three-quarters of an inch in diameter. The skull was X-rayed before being emptied, and nothing unusual, such as a bullet, was identified. No exit holes were present, and the orbital plate and nasal bones were present, ruling those out as exit routes for a bullet. X-rays did not reveal any fracturing around the hole in the skull. Upon cleaning the skull, it was noted that the opening was slightly wider on the inside surface of the skull than the outside. The X-ray technician, Dr. A.C. Singleton, observed that the hole had "rather smooth even margins as though this button of bone had been removed by a surgical instrument." Dr. Sharpe concluded that the hole in the skull was not produced by a weapon, but was the result of surgical trephining, a procedure usually undertaken to relieve pressure on the brain after a head injury.

Eleven years later, Sharpe was called upon to comment on the case again, this time by by F.L. Wilson, Ontario's deputy attorney general. Unfortunately, Sharpe's response did not clearly indicate what the attorney general's office wanted to know about the case. The tone of Sharpe's letter does suggest that there were some questions regarding the initial exhumation of the remains, perhaps in response to renewed calls to establish the contents of Thomson's grave in Leith definitively.

Sharpe explained to Wilson the events leading up to his arrival at Canoe Lake. Disturbing a grave was clearly not something that would be undertaken lightly, although in this case it would appear that official checks had broken down completely. "As far as I know," Sharpe offered, "no order for exhumation was ever given." Sharpe claimed that he was not aware no order had been given until driving away from the scene. Given how he was brought into the investigation, he may have assumed someone else had already received these directions. It is not entirely clear in his letter which decision he is suggesting lacked approval: the one made by the four men who initiated the dig or Corporal Rodger's decision to allow the continued exhumation of the remains. Given his explanation that "we assumed [the exhumation] had been necessary to rule out foul play," it seems he is referring to the involvement of initial explorers, some of whom characterized themselves as landscape painters, although why he would believe that a group of inexperienced amateurs on a weekend painting jaunt would be tasked with such a job is beyond reasoning. If he is referring to Rodger's later decision to continue allowing the disturbing of the remains without provincial government permission, the claim opens a veritable "can of worms" regarding what was found.

Sharpe suggests that the discovery of the remains was driven by the independent efforts of the four men involved: "the artist group who made the first dig." Perhaps making a pun, he declares, "Make no bones about it; they wanted [Thomson's] original grave opened."

Although rumours regarding Thomson's death and his burial place were apparently circulating around Canoe Lake, community members were upset by the artists' initiative. Sharpe reported, "There was some local feeling about a grave being disturbed." It would appear that the sanctity of a grave held higher importance for the locals than resolving any rumours about Thomson's burial place. Sharpe recorded that "[t]here was even talk about prohibiting the artist group from Algonquin Park as a result" of their work in October 1956.

Sharpe stated that when analysis of the remains was finished, they were given to Corporal Rodger to rebury at the location in which they were found. Sharpe's understanding was that Rodger had placed a wooden marker at the spot.

Sharpe continued to stand by his assessment, stating again in his 1967 account that "I am quite satisfied that this was an unknown Indian and that were no signs of foul play." He believed "it quite possible he was buried in Tom Thomson's original empty grave and the coffin could have been the one used for him at the first burial."

Whatever the attorney general's office's interest in the remains, Sharpe's comments appear to have provided assurance enough that no further action was taken.

In June 1970, Dr. Noble Sharpe made public his observations regarding the remains. Writing in the esoteric *Canadian Society of Forensic Science Journal*, Sharpe's comments did not reach a wide audience. Nonetheless, his observations and reflections more than a decade after the case are important to note.

Sharpe surveys some of the popular rumours circulating regarding Thomson, suggesting that these elements had become regarded as realities of the case. He noted that Winnie Trainor had told him in 1956 that she and Tom were engaged. He mentioned rumours that Tom had quarrelled with Martin Blecher Jr., who was interested in Winnie. He stated that Tom's offer to volunteer for army service had been refused, and that Blecher was a deserter from the U.S. Army. He also repeats Little's suggestion that Blecher had threatened Thomson the night before Thomson disappeared. Introducing a new wrinkle, Sharpe added that "a shot had been heard coming from the direction Tom had taken when he was last seen."

Sharpe gave a brief review of Dr. Howland's examination of Thomson's corpse. He suggested that an internal examination — which Howland did not undertake — would not have been particularly useful, as "decomposition would have masked indications of drowning." Sharpe did respond with some puzzlement to Howland's mention of bleeding from Thomson's ear. He noted that dried blood would imply some time had passed before the body was immersed in water. If the bleeding took place underwater, however, the blood should likely have been washed away.

Discussing the exhumation of the remains found in 1956, Dr. Sharpe noted that, along with the skeleton, also discovered were coffin handles, a metal plate, a small piece of canvas, and a piece of woollen sock "attached to a foot bone." Sharpe added that "most fabrics of this nature disappear in about twenty years in this type of soil."

Sharpe confessed that the initial belief among the men was that they were dealing with Tom Thomson's remains, found in his original grave, and that he might have died from a gunshot to the head. X-rays showed no projectiles within the skull and no fractures radiating from the hole, and bevelling — which he stated is expected for bullet wounds — was absent. He stated that a neuropathologist, Dr. Eric Linnell, agreed that the hole "resembled a trephine opening" more than a bullet entrance wound.

Having concluded their work, Sharpe stated that the remains were "returned to the grave." A marker was placed at the spot "to deter further interference."

Closing his report by considering if the remains could possibly be those of Thomson, Sharpe reviewed the differences between Thomson and the body found in the unmarked gravesite. Working with photos of Thomson's face and profile in 1956, Sharpe "found no evidence of Mongoloid bony points nor of agreement of bony points."

Additionally, Sharpe makes the simple observation that if an experienced doctor such as Howland was confronted with a corpse which had a relatively fresh hole in its skull — comparable in size to the hole found in the 1956 specimen's skull — he simply could not have overlooked it.

Through the 1970s, Sharpe continued to think about the case, conferring often with his associate Dr. Doug Lucas, who had become director of the provincial Attorney General's Laboratory (now the Centre of Forensic Sciences) in 1967. Although most of his writing would retrace observations he had already made, one notation in a November 1973 letter provides a useful clarification regarding the mechanics of exhuming a body in the Mowat Cemetery site. In this letter, Sharpe stated that "at our dig, only one man [could] work at a time. Yet we even did sifting and were through in about one hour." Sharpe's claim provides a useful benchmark for how long it might take a man to "re-dig" a recently excavated grave-size hole in the soil near Mowat Cemetery.

The October 1956 discovery of buried human remains just beyond the fence surrounding Mowat Cemetery generated mixed responses. Some Canoe Lake residents were appalled at what they saw as the desecration of a burial site by attention-seeking, callous curiousity hunters. The four men who engaged in the dig certainly seemed to believe that they very well might have discovered proof that many of the rumours they had heard about Tom Thomson's death and burial were true. Dr. Sharpe and his peers concluded, however, that the remains were not those of Tom Thomson but rather those of a younger Aboriginal man.

William Little was not willing to accept the degree of chance or complexity that Sharpe's explanations offered. Rather, he continued to pursue his theory that the remains he and his friends had discovered were those of Thomson. On the basis of his theory, Little also argued that the hole in the skull discovered in 1956 surely indicated that Tom Thomson had been murdered.

Despite Sharpe's forensic experience (and agreement among his equally learned peers), the sheer novelty of Little's claims — the prospect of conspiracy and heinous crime — would gather more traction in writing about the case. Starting with Little's analysis of the case, during the 1970s proposals of conspiracy and dark dealings would come to dominate the story of Tom Thomson's death.

Algonquin Park Visitor Centre Collection, APMA #3396

Tom Thomson as a young man. Joan Murray suggests that this photo was taken around 1893. However, S. Bernard Shaw suggests that it was taken around 1900.

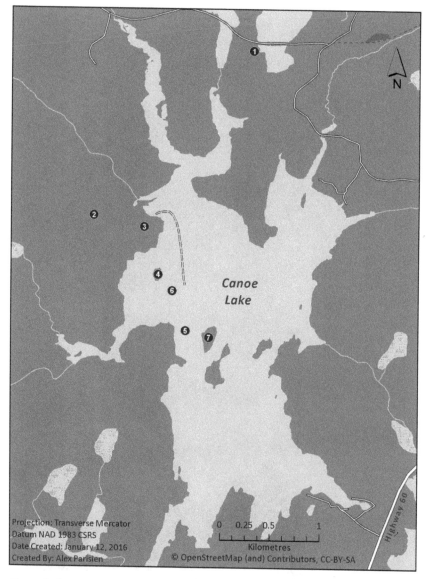

Canoe Lake, 1917

1. Mark Robinson's ranger hut
2. Mowat Cemetery
3. Mowat Lodge
4. Little Wapomeo Island (where Dr. Howland was cottaging)
5. Approximate location where Thomson's canoe was discovered, July 8
6. Approximate location where Thomson's body was discovered, July 16
7. Big Wapomeo Island
=== Approximate route of Thomson's canoe on July 8, as described by author
    Blodwen Davies in 1935.

Algonquin Park Visitor Centre Collection, APMA #184

Mark Robinson, undated. Between 1907 and 1936 Robinson worked in Algonquin Park, serving as ranger, chief ranger, and eventually superintendent of the park. Robinson's records of the search for Tom Thomson's body, and the testimony he provided in the 1930s and 1950s regarding the events at Canoe Lake in 1917 are a key element in most theories concerning Thomson's death. Robinson passed away in December 1955.

Shannon Fraser and the repurposed hearse he used to transport guests between the Canoe Lake train station and Mowat Lodge, which he operated with his wife, Annie. Records indicate that Fraser was the last person to see Tom Thomson alive. Fraser's suspicious behaviour after Thomson's death has led to speculation that he might have been involved.

Algonquin Park Visitor Centre Collection, APMA #3010

Algonquin Park Visitor Centre Collection, APMA #48

Shannon and Annie Fraser (far left, back and front row) with friends at the Canoe Lake train station. Rose Thomas is at the far right, front. Thomas told Ottelyn Addison that she had seen Tom Thomson on the morning of his death.

Algonquin Park Visitor Centre Collection, APMA #2500.

Winter 1916–17: A horse-drawn sled leaves Mowat Lodge to pick up mail at the Canoe Lake train station. The woman at the back of the sled has been identified as Daphne Crombie. In the 1970s, Crombie's stories about things she had been told by Annie Fraser, proprietress of Mowat Lodge, would fuel speculation that Tom Thomson had been murdered.

Algonquin Park Visitor Centre Collection, APMA #186

Mowat Lodge, as it appeared during Thomson's days at Canoe Lake.

The area of the chipyard at Canoe Lake, where the Gilmour Lumber Company dumped detritus from the sawmill to create a dry foundation for stacking logs. The area is still quite shallow, and worked wood samples are easy to find. The upper image closely resembles the conditions recorded by Thomson; the lower image shows conditions looking south, toward Mowat, in 2008.

The chipyard today.

82565940123

In May 1931, Dr. A.E. Ranney, the coroner who conducted the inquest into Thomson's death, provided author Blodwen Davies with notes derived from his files.

George Thomson, one of Tom's brothers, wrote author Blodwen Davies in June 1931. He related what he describes as the coroner's notes from the inquest. The tone of the notes suggests that they are far more likely those of Dr. Howland than of the coroner, Dr. Ranney.

In late September of 1956, four men excavated what they believed was Tom Thomson's original burial plot at Canoe Lake. They discovered human remains, which seemed to show indications of foul play, suggesting Thomson did not die by accident.

Algonquin Park Visitor Centre Collection, APMA #6754

Leonard "Gibby" Gibson, digging just outside the fence on the northwest side of Mowat Cemetery, September 1956. Photos of the exhumation (see p. 125) do not show the fence or tree, suggesting this is one of the first two pits the men dug. The photographer is likely William Little, whose 1970 book, *The Tom Thomson Mystery*, spurred new speculation about Thomson's fate and the final location of his remains.

The men in the photo are, from the left: Leonard "Gibby" Gibson, William Little, Frank Braught, and Jack Eastaugh.

October 1956: Dr. Harry Ebbs and an unidentified man exhume the human remains discovered outside Mowat Cemetery. Ebbs is sifting the remains. Note the cardboard box beside him, which may have been used to hold the remains as they were discovered.

The human remains exhumed in October 1956 from near Mowat Cemetery at Canoe Lake included a skull with a perplexing hole in the left side.

Canoe Lake's Mowat Cemetery, viewed from the south side. On the other side of the fence, between the tree and the photographer, lie the headstones for the cemetery's two marked graves.

Present-day visitors to Canoe Lake will find this small cross a few metres north of the fence surrounding Mowat Cemetery.

Gregory Klages

The expanse of Canoe Lake where Thomson's body was discovered. On the left is the northern side of Big Wapomeo Island. On the extreme right is the Little Wapomeo Island cottage where Dr. Howland was staying. Thomson's body was discovered somewhere between the two.

Gregory Klages

Tom Thomson is buried in a family plot at Leith United Church cemetary, north of Owen Sound, Ontario. The headstone includes the names of Tom, Tom's infant brother (James), who died in 1883, and his maternal grandfather Kenneth Mathison, who died in 1879.

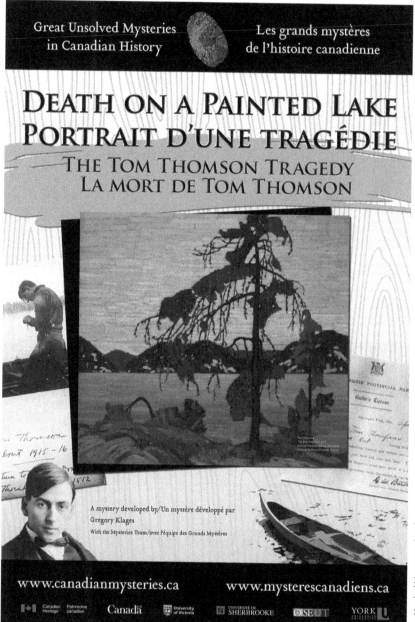

In April 2008, Great Unsolved Mysteries in Canadian History launched the website *Death on a Painted Lake: The Tom Thomson Tragedy*, of which the author of this book was research director. The fully bilingual site contains transcribed documents, photos, artworks, maps, and analysis related to Thomson's death. It has helped to generate international interest in Thomson's case.

7

AN ACCOMPLICE CONFESSES

In these accounts there is always the mysterious hint of something
known but withheld. If the grounds for these suspicions of murder or
suicide could be stated, the matter might lose its false air of mystery.
I suspect that the accidental verdict would stand.
— R.H. HUBBARD, *TOM THOMSON,* 1962

——— ———

IN 1962, R.H. HUBBARD published a brief biography of Thomson, the first
to be released since the 1930s. Although Hubbard gave little credence
to the idea that Thomson did not die accidentally, his biography does
show that a tremendous amount of ill-founded speculation and gossip
had become incorporated into the story of Thomson's life.

For instance, Hubbard lifts freely from Mark Robinson's unsupported
stories of the artist's intention to record the changing weather and seasons
around Canoe Lake during spring 1917. Using R.P. Little's mid-1950s article as a source, Hubbard relates how Thomson's canoe was brought in off
the lake by his friends as soon as it was discovered: Thomson's empty canoe
"was taken in by neighbouring summer cottagers the same day [he departed
from Mowat Lodge] and seems to have spent a day or two in their boat
house before it was identified as Tom's by a friend from Ottawa."

Despite accepting so much weak testimony regarding Thomson's death,
Hubbard rejected the speculation regarding foul play that had been resur-
rected by the 1956 exhumation. He noted:

Much has been made by Miss Davies and the writers of recent newspaper articles of the supposed lack of water in the lungs, the bruise on the head, and some copper fishing wire tangled about one ankle. In these accounts there is always the mysterious hint of something known but withheld. If the grounds for these suspicions of murder or suicide could be stated, the matter might lose its false air of mystery. I suspect that the accidental verdict would stand.

What Hubbard's complaint points to is that the foul play theory was grounded in "evidence" that could not be confirmed: statements of "gut sense," contradictory testimony, and refusals to accept expert analysis.

Hubbard's conclusion — that Thomson's death could still only be plausibly explained as accidental — was being reached by others as well.

In 1966, Thomson's former studio mate, friend, and fellow artist, and former member of the Group of Seven, A.Y. Jackson, was trying to have Blodwen Davies's second biography of Thomson republished to mark the fiftieth anniversary of Thomson's death. Jackson's choice is odd given his own apparent lack of faith in Davies's conclusions.

Jackson had strong doubts about the murder theory. He had edited some passages out of A *Study of Tom Thomson* to downplay inflammatory speculation about Thomson's death. Jackson suspected one publisher had declined to republish Davies's book because it was hesitant to give a platform to her unsupported, fantastic claims.

Privately, Jackson recalled to his friend, artist Yvonne Housser, that Dr. MacCallum believed Thomson had committed suicide. "They brought in a verdict of accidental death to make it easier for the family," he offered, without, however, addressing what sort of evidence might exist to support the observation. As Davies had never mentioned this theory, it did not appear in the republished work, and Jackson did not raise it in his introduction.

Perhaps inspired by the republication of Davies's work, in 1969 the Ryerson Press published *Tom Thomson: The Algonquin Years*. Mark Robinson's daughter, Ottelyn Addison, wrote an account of Thomson's life, with collaborator Elizabeth Harwood. In its use of primary sources, this work constituted the most trustworthy approach to Thomson's last days published to that time.

Rather than building their narrative upon the recollections of people who claimed personal knowledge of the events, Addison and Harwood accounted for Thomson's activities in Algonquin Park during the spring of 1917 by quoting at length from letters he wrote to his family and friends. Many of these letters had not previously been available to the public. Addison also provided new insights by including substantial excerpts from her father's journal that recorded his thoughts and observations during the search for Thomson at Canoe Lake between July 10 and July 19, 1917. This information had also never been made publicly available.

The book's endnotes indicate that the authors consulted the Thomson-related correspondence that Blodwen Davies had deposited with Library and Archives Canada, as well as the collection of letters and other materials that Dr. MacCallum had given to the National Gallery. In addition to personal records, Addison and Harwood's book included copies of official documents related to Thomson's death, such as the temporary death certificate signed by Dr. Howland, a July 19 letter from Dr. Ranney to Mark Robinson that accompanied the official death certificate, the certificate to take possession of a body, and the burial certificate.

Addison relates a few claims contained in a letter she received from Rose Thomas in February 1956. During 1917, Rose's parents operated the Canoe Lake train station. Thomas reported that the weather on July 8 had been hot and "sultry." She had seen Thomson and Fraser walk together past the train station about noon that day. Thomas also suggests that upon finding Thomson's canoe floating in the lake, the Blechers took it to Shannon Fraser's. Although the letter had been written in 1956, Addison did not release this account until publication of her book. Addison and Harwood may have had some doubts about the trustworthiness of Thomas's testimony, though, as rather than incorporating her account into their narrative of Thomson's last day, they inserted it as an endnote.

It is not surprising that Addison's book repeated many claims her father had made in the years after Thomson's death, including the story of Thomson's painting-a-day plan for the spring of 1917. She also related how Thomson had approached Robinson in early July hoping to exhibit the series of sketches he had made in the ranger's cabin. Establishing a sense of foreboding, Addison added that this was the last conversation Robinson would have with Thomson. Inexplicably, Addison and Harwood overlooked Robinson's mid-1950s claim that Thomson had spoken to him on the day of his disappearance.

When discussing the "mystery" of how Thomson had died, Addison and Harwood struck a tone very similar to A.Y. Jackson's. They observed that there were "a number of troubling circumstances which might have been explained immediately had sufficient time and care been taken at the inquest." Without evidence, however, these circumstances gave rise to "a host of rumours" including "claims of foul play." Addison and Harwood suggested that "[m]any of these [rumours] are far-fetched and misleading," but — inserting just a hint of ambiguity — they stated that "facts to support any theory are almost impossible to obtain." In the absence of facts, they concluded, the exact circumstances of Thomson's death would likely remain unknown.

Addison and Harwood's book included an abundance of rare photos of life in Algonquin Park, including images of some of the key persons involved in Thomson's life around Canoe Lake, as well as photos taken by Thomson himself. One of these images is particularly important because of its role in further confusing the Thomson story. The photo shows a woman in a long, high-necked plaid dress, her left hand holding a fishing rod, and a string of fish in her right. Under the image is the caption, "Winifred Trainor (1884–1962)." When it was published, the image did not produce any comment, though the identification of Trainor would eventually be questioned.

The Thomson photos and correspondence introduced in Addison and Harwood's book (which would be included in several other publications in the late sixties and early seventies) may have entered circulation as part of a "housecleaning" by Thomson family members. In 1967, Mrs. F.E. Fisk, the daughter of Tom Thomson's sister Elizabeth and T.J. Harkness (the executor of Tom's estate), discovered a series of forty photographic negatives stored with Tom's belongings. In 1970, the National Gallery of Canada published the photos, along with commentary by Dennis Reid, the gallery's curator of post-Confederation Canadian art.

Reid did not address Thomson's death in his comments. He did make observations about two photos of the woman Addison and Harwood had listed as Winnie Trainor. Reid noted that the identification had come from Mrs. Fisk. He alluded to the importance of Trainor in Thomson's life in a subtle footnote, suggesting: "The three rings on the third finger of her left hand ... have not been explained."

The publication of Addison and Harwood's book, and the reprinting of Davies's, drew new attention to complex and unresolved questions about Tom Thomson's death. The public interest in these works suggested to William Little that he might find new interest in his theory that Thomson was murdered and his remains buried in Algonquin Park. During 1968, Little worked with producers at the Canadian Broadcasting Corporation to produce a television docudrama regarding the Thomson case.

The program's producers consulted experts, including Dr. Noble Sharpe, the forensics expert who had concluded that the remains found by Little and his friends in the park in 1956 were not Thomson's. Sharpe was given a draft outline of the program with the hopes that he might like to contribute to it. He responded with five pages of written notes, providing some provocative observations regarding his involvement in the 1956 events.

Sharpe informed the producers that his mandate for assessing the remains in 1956 was not to identify the remains — the "only real concern of the Attorney General's Department," Sharpe stated, "was to look for evidence of foul play."

He recollected that the anthropologist who assessed the skeletal remains was not given any information regarding who they might have belonged to. He also stated categorically that the anthropologist and X-ray technician consulted on the case agreed the hole in the skull was produced by trephination, a process, he added, that "did not become common until after Tom Thomson's death."

Along with providing his first-hand, expert knowledge concerning the remains found in 1956, Sharpe also addressed the 1917 examination of Thomson's corpse. Addressing the idea that the absence of water in

Thomson's lungs might prove that he did not drown, Sharpe clarified that "decomposition after days in warm water would mask all signs and it would not be possible to be sure of drowning as a cause of death." He also spoke in support of Dr. Howland's skills. With a bit of grammatical butchery, Sharpe stated, "I do not think he would not distinguish between a bruise and a bullet wound" (a difference that would not seem to require medical certification to recognize, regardless).

Was Tom Thomson Murdered? aired on February 6, 1969. Using re-enactments of key scenes, the program speculated that Thomson had been a victim of foul play, and that his remains might very well stay in Algonquin Park.

Just as the 1956 exhumation upset Canoe Lake locals, newspaper reports suggest the CBC's very public speculation about one of Owen Sound's "hometown heroes" was not appreciated there. Two days before the program aired, Owen Sound's *Sun-Times* noted with some disgust that a CBC producer was seeking to have Thomson's grave in Leith dug up on the grounds that Thomson's remains might not be buried there, or that his grave might contain some evidence that Thomson was murdered. The *Sun-Times* intimated the idea was rooted in "mud-raking" of an innocent situation that served to "splash mud on both the memories of the principals and ... their families and friends." The article stated that until conclusive proof for the claims could be supplied, Thomson's grave should remain undisturbed.

The response following the broadcast of the CBC program was no friendlier. According to a second article in the *Sun-Times*, the broadcast produced "considerable revulsion" among local citizens and upset Thomson's relatives.

The *Sun-Times* also published comments on the CBC program by a number of local prominent citizens. One observed, "Instead of watching what we thought would be a tribute to the wonderful art of Tom Thomson, we watched a group of ghouls at work." Another suggested that "the CBC, in their stupidity, have deliberately tried to destroy the image of this revered artist which is causing anguish for the Thomson family." Echoing concerns similar to those that had been raised by Frank Braught in 1956, a member of the town's art gallery committee suggested that the speculation might be part of an effort by the McMichael Canadian Art Collection to have the remains of the members of the Group of Seven (a well as Thomson, it would seem) buried together. The head of the art department for one of the local secondary schools offered a provocative comparison when he said, "Christians do not feel they need to know beyond doubt where Christ is buried before they can honor him, so why should we feel we need to know the location of Tom Thomson's grave in order to honor him?"

Concerned with the proposal that Thomson's grave in Leith be opened to prove that his remains were indeed buried within, Thomson's nephew, George Jr., reported that he and his two surviving aunts would not give permission for such a gruesome exercise.

Introducing a new claim regarding his great-uncle's last days, George Jr. indicated that his father had been told, "Tom had suffered a sprained ankle just before his disappearance." According to George Jr., his father "was of the opinion Tom had stepped out of the canoe onto his injured foot, had slipped, hit his head on a rock and rolled unconscious into the water to drown." His father had also vowed that Tom's body was in the casket brought out of the park from Canoe Lake.

On February 10, the *Sun-Times* published a third article concerning the CBC documentary. The piece related a new account provided by "two elderly ladies [the McKeen sisters] who were childhood neighbours of Tom Thomson and his family." The ladies' niece reported that they recalled their cousin visiting the Thomsons' Owen Sound home during the period when Tom's coffin was there. The man witnessed how Tom's father insisted on seeing his son's remains despite the undertaker's protestations, and was present when the coffin was opened.

The local newspaper's coverage reveals that the CBC program *Was Tom Thomson Murdered?* generated a tempest in Owen Sound. The program also generated popular interest but significantly less critical discussion beyond the town. For instance, provincial records show that a classroom of primary school students wrote individual letters to the attorney general weighing in on the issue, most asking for Thomson's grave in Leith to be opened.

The program did not produce the type of result that William Little had likely hoped for. Thomson's grave was not reopened. Little, however, was heartened by the interest his ideas received. Within a year of the program's broadcast, he published his account of Thomson's death and his involvement in the 1956 discovery of remains in Algonquin Park. Titled *The Tom Thomson Mystery*, the book was the first exclusively devoted to discussing Thomson's death. The lengthy work certainly, for better or worse, has become one of the critical references for anyone hoping to discuss the case.

Little's book is divided into two parts. The first discusses Thomson's death. The second explores the 1956 discovery and analysis of the remains found outside Mowat Cemetery.

Little's claims are straightforward. He believed that Martin Blecher Jr. murdered Tom Thomson by striking him over the head with a paddle. He suspected that the two men had fought over their expectations of who would win the war, or perhaps over Winnie Trainor. Little states that Thomson and Winnie were engaged, and that Thomson likely planned to marry Winnie at the end of summer 1917. Finally, Little also believed that Thomson's remains had never been removed from Algonquin Park.

Little provided readers a service by bringing together a number of accounts that had not received significant attention, such as R.P. Little's 1955 article, Addison's excerpts from her father's diary, several letters Little had received about the case, and the memories of Thoreau Macdonald (the son of Group of Seven member, J.E.H. Macdonald) regarding Thomson (handwritten in 1958), which had also been included in Addison and Harwood's recent manuscript.

It seems Little had engaged in some archival research. His notes suggest he consulted the Thomson-related materials that Davies had deposited with Library and Archives Canada, as he quoted from a number of letters she received in the 1930s, as well as a letter that she received in the 1950s. These had not previously been published. Additionally, he produced a transcript of a talk by Mark Robinson from the 1950s. (He dated it to October 1953, but the Algonquin Park Museum and Archives dates the audio recording to 1955.)

Little complicates consideration of his argument, however, by mixing observations drawn from historical testimony with his own speculations and imaginative recreations. Writing more than fifty years after

Thomson's death, he narrated events that had not been described in any previous accounts.

For instance, Little suggested that on the night of Saturday, July 7, a few of the men around Canoe Lake — Shannon Fraser, Thomson, and Blecher Jr., included — gathered to drink a "modest amount" of "bootleg" liquor at one of the guide's huts. Not surprisingly, at some point late in the evening talk turned to the war. Little claimed that Blecher was strongly pro-German, a position that he suggested raised Thomson's ire. (Little related that Thomson had unsuccessfully tried to enlist "at least" two times.) Harsh words were exchanged between the two men, who were only kept from exchanging blows by their friends, who were, "for the most part solidly behind Tom." In the end, Little suggested that Blecher had stalked off, but not before warning Thomson to, "Stay out of my way if you know what's good for you."

While a few previous accounts had mentioned that Thomson might have had some conflict with a local Canoe Lake man, none had ever mentioned any particular events. Certainly, no previous accounts had described a party or fight the night before Thomson died, or identified that threats were made toward Thomson.

Little's scenario provides support for a theory that had previously been mentioned by Robinson and Davies. Little asks, "Did [Blecher] meet Tom Thomson on the lake or at the Gill Lake portage that Sunday afternoon? Did he have any knowledge as to how Tom received that cruel blow on the temple which so resembled the smash of a paddle edge?"

The impression Little's rhetorical questions might make really depends on an imagined scenario. Perhaps recognizing the flimsiness of his speculation, he provided an alternative conflict that might have led to Thomson's death. This theory is similarly weak, though, as it reflects decades of unsupported gossip.

One of the important components of the idea that Thomson was injured in a fight is the notion that Thomson needed money to cover the costs of getting married to Winnie Trainor. The prospect that Thomson was engaged to Trainor was based on the testimony of two persons who assured Little their stories were true. An unidentified source told Little that a honeymoon cabin had already been arranged for late summer.

Another, Winnie's nephew, assured Little that he had letters written between Tom and Winnie that proved the two were engaged. Since 1970, the nephew has never produced the letters, however, despite requests by multiple researchers. Nonetheless, Little states that after Trainor's death the couple's engagement became "known authoritatively."

This claim is not entirely supported by testimony of people who were living at Canoe Lake in 1917. At least two people — Bud Callighen, a ranger friend of Thomson's, and Irene Ewing, a close friend of Winnie's — attested that Winnie was more interested in Tom than he was in her, and that Tom was not interested in marriage.

Along with his own speculation, Little's storytelling owes much to Mark Robinson's account recorded during the 1950s. Robinson's influence is particularly obvious in Little's description of the events of Sunday, July 8. Little stated that Tom rose early and walked to Colson's Algonquin Hotel on Joe Lake. On the way there Shannon Fraser joined him, or Fraser met him at the hotel. On his return, Tom and Fraser stopped to fish at Joe Lake Dam. Tom almost caught a fish and proceeded to conceive of catching a different fish to fool Mark Robinson. As he finished talking through his idea, Thomson spotted Robinson watching them. He waved at Robinson and said, "Howdy." Despite having been overheard, it seems Tom intended to follow through with his idea. Little reported that Thomson stopped by the "mess," where Little claims he was staying, while Shannon fetched some food from the lodge. Shannon watched Tom leave from Mowat Lodge dock at 12:50 p.m. Visitors at the lodge saw Tom depart, and they watched Tom boat round "the southern tip of the larger islands a scant three-quarters of a mile away."

Borrowing further from Robinson's accounts, Little reported that before preparing Thomson's body for burial, Dr. Howland examined the body, accompanied by Robinson. Little provided a transcript of testimony from Robinson, noting sixteen or seventeen coils of fishing line wrapped around Thomson's left leg.

The challenge in repeating elements such as Robinson's final exchange with Thomson, as well as the story about the coiled fishing line, is that these details have no corroborating evidence and do not appear in any of Robinson's earlier versions of the story. Little, however, reported them as if they were uncontroversial facts, even when material included elsewhere in his book offers alternative accounts.

Little's creativity in reporting "facts" and his questionable process for discriminating between available evidence would deeply influence later narratives written about Thomson's death. A number of his assertions that might seem incidental deserve attention by virtue of how often they have been repeated. For instance, Little indicated that Charlie Scrim and George Rowe examined Thomson's canoe when it was discovered. They noted, he claims, that Thomson's "working paddle" was missing, and that his spare paddle was tied into the canoe, although it was "knotted in a most unorthodox way." This is the first published account that suggests Thomson might have been using three paddles, and is also the first to suggest that the way Thomson's paddles were tied in to the canoe might have caused any suspicion.

Little notes that the searchers gathered at Mark Robinson's cabin each night to report on their day and to plan the next day's search. Little suggests that George Thomson sat in on some of these meetings while he was at Canoe Lake between July 12 and 14. Not arriving at any clearer notion of what had happened to his brother, George apparently talked to Hugh Trainor, packed up some of Tom's sketches, and headed back to Owen Sound. No previous accounts mention these meetings, suggest George Thomson was meeting regularly with searchers, or indicate that George Thomson met with Hugh Trainor.

On the evening of July 17, the coroner A.E. Ranney arrived on the 8:00 p.m. train from North Bay. Little reports that Martin Blecher Sr. met him at the train station and took the doctor to his house. Robinson followed along later, by Little's account, and identified who he believed should be present at the inquest, including Dr. Howland, George Rowe, Larry Dickson, Shannon Fraser, Martin Blecher Jr., and Bessie Blecher. The inquest began about 9:30 p.m. at the Blecher house.

Little expressed concern over the choice of location, as he suggested the younger Blecher's hostility to Thomson might have biased the proceedings. His concern would be legitimate, were it not entirely based on his own imagined account of a fight having taken place between Thomson and Blecher the night before Thomson disappeared.

Intriguing details in Little's story of the exhumation of Thomson's body also differ from those included in previous accounts. The body having been shipped out on the train to Owen Sound on the morning of July 19, Little claimed that George Thomson and an undertaker received the body in Owen Sound early that afternoon. Aside from the improbability that a train could travel the distance between Owen Sound and Algonquin Park in such a short period of time, Little's claim is the first to place George Thomson at the Owen Sound train station on July 19.

Taken on its own, Little's conclusion that Thomson was murdered rests on flimsy evidence. Supporting his belief, though, he summarized the opinion of three people whose views are important. Little states that Mark Robinson, Shannon Fraser, and George Rowe all agreed on three facts. The first: "Thomson did not die a natural death." The second: he "died from a blow on the temple from a paddle." The third: that "his body rests on the Canoe Lake hillside where it was buried."

Weighing in with his own assessment, Little took issue with the finding that Thomson drowned by accident. He stated that "those who subscribe to the 'accidental' view are those who were not associated with Tom during the period preceding his death." Little also complained that the coroner never saw the body, instead accepting "the interpretation of important circumstances given by a medical doctor who never met Tom Thomson." Why the coroner or doctor would have to have known the person whose death they were assessing is not clear. He may have been suggesting that those who knew Thomson would have found the idea he drowned accidentally very hard to rationalize.

Little made the strange observation that the "doctor had conducted a post-mortem examination without having access to many facts that became available after the official inquest had been held." Clearly, *during* his examination the doctor could not take into account facts that became available *after* his examination. Little might have been suggesting, however, that if Howland had waited to allow the coroner to conduct the examination, other possible conclusions might have been more carefully considered.

Taken at face value in 1970, Little's book certainly made a compelling case for the prospect that Thomson might have been murdered. Much of the evidence that Little drew upon was not widely available, making it difficult to identify where he was working from historical facts and where his argument might rest upon speculative interjections. His consideration of Thomson's death was really, in many respects, merely a set piece for discussion of the remains Little was involved in discovering near Mowat Cemetery in 1956.

The second part of Little's book provided his account of how the remains were discovered and exhumed. Some differences between Little's and Frank Braught's account, which was recorded more than a decade earlier, point to Little's efforts to recast what had occurred in the fall of 1956.

Establishing how he became interested in Thomson's death, Little recalled Mark Robinson's belief that Thomson's body was never removed from Canoe Lake, a claim Robinson made "as far back as 1930." Little reported posing the simple question to his friend Jack Eastaugh in 1956, asking, "Why don't we check, and find out if this grave still exists?"

The men conferred with two others, Braught and Gibson, and decided they would establish whether rumours that Thomson's remains were still in the park were true. As Little records:

> If we found no evidence of a rough box or casket, then we would know that the official version (now firmly accepted by the Thomson family, the Department of Lands and Forests, and the Attorney General's Department) was indeed a fact. This would, we believed, forever stifle those unbelievers, including ourselves, who seriously questioned whether the alleged exhumation had ever taken place.

Little stated the men knew that any remains they discovered would be Thomson's, as "[w]e knew no other graves had been dug, or burials recorded other than those of the Hayhurst child, the millhand from Parry Sound, and Tom Thomson." Discovery of a grave, "complete with casket and body," in the location where Robinson reported Thomson was originally buried, would indicate that the rumours had always been correct, that Thomson's remains had never been exhumed.

Little suggested that aside from testing the idea of whether Thomson's remains were buried in the park, the men were also interested in resolving if Tom Thomson had been murdered. Of course, answering this question would really first require finding remains.

Little recounted that Robinson had suggested to him that Thomson's original burial place was "just to the north of the other two" marked graves. The men concluded that any grave would likely be within twenty feet of the existing cemetery enclosure. After clearing underbrush from the north side of the cemetery, they began to dig in the first spot they expected a burial might have been made. Little noted the soil was sandy and "easily moved save for a variety of tenuous roots." By the time they reached a depth of six feet, they had only encountered "clean stratified sand and loam." When a second hole did not produce any promising results either, the men began to rethink their faith in the rumours.

Diverging from Braught's account, Little stated that Jack Eastaugh spotted a depression in the ground further away from the cemetery. The hole was about two-and-a-half feet across, underneath a spruce Little estimates to have been about twenty-five feet high. The depression, Little reported, "extended from one side of the tree's branches to the other. The tree trunk lay dead centre in the depression. Checking due south of the location we noted that the ends of the depression lay in exact line with the two graves and our recent excavations."

The men began digging. In Little's version of the story, he was the man who made the first discovery of any signs of a burial. As he described it:

> Digging with my hands I felt a smooth piece of board. As I pried it free from the soil a hollow space that could only be the exposed end of a coffin was revealed. I jumped out of the hole and handed over the piece of board which was in an advanced state of decay but readily recognizable as a machine-finished piece of wood. I explained what had been exposed at the bottom of the pit. Gibby jumped down head first to explore the opening. He thrust his hand into the aperture and pulled out a bone which appeared to be a foot bone of a human body.

Only upon this discovery, Little stated, did the men remove the spruce tree over the site and open the grave further. They discovered an oak casket that had collapsed under the weight of the earth and tree above it. Seeking to confirm that they had indeed discovered human remains, which they strongly expected were the corpse of Tom Thomson, the men sought out the expertise of Dr. Harry Ebbs. Ebbs suggested that the bones were those of a human who was likely about six feet tall.

Little provided few details about what occurred at Canoe Lake after this point. The challenge he faced in relating the details regarding the police exhumation is that he had returned to his home after the weekend discovery. His account of the exhumation had to depend on the observations of others. Essentially, Little summarized the affair as the police boxing the remains and taking them away for study "after some cursory examination and discussion."

The brevity of Little's description of the exhumation also suits his conclusions. By giving the impression that the exhumation was not given the degree of attention it deserved, he lends credence to his suggestion that the resulting analysis of the remains was flawed. Noting that the official position was that the remains discovered by him and his friends were those of an Aboriginal, Little claimed the conclusion was unsatisfactory. It overlooked, he suggested, an abundance of facts, and flew in the face of logic. The remains, he left his reader suspecting, must be Tom Thomson's, and their condition clearly pointed to Thomson having been murdered.

Regardless of the shortcomings in Little's work — using flawed or unknown sources to create fictional accounts of scenes — at the beginning of the 1970s Little's book was provocative enough to stir significantly wider interest in Thomson's death. The discovery of remains in 1956 was critical in challenging the idea that the accepted version of Thomson's death might be wrong. The questions produced by the discovery might have faded into obscurity, however, had Little not made his startling claims in The Tom Thomson Mystery. His book certainly inspired a generation of speculative, and sometimes rather fantastic, discussion.

By the mid-1950s, Tom Thomson's death was considered a sad footnote to the life of a painter whose reputation was becoming increasingly heroic. With the discovery of remains in what was believed to be Thomson's original burial site — a site in which no remains were supposed to lie — discussion of the circumstances of Thomson's death gained new impetus. When police investigators reached the conclusion that the remains were not those of Tom Thomson, interest quickly subsided again. Writers such as Hubbard indicated that any conclusions other than Thomson dying by accident simply lacked evidence. It was not until the late 1960s, particularly with the 1967 republication of Blodwen Davies's 1935 book speculating that Thomson was murdered and William Little's similar proposal published in 1970, that full-fledged, serious discussion about whether Thomson might have been murdered begin to emerge. The characteristics of these works — facts mixed with gossip and speculation, capitalizing on foggy memories, and working from limited access to historical records — set an unfortunate standard for researchers into the case. These qualities would become the hallmarks of much of the next few decades of writing about the tragic events at Canoe Lake.

8

THOMSON AS A FATHER

The Tom Thomson legend doesn't come from facts, it comes from mystique, from the raw naïveté of the park people, the removal of the body at midnight, and the bizarre web that knit around Winnie Trainor until she died.

— ROY MACGREGOR, "THE GREAT CANOE LAKE MYSTERY," *MACLEAN'S,* 1973

———

BY THE LATE 1960s, discussion of Thomson's private life, and the ideas about his death that his family had been unwilling to countenance, were being widely debated in the country's newspapers, magazines, and television programs.

The speculation did not diminish Thomson's reputation, though. Growing interest in Thomson's life (and death) was both fed by, and fed respect for, his creative genius. The new Canadian cultural nationalism of the 1960s — spurred by the country's centennial — encouraged identification of unique, particularly Canadian heroes. Thomson was an ideal candidate, with his love of Canadian nature, his turn away from war, and his style of painting that broke with staid European traditions. The prospect that Thomson had died of unnatural causes, whether through accident or foul play, appealed to a typically Canadian romantic pessimism.

Publication of Addison and Harwood's text and the discovery of never-before-seen photographs and documents that the Thomson family had begun to share with select researchers offered an expanded view into Thomson's creativity as well as his activities.

Reconsideration of many facets of Thomson's life was aided by the fact that most of the family members and friends who had played key roles in Tom Thomson's life and final months had passed away. Respectful silence about unseemly aspects of the man's life no longer seemed to be called for. Republication of Davies's book, the CBC television special, and soon thereafter, the publication of William Little's provocative manuscript invited speculation regarding seamier, titillating aspects of life at Canoe Lake.

The public interest in Thomson's life and death that emerged during the late 1960s would motivate some of the few remaining living persons who had been in Canoe Lake during 1917 to share their recollections. During the 1970s, several witnesses provided new testimony regarding Thomson's last days.

Additionally, journalists, art historians, and others with attachments to the Canoe Lake region began to step forward to offer their own interpretations of the evidence, and to offer proposals for what might have happened to Tom Thomson.

By 1971, the Art Gallery of Ontario (AGO) organized an exhibition devoted to Thomson's work. The exhibition offered an unusual view into Thomson's creativity by paying significant attention to his rarely considered design work. Joan Murray, then curator of the AGO's Canadian collection, wrote the catalogue text.

While a relatively brief document, Murray's work is a good view of what was believed about Thomson's life, and death, by the early 1970s. It would seem reasonable to expect that within the context of an art exhibition, interest in Thomson's death would remain secondary to discussion of his creative work. Murray's essay reveals, however, that consideration of Thomson's death was becoming an integral aspect of attempts to make sense of his aesthetics.

Murray devoted singular attention to the works that Thomson produced during the last four months of his life. Noting his use of colour and line, and his handling of paint in these works, she boldly offered the conclusion that the "calm serenity and certitude of mood" in these works are something "which no potential suicide could possibly capture." Noting the strength of the forty known Thomson sketches from this period, she lamented that another twenty or more that he produced were missing.

Murray developed her narrative using a mix of sources, some more trustworthy than others. She consulted archival documents held by institutions such as the McMichael Canadian Art Collection. She was also in contact with surviving members of the Thomson family, and gained access to letters and other material from Thomson's life that they still held, and which had been discussed by few researchers (other than, perhaps, Ottelyn Addison and Elizabeth Harwood).

Along with historical evidence, Murray used less credible claims made by other researchers. Murray estimated how many of Thomson's last sketches were missing using the transcription of Mark Robinson's 1950s testimony provided in William Little's The Tom Thomson Mystery. She does not seem to have considered that only one person, Mark Robinson, had ever testified to Thomson producing a series intended to "record" the changing season, and that the first time Robinson had provided the detail about the number of works Thomson produced in that series was during the 1950s, more than three decades after Thomson's death.

By the early 1970s, writing about Thomson's death required distillation of the growing number of varied stories to create any cohesive, unified narrative. Murray's case was predominantly developed using information drawn from often flawed secondary accounts. Working from these sources, she may not have even realized that her assertions regarding Thomson's artistic output were based on untrustworthy evidence. Nonetheless, even if later research has revealed many of her claims to be unsupportable, she has continued to stand by her conclusions. Since the early 1970s, she has built upon the preliminary narrative she produced for the exhibition catalogue in multiple books devoted to Thomson and his art. Through frequency of repetition, and in the absence of any sustained and forcefully delivered contradiction, Robinson's 1950s claim, taken up and repeated by people like William Little and Joan Murray, took on the appearance of fact.

The increasingly wild storytelling about Thomson's death cannot be blamed solely on weak scholarship. During the 1970s, several of the people who had been at Canoe Lake in 1917 offered their insights for the first time, capitalizing on the media attention and further confusing the historical record.

In 1972, Charles Plewman wrote an article for the Canadian Camping Association's quarterly magazine. Titled "Reflections on the Passing of Tom Thomson," the article was motivated, Plewman claimed, by his desire to dispel some of the myths about Thomson's death that were gaining currency.

Plewman began his story by relating his arrival at Canoe Lake as a convalescent between the time Thomson's body was discovered and the day it was buried. He described arriving to a "tense atmosphere," where the dominant topic of conversation was Thomson's death. Many wondered how a man as experienced as Thomson could accidentally drown in a small, calm lake that he knew well.

Plewman was staying at Mowat Lodge during July and August of 1917, and suggested that during that time he came to share the confidence of Shannon Fraser. He described what Fraser had told him about Thomson's last days.

Fraser indicated that Thomson was engaged to Winnie Trainor, who was pressing Thomson to finalize the promised union. According to Plewman, Fraser reported that Tom "had come to the conclusion that a settled, married life was not for him, but that he could not say so to Miss Trainor." Fraser's suspicion was that Thomson had considered committing suicide "on earlier occasion but had not mustered sufficient courage." This time, Fraser seemed to believe, Thomson had. Plewman added that he later learned Fraser had stated his conclusion to George Thomson.

Plewman noted that only one person voiced concerns that Thomson had been murdered: Winnie Trainor. Describing her as Thomson's "girlfriend," Plewman stated that Trainor arrived at Canoe Lake after Thomson's body had been discovered. She demanded to see his remains, as she could not accept that he would have drowned accidentally on Canoe Lake. Mark Robinson refused her demands, though, which Plewman suspects was intended to protect her from the extreme unpleasantness of seeing Thomson's decaying corpse.

Closing his memories of Canoe Lake, Plewman stated that he understood Thomson to have been a pacifist who had given up hunting and who had no inclination to enlist in the army. He also stated that there was a multitude of Thomson's sketches still at Mowat Lodge at the time of Thomson's burial.

As for the possibility that the remains discovered in 1956 at Canoe Lake might be Thomson's, Plewman offered some intriguing suggestions. Plewman claimed to have been enlisted as a pallbearer for Thomson's funeral. Noting that the discovery was made outside the fenced-in area of Mowat Cemetery, he said, "To the best of my knowledge, I would have to say that we buried Thomson inside the area enclosed by a small fence." He also shared that "I am told that an Indian was buried in this cemetery around 1894 and probably other persons too." Of course, only two burials in the area of the cemetery have markers, one a lumberman buried in 1897, and the other a boy buried in 1915.

In October 1973, Plewman spoke with Dr. Doug M. Lucas, director of the Attorney General's Laboratory, at a meeting of Toronto's Forest Hill Rotary Club. Plewman apparently told Lucas that he was confident Thomson's body had been removed from the park for burial in Leith. His reason for this, Lucas related in a letter to Dr. Noble Sharpe, was that at Winnie Trainor's insistence Hugh Trainor (Winnie's father) and her brother had helped the undertaker to exhume Thomson's remains. Plewman also repeated his claim that an "Indian" had been buried in the cemetery during the 1890s.

Plewman's perspective further complicated what had already become — particularly with publication of William Little's work — a complex pack of theories regarding the end of Thomson's life. The prospect that Thomson had committed suicide had not really been given much credence in writing about Thomson's death. Without some reason to suspect Thomson was depressed or emotionally desperate, there was little reason to consider suicide. Plewman's claims suggested that Thomson might well have felt quite desperate about Trainor's demands to marry — desperate enough to consider suicide more than once.

As an option that had previously received little attention, the idea that Thomson might have committed suicide offered writers a rich new field for speculation.

By 1973, Roy MacGregor, having just completed his journalism diploma at the University of Western Ontario, managed to interest *Maclean's* magazine editor Peter Newman in an article on Tom Thomson's death. MacGregor's work "The Great Canoe Lake Mystery" included a number of never-before-reported narrative elements. Some of these were attributed to new sources, while many were not attributed at all.

MacGregor had a personal interest in Thomson. As he stated in 1973, Thomson was not only his "first Canadian hero," but Winnie Trainor was his "aunt's sister" (a distant relative by marriage rather than blood). He suggests his grandfather knew Thomson, though, and had little respect for the man, characterizing him as a "lazy bum." MacGregor was also familiar with the Canoe Lake area, as his father had worked for decades in the region for a lumber company.

In his lengthy piece, MacGregor wove together his own memories of Trainor with elements of the Thomson story that, by the early 1970s, had become commonly accepted as facts. He also offered a number of insights gained through his personal contacts with the Canoe Lake locals. Unfortunately, much of MacGregor's work is hung on the flimsy claims that had been offered by William Little in *The Tom Thomson Mystery*.

Early in his account, MacGregor connected Tom Thomson and Winnifred Trainor. He breezily asserted, "of course they were engaged." As proof, he offered that Thomson had booked a cottage for a "fall honeymoon." Given that no one had ever been able to prove Thomson and Trainor were engaged, and that William Little had been the only person to have made such a claim, it is rather surprising that he passes over it so quickly.

MacGregor lifted another Little speculation in his description of how Blecher was Thomson's only enemy, and how the two men had fought while drinking at a guide's cabin. He described how they argued about the war, and noted that Blecher had threatened Thomson. He also repeated Little's unique claim that one paddle was sloppily tied into the canoe, and that Thomson's "favourite ash paddle was never found."

Along with his uncritical repetition of Little's imaginative speculations, MacGregor introduced some of his own rhetorical flourishes. His interjections are overwhelmingly weighted toward building a sense of suspicious dealings, while giving a false sense of journalistic balance and objectivity. For instance, he stated that fishing line was wrapped around Thomson's ankle. MacGregor may have believed this to be true. When he noted that it is not known "whether he had entangled himself or someone had tied him," MacGregor communicates a false sense of journalistic balance and objectivity. He admitted that the line might not have been related to Thomson's cause of death, while handily dismissing alternative, innocent explanations such as the line getting tangled in the water post-mortem or having been used to tow Thomson's body to shore.

MacGregor takes a similarly tricky approach when discussing the exhumation of Thomson's body. Noting that an undertaker arrived to arrange shipment of the body to Leith, MacGregor stated, "No one in the Thomson family has ever said they ordered this but it was done ... " MacGregor doesn't note, of course, if anyone had ever actually thought it *necessary* to ask the Thomson family to prove that they had approved exhumation of Tom's body.

Feeding the sense of mystery, MacGregor suggested that "if" the body was exhumed, the undertaker "spent less than three hours at his task." He attributed this time frame to Shannon Fraser. Fraser, though, had not written any account of his interactions with the undertaker, and was long deceased by the time MacGregor wrote his story. At best, then, it would seem MacGregor is reporting hearsay as fact.

MacGregor takes speculation about the case to a radical new level. MacGregor is the first author to raise the possibility that Trainor had become pregnant by Tom. Having introduced the idea, he quickly backs away from it, however, mentioning that Winnie's long-time physician, Dr. Pocock, reported that she never mentioned either having had a baby or an abortion. On what grounds MacGregor might have based his speculation, then, he does not clarify.

MacGregor does not seem to have been concerned with whether many of the details of his story were verifiable, or to have applied much critical thinking in his research. He lifts liberally from William Little's book, which, in turn, depended on Mark Robinson's sketchy 1950s testimony. However, MacGregor apparently recognized that Robinson's later accounts might be less than trustworthy. Writing about Robinson, MacGregor stated, "In his later years ... he began earnestly applying yeast to the mystery." Given his observation, to have derived so much of his story (indirectly) from these "yeasty" accounts challenges comprehension.

Even when he turns to other sources, though, MacGregor's critical judgment is questionable. He advised his readers that he had gained from talking to Leonard "Gibby" Gibson, one of the four men involved in the 1956 dig at Mowat Cemetery. Gibson indicated to MacGregor that he was the man who had first identified finished wood in the third hole the men dug, and that it was he who had pulled out a foot bone. Clearly having consulted William Little's book, MacGregor doesn't seem to have noticed that Gibson's account varied significantly from Little's.

Having built up events at Canoe Lake as a web of shady and suspicious dealings, MacGregor rather surprisingly suggested that the mysteries may have been largely generated by the desire of simple people to make a sad event a little more exciting. He stated, "The people of the lake, looking for an answer, would pounce on the wildest theories. You can't blame them. Facts are boring; they rob the imagination." (The same might be said for young journalists seeking a big break.)

Backpedalling on the suggestion that all of these stories might have been produced by overworked imagination, MacGregor introduced another wild theory into the mix. He reported a tale he had been told by Jimmy Stringer, a seventy-three-year-old, long-time Canoe Lake resident. Stringer claimed that when some of Thomson's Canoe Lake friends heard that his body would be removed from the park, they took matters into their own hands. Before the undertaker arrived from Huntsville to take Thomson's body back to Owen Sound, these friends exhumed it and relocated it within the park. With a final flourish, MacGregor closed his story with Stringer drowning accidentally before he was able to show MacGregor the location of Thomson's "real" grave.

On the whole, the selection of stories and ideas included in MacGregor's article seems intended to excite curiosity more than to convey facts about the case, as the controversial CBC documentary had a few years earlier.

MacGregor's article provoked a response from some of Thomson's relatives. Researchers working on a book about Thomson interviewed Tom's sister Margaret in 1973. She told them that she had phoned *Maclean's* magazine to complain about MacGregor's article. She suggested that the magazine and MacGregor could be sued for slander, presumably against Tom. She understood publication of the article as being motivated by a simple desire to be shocking in order to make money.

Margaret had only met Winnifred Trainor once, at the 1917 Canadian National Exhibition in Toronto. From this meeting and through exchange of several letters about Tom's passing, she had concluded that Winnie's "mind was gone." The insinuation would seem to be that any information coming from Winnie, or perhaps even from any of her relatives, would be untrustworthy.

Another Thomson family member, Elva Henry, told the same researchers she was hesitant to speak to anyone about Thomson for fear of feeding the upsetting media interest in Tom's death. The family was becoming very concerned with rumours and "lies" circulating, and insistent that any research they assisted in would have to be "the truth."

Aside from confirming the Thomson family's growing consternation with the coverage of their famous relative, the Henry interview also reintroduced an element into the story that had only been mentioned once before: the claim that Tom Thomson had a sprained ankle when he died.

In 1969, George Thomson's son, George Jr., had made this claim to an Owen Sound *Sun-Times* reporter. In 1973, Henry suggested the same. She repeated George Jr.'s claim, adding that George Jr. suspected Tom had simply "missed his footing getting out of the canoe and hit his head on a rock and died." Tom's brother, according to Henry, had mentioned several times that Tom had likely fashioned a "backwoods treatment" for his ankle, and "tried to bind it up somehow with the fishing line."

If Thomson had a weak ankle, the possibility that he slipped on a wet rock would be higher. If he had tried to splint the ankle with fishing line, this could explain why it was wrapped neatly and so many times (if Robinson's 1950s account is to be believed). That this claim did not surface until 1969, however, raises some questions about its trustworthiness as an explanation for Thomson's death.

Within a few years, despite the Thomson family's wishes to stop what they believed were wild and unfounded stories about Tom, several more poorly supported theories were offered regarding Thomson's death.

In 1975, Dr. Harry Ebbs, the man who had provided the initial contact between provincial authorities and the group of men who discovered remains in Mowat Cemetery in 1956, proposed that Thomson had been shot in the head.

In an interview with Algonquin Park historian Rory Mackay, Ebbs outlined his belief that the remains found in 1956 were Tom Thomson's. Ebbs concluded that the hole in the skull discovered in 1956 was the result of a bullet. At some point after 1956, Ebbs related to Mackay how he had spent some time informally investigating his ideas around Canoe Lake. His work led him to conclude that Martin Blecher had shot Thomson from the Blecher boathouse. Ebbs hoped to one day publish his theories about Thomson's death, planning to use the title "Yes, Tom Thomson was Murdered."

In 1977, Ronald Pittaway, who was researching the history of Algonquin Park, was conducting interviews with people who might offer unique insights into park life. Daphne Crombie had come to Canoe Lake with her husband, Lieutenant Robin Crombie, during the fall of 1916. Having sustained a war injury, Crombie's husband had been told his lungs might benefit from the cool, clear air of New Ontario. Settling in at Mowat Lodge during the first half of 1917, the Crombies spent their days quietly watching the lake, resting, and chatting with the locals.

What has been preserved of the audio version of Pittaway's interview with Crombie suggests that his primary, if not sole, interest in Crombie's testimony was to hear any observations she might make about Tom Thomson. At the beginning of the recording, she asks Pittaway, "What am I saying that would be worthwhile?" His response is that she is one of the few people still alive who knew Tom Thomson. As interest in Thomson's life was high, Pittaway suggests that many people might be interested in Crombie's memories.

Pittaway's first request of Crombie was to share what she knows about the relationship between Tom Thomson and Winnifred Trainor. Without pause, Crombie launched into a somewhat convoluted tale chocked with unique revelations.

While at Canoe Lake, Crombie reported, she and Shannon Fraser's wife, Annie, became friends. Annie confessed to Crombie that she had read the last letter Tom received from Winnifred Trainor. In the letter, Trainor told Tom she was coming to see him during the next week, and begged him to get a new suit because "we'll have to be married." By the time Trainor arrived at Canoe Lake, Crombie reported, Tom was dead.

In response to the letter, Crombie suggested, Tom approached Shannon Fraser during a drunken party on the night of July 7, asking Fraser to repay a loan so that Thomson could cover his wedding expenses. Fraser punched Thomson. Crombie claimed Thomson fell, hit his head on a fire grate, and passed out — all of which she said she learned from Annie Fraser. She also stated that Dr. MacCallum was aware of the fight.

Having to make sense of their stories, Crombie's conclusion was that Shannon and Annie Fraser had panicked, thinking Tom was dead. She surmised they had placed his body in his canoe, then dumped the body in the lake.

Crombie gave little credence to the theory that Thomson had committed suicide. She indicated that sometime soon after Thomson's death, Dr. MacCallum asked her opinion whether Tom might have killed himself. She responded, "Utter bosh rubbish." In Crombie's words, Thomson "told me with great big round eyes how he'd just sold [a painting] to the government for $500. He was all up in the air about his paintings." Her assessment was that Thomson was excited about his future, certainly not despondent.

She also stated her opinion that there was nothing romantic going on between Martin Blecher and Trainor. In her assessment, Blecher was unattractive and "blowsy," with a German accent.

Crombie's provocative claims were, not unsurprisingly, quickly publicized. Rather more surprising, though, is that they did not receive more scrutiny. Crombie's testimony is laced with impossible claims.

Speaking of what occurred when Thomson's body was found, Crombie clarified that she couldn't provide any facts about that because she wasn't at Canoe Lake at the time. She added, however, that "we were there shortly before that, and I went down to MacCallum. The first thing that MacCallum said was, 'You don't think he committed suicide, do you?'" While MacCallum could possibly have met Crombie during his May 1917 visit to Canoe Lake, he would not have been speculating as to whether Tom had committed suicide over a month before the man disappeared. As there is no record of him later visiting Canoe Lake, Crombie's "memory" must be treated with doubt.

A few months after Pittaway interviewed Crombie, Thomson's artwork was the focus of a widely publicized book, *Tom Thomson: The Silence and the Storm*, written by art critic David Silcox and respected Canadian painter Harold Town. Town's intention was to "rescue" Thomson's sullied reputation from the "club-footed ghouls" speculating about Thomson's death, who were distracting people from what was important: Thomson's art. Town and Silcox were both certainly keen to downplay any whiff of tawdry tabloid sensationalism in their discussion, and worked to minimize consideration of Thomson's death. Nonetheless, that they gave any attention to the stories regarding Thomson's demise at all provides an indication of how the mystery was coming to play an integral role in understandings of Thomson's life.

As part of their effort to explain the mystery away, Silcox advanced a radically simple explanation for Thomson's death. Working from information gained during the 1973 Elva Henry interview, Silcox claimed that Thomson had sprained his ankle in the days leading up to July 8, 1917. He suggested that if Thomson had stood up in his canoe — perhaps to urinate — and put too much weight on his bad ankle, he might have slipped, hit his head on the canoe's gunwale, and drowned.

In a direct inversion of how the overwrought speculations of many writers gained widespread attention, Silcox's rather simple explanation was met with silence. For many of his readers, perhaps, the remonstration to avoid thinking about Thomson's death was enough to render explanations unnecessary.

In 1977, Roy MacGregor was inspired to revisit the story of Tom Thomson's death by publication of Silcox and Town's book. He had also recently become aware of Daphne Crombie's testimony, and drew heavily upon her claims to support the flimsy theories he had offered in 1973.

Simply titled "The Legend," his article in *The Canadian* magazine echoed Joan Murray's suggestion that we must understand Thomson's death if we are to understand his painting. Implying a challenge to Harold Town's dismissal of those interested in Thomson's death, MacGregor confidently stated, "We know the man's work and his story are inseparable."

MacGregor is free with his criticism, pointing out errors, oversights, and what he saw as the foolishness of most of the writers who had tackled the subject of Thomson's death since the late 1960s. One of the few writers he does seem to respect is William Little and his theory that Martin Blecher Jr. murdered Tom Thomson. MacGregor stated that Little "built a much-researched and complicated case," and identified no flaws in his research or argument.

MacGregor directed most of his criticism toward Silcox and Town's recently published *The Silence and the Storm*. He took issue with their knowledge of the history of Algonquin Park. Silcox had suggested that Thomson's complaint about Muskoka — in particular, that the social environment of his patron's Georgian Bay cottage was getting too much like Toronto's tony North Rosedale neighbourhood — could also apply to Canoe Lake. MacGregor implied his superior historical knowledge when he assured his readers that in 1917 Algonquin Park was "as much like North Rosedale as Canoe Lake was like the Atlantic."

Criticism of their grasp of social history aside, MacGregor suggested Silcox and Town did not carefully enough consider the sources for some of their key evidence. In his opinion, Silcox and Town gave Charles Plewman's comments about the relationship between Trainor and Thomson too much weight. MacGregor reminded his readers that Plewman was not at Canoe Lake when Thomson was alive, and had probably never spoken to Trainor. On this basis, he suggested, the credibility of Plewman's testimony regarding Thomson and Trainor's relationship, and the relationship's effect on Thomson's state of mind, is weak.

How, exactly, MacGregor thought Plewman's testimony might have led Silcox and Town astray is unclear. Silcox did not accept Plewman's theory that Thomson had committed suicide in order to avoid marrying Trainor. Silcox's theory was that Thomson had accidentally fallen out of his canoe and struck his head. This theory could easily coexist with MacGregor's suggestion that Winnie and Thomson were intending to marry soon.

Regardless, MacGregor is direct and brief in his assessment of Silcox's theory that Thomson fell due to a weak ankle: "Cute, but facile," he stated. "No one who was there ever mentioned Thomson having an open fly or a sore ankle," MacGregor pointed out.

When MacGregor turned to offering his own analysis, however, his position suffered from the same weaknesses he drew attention to in the work of others.

He suggested that Silcox and Town's version of the story gave the impression of wide agreement on the facts. MacGregor noted that key elements in the story are unresolved, however. For instance, he asked, "Was the canoe upside down or upright? Did they find it one or two days later?"

A survey of the primary documents held by the Thomson family, Mark Robinson's diary, and the materials collected by Blodwen Davies in the 1930s would have revealed quite clear answers to these questions. MacGregor, however, had already angered members of the Thomson family with his 1973 article. Even if he had asked for access to the important documents they held, they would not likely have granted him permission. The other two collections were available, though. A transcript of Robinson's diary had been published, after all, in Addison and Harwood's book almost a decade before, and was republished in Little's book in 1970. Davies's materials had been in Library and Archives Canada for at least a decade or more.

Having noted ongoing disagreements regarding aspects of the case, MacGregor then inexplicably suggested that other, highly contentious elements are commonly accepted without question. He stated, "The only things they all agreed on were that Thomson's favorite paddle was missing and couldn't be found, despite repeated searchings of the shoreline, and that his spare paddle was strapped awkwardly into portaging position, not at all the way Thomson would have had it."

This assertion defies logic. All of the 1917 accounts indicate two paddles were tied into the canoe, and none mention anything about sloppy knots. Robinson had given contradictory testimony on the issue. It is noteworthy, though, that the only time he mentioned a sloppily tied paddle was in the 1950s, his last recorded testimony on the topic. Before MacGregor's 1977 article, the only other published versions of the story to make such a claim about a sloppily tied-in paddle were Noble Sharpe's 1970 article in the *Canadian Society of Forensic Science Journal*, and Charles Plewman in his Canadian Camping Association magazine article in 1972.

Along with questionable research, MacGregor again subtly misrepresented facts so that they would seem incontrovertible. He described the "bruise" that Robinson and Howland had identified on Thomson's temple during their 1917 examination as "a violent mark." The choice of adjective is significant. Robinson's July 1917 examination notes state: "We found a bruise on left temple about four inches long, evidently caused by falling on a rock. Otherwise, no marks of violence on body." Howland similarly described "a bruise on right temple size of 4 [inch] long, no other sign of external marks visible on body." Clearly, MacGregor was applying artistic licence to his description of Thomson's corpse, exaggerating the possibility that the body had suffered from violence.

The selective and misleading approach to reportage pursued by MacGregor groundlessly inflated the possibility that Thomson had been murdered. To MacGregor, perhaps, the presumption of conspiracy was permissible. He bluntly stated, "All who knew [Thomson] well discounted both accident and suicide." The criteria of "knowing Thomson well" was perhaps intended to undermine the credibility of professionals such as Dr. Howland. MacGregor's statement is certainly difficult to reconcile with the fact that both George Thomson and Dr. MacCallum rejected any explanation for Tom's death outside of "accidental drowning."

If MacGregor's patently false claim that accident or suicide were implausible explanations for Tom Thomson's death is accepted, the only thing missing, he assured his reader, was a plausible murder theory. Missing, that is, until Daphne Crombie provided her testimony.

MacGregor's article put Crombie in a far-fetched role, suggesting that she was "the Forgotten Lady in the Tom Thomson story." Forgotten, he suggested, because she had a story to tell but had not spoken publicly. This was in part, he claimed, "because no one — until I came across her — has ever asked her."

Here, yet again, MacGregor's claim does not stand up to simple analysis. His suggestion that he had "discovered" Crombie independently, by chance, only a few months after Pittaway, is wrong. When he interviewed her, Pittaway did not ask Crombie about Thomson being murdered. He had sought her out — as one of the few surviving persons who knew Thomson during his time spent on Canoe Lake — to record her reflections on Thomson's personality and Thomson's relationship with Winnie Trainor. Pittaway recorded Crombie's story about Annie Fraser's confession, and her speculation that Thomson had been murdered. MacGregor certainly did not rescue Crombie and her testimony from being "forgotten," as Pittaway had already recorded it. MacGregor did, though, elevate her story into much wider attention.

MacGregor's 1977 description of his relationship with Crombie, and the singular importance of the story she told him, is also undermined by his 2010 description of how he came to interview the woman. In *Northern Light*, MacGregor explains that in 1977 an Algonquin Park staffer alerted him to the audio recording of an interview Pittaway had recently had with Crombie. After listening to the recording, and being shocked by what she had told Pittaway, MacGregor sought out his own interview. This version of the story is a far cry from the assertion he made in 1977. It is also one that is hard to explain as "artistic licence" or lapsed memory, and raises the question of what other aspects of MacGregor's 1977 account might be misrepresented.

For instance, when MacGregor quoted Crombie, her words often differ only slightly from those recorded by Pittaway. Frequently, full sentences are verbatim matches. The amazing synchronicity between the language and phrasing that Crombie used in telling her story to Pittaway and as reported by MacGregor — particularly given that ten months had passed between the two interviews — suggests that she either had much more practice telling her story than she admitted to, or that MacGregor offered significant portions from Pittaway's recording as his own interview. Neither option undermines Crombie's testimony, but this once again suggests that care needs to be taken with the second record of Crombie's accounting of the events.

The version of the story Crombie told MacGregor in October 1977 *did* differ in some details from the one she had told Pittaway ten months earlier. She was consistent in stating that she was relating only what Annie Fraser had told her: Winnie Trainor wrote Thomson telling him to get a new suit, and that they would have to be married. In her first interview, Crombie added that Trainor had also instructed him to ask Shannon Fraser to repay his debt to Thomson.

In her second account, Crombie reportedly claimed that Annie Fraser had confided in her not once, but twice. The first time, she told MacGregor, was to gossip about Trainor's letter. MacGregor suggests this conversation happened before Thomson's body was discovered because Crombie had left Canoe Lake by that time. The second conversation occurred several weeks later, after the exhumation of Thomson's Canoe Lake grave, by which time Crombie had returned to the region. In this second conversation, according to Crombie, Annie confessed that she and her husband had disposed of what they believed to be Thomson's corpse.

MacGregor noted that if Crombie's story is to be believed, it raised the issue that anyone who had reported seeing Thomson on the morning of Sunday, July 8 — including, at minimum, Shannon Fraser and Mark Robinson, and perhaps the Colsons as well as some guests at Mowat Lodge — were either sorely mistaken or lying.

Surprisingly, he does not raise the key questions that would seem just as obvious: Why would Annie confess to someone that her husband had murdered Thomson several weeks before? That she and her husband had conspired together to hide Thomson's body? That they had decided to deceive Thomson's family, friends, as well as the park and provincial authorities? Additionally, why would Crombie not report the confession of such a heinous crime to authorities as soon as she became aware of it, rather than wait sixty years to confess it to an Algonquin Park historian?

Regardless of the improbabilities in Crombie's testimony, MacGregor gave her statements credibility, even as he admitted that what she was confiding in him was entirely hearsay. He reported that she assured him, however, "I'm only telling things I'm absolutely sure of." She could only be sure of what Annie Fraser had told her, though, and not the truth behind what Annie claimed.

In 1980, MacGregor returned to the Thomson story for a third time, treating the tale through the lens of what might today be called historical fiction. In *Shorelines*, MacGregor avoids providing a definitive answer to the question of how Tom Thomson died at Canoe Lake. Even when treating the story as fiction, MacGregor highlights many of the thinly justified claims, while struggling to reconcile competing theories and speculation. For instance, he described Thomson attending a drinking party on the night of July 7, 1917. To ensure that neither the Blecher nor Fraser mystery are entirely discounted, he included Thomson both bullying Martin Blecher and receiving a head wound in a fight with Shannon Fraser.

The core of MacGregor's story, however, are the repercussions of Thomson's death for Winnie Trainor. Janet Turner (a fictional stand-in for Trainor), pregnant by Thomson, flees to Philadelphia. There she has a daughter, who is given over to a local family. The daughter returns to the Huntsville area in 1961 to learn about her birth parents, and discovers that she is the child of Tom Thomson and Janet Turner. When the book was reprinted in 2002 under the title *Canoe Lake*, MacGregor included an author's note indicating that, to no one's surprise, Trainor was his model for the Turner character.

Telling Thomson's story by adapting it as a fictional work allowed MacGregor to riff on his theories, to fill in gaps in the documentary record, and to pursue a "good story" where facts might get in the way. His narrative breaks fundamentally with what the historical records show can be confidently stated about Thomson's death, though. In this regard, *Shorelines* — while admittedly a work of fiction — should not be trusted to in any way shed light on actual historical events.

Very few elements of MacGregor's work reflect facts contained in documents produced at the time of Thomson's death, or even information produced by those involved within ten years of the events described. As an accessible, entertaining version of what was believed by many to be a historically grounded story about Thomson's death, *Shorelines/Canoe Lake* helped to further cement particular flawed beliefs about Thomson's death into popular culture. These flawed claims, it might be added, had largely been advanced by MacGregor in the two magazine articles he had written during the 1970s.

Three decades would pass before Roy MacGregor returned to the Thomson story for a fourth time. In 2010's *Northern Light: The Enduring Mystery of Tom Thomson and the Woman Who Loved Him*, MacGregor proposed (again) that Thomson's death was not accidental. He repeated his suggestion that either Shannon Fraser or Martin Blecher Jr. had killed Thomson. He also concluded that Thomson's body was not removed from the park in 1917, based on analysis of photographs of the remains found at Canoe Lake in 1956. MacGregor's work — with its compelling narrative, evocation of his personal acquaintance with personalities around Canoe Lake, and reference to advanced science — generated significant attention from Canadian media. Unfortunately, *Northern Light*'s argument for foul play is entirely contingent on MacGregor's continued sloppy use of untrustworthy evidence. Instead of correcting misinformation associated with the case, MacGregor's book unfortunately further muddles our understanding.

As he noted in the acknowledgements for *Northern Light*, MacGregor made use of the transcriptions on the *Death on a Painted Lake* website to save himself significant research time, travel, and costs. The temptation to work from some of his previous writing on the topic, and the convenience of using freely available, digital transcriptions of some sources, may have led MacGregor to overlook alternative, unpublished evidence, and to not consider some of the contradictions within and between some of the primary sources.

In developing his account of Thomson's last days, MacGregor stitches together select accounts offered decades after the artist's death. MacGregor uses details from each of Robinson's three accounts, presenting the selections as a coherent whole that remained consistent over time. That Robinson's testimony evolved significantly over thirty-five years, and that contradictory elements existed between his accounts, is not identified. In granting Robinson's accounts the veneer of consistency and credibility,

MacGregor gave parts of Robinson's testimonies far more authority than they merit.

For instance, in 1917, Robinson did not record how many paddles were found in Thomson's canoe. In 1930, he stated that one paddle was found. In the 1950s, he claimed two. MacGregor repeats the third version of Robinson's story, avoiding even mentioning the two earlier, distinctly different accounts. This decision also ignored primary evidence, produced by Shannon Fraser in July 1917, claiming that both of Thomson's paddles were found in his canoe. MacGregor's position regarding Thomson's death, however, was deeply invested in a paddle being missing. During the 1970s, MacGregor had built his theory of Thomson being killed on a "lost paddle" narrative. Stressing the fact that the primary sources suggested no alarm over the number of paddles found and that Robinson's testimony was inconsistent would have seriously undermined MacGregor's theory.

As discussed earlier, MacGregor would not likely have been granted access to records held by the Thomson family during the 1970s, and so he cannot be faulted for overlooking accounts he could not be aware of. By the 1990s, however, the Thomson family documents were publicly available in the Library and Archives Canada collections. By 2011, MacGregor's strange choice of evidence cannot be explained by lack of access to the historical records.

MacGregor made a similarly questionable judgment in his account of Mark Robinson's last words with Tom Thomson. In the 1950s, Robinson claimed to have watched Thomson and Fraser fishing and to have overheard Thomson's plan to play a practical joke on him. He also mentioned that Thomson saw and spoke to him. Robinson's account provides a charming anecdote of how bucolic life in the park might have been. As testimony, though, this story is untrustworthy. In 1930, Robinson mentioned seeing Thomson and Fraser from afar on the morning of July 8, but did not state that he heard their conversation or spoke with Thomson. As their last meeting, this would seem to be something significant to share when relating his memories to people. The first — and only — time Robinson mentions speaking to Thomson and overhearing Thomson's conversation with Fraser that morning was in the 1950s. Fraser never attested to the story, and Robinson never mentioned it earlier to George Thomson or to researchers such as

Davies. MacGregor never suggested that any different version of Robinson's story exists, though, once again giving Robinson's final version more credibility than it deserves. Why MacGregor used Robinson's very suspicious claim as the accurate description of the events of Thomson's last morning is confounding, and it's something that he never explains.

Perhaps recognizing that Robinson's accounts are not consistent, MacGregor attempts to support them with references to testimony he says was provided by Shannon Fraser and Martin Blecher Jr. This clearly misrepresents the facts. Much of what MacGregor credits as Fraser's and Blecher's testimony is drawn from Robinson's 1930s and 1950s "reporting" of what these men testified at the 1917 inquest. Blecher never spoke out publicly regarding Thomson's death. The only communication we have from Shannon Fraser about the events surrounding Thomson's death are the few telegrams and short letters sent to Thomson family members and friends during 1917. Through patently false claims about testimony that agrees with Robinson's story, MacGregor gave the impression that Robinson is a trustworthy source. The testimony he turned to, however, derived from Robinson himself.

Although it provided a compelling narrative, MacGregor's account of Thomson's last days mostly contains assertions polished to cover up inconsistent and hearsay evidence provided by one man over the course of almost four decades. On its own, this would undermine the credibility of his claims. Unfortunately, MacGregor's work suffers from a number of additional flaws.

MacGregor repeats the strategy he employed in 1977, using *Northern Light* to suggest that a woman was the "forgotten" figure in Tom Thomson's life. In 2010, however, the overlooked protagonist is not Daphne Crombie but Winnifred Trainor. MacGregor argued that the woman pictured in two undated Thomson photographs, likely taken between 1912 and 1914, had been incorrectly identified as Winnifred Trainor. One of the photos was published in Addison and Harwood's 1969 book, and both were included in a 1970 National Gallery of Canada periodical. The Thomson family provided the negatives for the photos, and one of Tom Thomson's nieces identified the woman as Trainor. She had met Trainor only once, in 1917.

MacGregor assured his readers that he knew what Trainor looked like because she was his aunt's sister, lived close to his childhood home, and, as he spent much of a chapter relating, she regularly visited his family well into his teens. He does not explain, though, why after writing three lengthy magazine articles and a book exploring Thomson's death, it took him forty years to realize that someone he claimed to be so familiar with was misidentified in photos. Regardless, as interesting an issue as this is, MacGregor's identification of the "correct" Winnifred Trainor does not tremendously alter the central questions concerning the narrative of Thomson's death, or MacGregor's answers to them.

Another facet of *Northern Light* is MacGregor's efforts to ascertain whether the remains found in 1956 at Mowat Cemetery could be those of Tom Thomson. This effort is based on MacGregor's doubts about the provincial police crime lab's conclusions regarding the remains. MacGregor reasoned that the chances of William Little and his friends discovering an unknown burial were slim to none. On this basis, he concluded that the provincial investigators might have erred in their assessment that the body was that of an Aboriginal man.

Encouraged by two Ottawa dentists engaging in what he called "admittedly amateur forensic work," MacGregor approached Ron Williamson of Toronto's Archaeological Services, Inc. He described providing Williamson with photographs of Thomson as well as of the skull exhumed in 1956. MacGregor also shared a transcription of the 1956 forensic report.

MacGregor related that Williamson's perspective was that Dr. Sharpe's conclusion reflected knowledge current for his time. On the basis of his own experience, however, Williamson could not support the conclusion that the remains were those of an Aboriginal man.

With Williamson's assessment in hand, and on a preliminary visual analysis of the photographs that suggested the 1956 skull and Thomson's skull shared some similarities, forensic artist Victoria Lywood was asked to render visually what the person whose skull was found in 1956 might have looked like. With the warning that he should "take a Valium" before he looked at Lywood's work, MacGregor was confronted with a drawing that seemed to very closely represent Thomson's face. On this basis,

MacGregor offered that the remains found in Mowat Cemetery in 1956 are very likely Thomson's, and suggested that this connection reinvigorates the murder theory.

The 1970s certainly saw an explosion of writing about Tom Thomson's death. New documents and new testimony fed the development of new ideas regarding the case. Departing significantly from evidence that had been drawn upon in the past, these new ideas — often suggesting much darker activities at Canoe Lake during 1917 — have served to propel speculation ever since. A few of the persons who first tackled the story of Thomson's death during the 1970s, such as Joan Murray, David Silcox, and Roy MacGregor, have continued to write about the case, returning to it regularly. Roy MacGregor's work has certainly steered popular thinking regarding the case, although both Murray and Silcox have also continued to advance their own unique perspectives. Based on their personal reputations, and through repetition, their analyses have taken on the impression of being the most advanced thinking on the case. However, their work was clearly flawed from the outset, and their reworkings of their original writings on the subject have repeated many of these problems over the following decades.

9

REPETITION MAKES THE STORIES TRUE

He is made stronger by what does not kill him.
And what kills him makes him stronger still.

— TROY JOLLIMORE, "TOM THOMSON IN HIS OFFICE, THURSDAY AFTERNOON," *TOM THOMSON IN PURGATORY*, 2006

SINCE THE 1980s, speculation about Tom Thomson's death has become a field of its own, fuelling websites, party games, Twitter accounts, books, art exhibitions, and plays. Many of these materials, however, depend on the tenuously supported mythology about Thomson's last days that blossomed during the late 1960s and 1970s.

In the last decade, an abundance of publications have provided newcomers to the case with a variety of approaches to the mysteries. Some of the work attempt to correct past writing on the topic and to provide new assessment of the evidence. Some treat Thomson's death as a symbolic reference point, as a launching pad for their own creative work. While many of these works make for fascinating reading, what is disappointing is that almost a century after Thomson's death, most of these recent works rarely pare away rumours, hearsay, and errors from Thomson's biography.

Writing about Tom Thomson and his death has also become a topic of study itself, as scholars investigate the development of Canadian identity, nationalism, and masculinity through works exploring Thomson's life, his painting, and his death. These works have helped to reveal how

Thomson has become incorporated into a national mythology, and how particular understandings of Thomson's death have in fact become integral to public appreciation of his value to Canadians.

During the mid-1970s, Tom Thomson and his art became a reference point for Canadian visual artists. Nationalist creators drew on Thomson's imagery, as well as his reputation, suggesting parallels between the Canadian identity and stories about Thomson's love of nature, avoidance of war, tragic love, and solitary personality. See, for instance, John Boyle's *Midnight Oil (Ode to Tom Thomson)* (1969), Joyce Wieland's *True Patriot Love* (1971) and *The Far Shore* (1976), Michael Snow's *Plus Tard* (1977), and General Idea's *Pharm@cology* (1994).

Tom Thomson has also recently received attention in popular Canadian music. His story serves as the basis for The Tragically Hip's 1991 song "Three Pistols" and lurks as a contributing element to the Rheostatics' 1995 instrumental work, *Music Inspired by the Group of Seven*.

The Hip's song begins with the direct reference "Well, Tom Thomson came paddling past/I'm pretty sure it was him." The song gives presence to a Winnifred Trainor–type character, "his little, lonely love/his bride of the northern woods," who keeps a vigil over Thomson's grave. Repeating a story that has circulated regarding the watch Winnie Trainor kept over Thomson's original burial site, Gord Downie, The Hip's lead singer, proclaims the "bride's" role in the song's last verse: "Well, little girls come on Remembrance Day/Placing flowers on his grave/She waits in the shadows 'til after dark/Just to sweep them all away."

In a less esoteric vein, during the late 1990s Gaye Clemson, who has written several books addressing Algonquin Park history, created the *Tom Thomson Murder Mystery Game*. The game involves players in assessing "evidence" related to Thomson's death, considering the personalities and interests of people who might have been involved, and arriving at a conclusion regarding how Thomson died. Clemson's web page advertising the game indicates her position: "Though some say it was an accident, those of us who've spent our lives on Canoe Lake in Algonquin Park know that it was really foul play at work." Regardless of how Clemson reached her conclusions, the history she draws upon in the game is liberally mixed with speculative and fictional elements. She notes that the "characters are all real, though some of the activities and feelings attributed to them are purely fictional." The fictional elements have been added "to make it fun," Clemson suggests. Of course, they also muddle understanding of the real story of Thomson's life for those who might not be clearly aware of what the "real evidence" is to begin with.

Tom Thomson's death has also served as the basis for a mystery story featuring two preteen detectives, Dani and Caitlin. Larry McCloskey's *Tom Thomson's Last Paddle* (2002) has the ghost of the murdered Tom Thomson seeking justice. At the end of the tale, Thomson explains to the two girls how he died. The ghost explains that he fought with Fraser and Blecher at a party on the night of July 7, when liquor, talk of the war, and the need for debts to be repaid led to heated exchanges. Incorporating characterization of Thomson as an early environmentalist, Thomson's ghost adds that he also fought with a man named Billy Bull, who worked with a local lumber company, over whether the lumber industry's work in the park should be stopped. Thomson's ghost also suggested that he was being pressured to marry a woman he did not love, and had lost someone that he might have been interested in marrying. None of these led to his death, however.

About noon on July 8, Thomson's ghost relates, he wrapped a sprained ankle in fishing line and took off in his canoe. Not paying much attention to his surroundings, he discovered that Billy Bull was approaching in another canoe. Suggesting that Tom's meddling in the lumber company's business was not appreciated, Bull swung his paddle at Thomson's head, hitting his right temple. Thomson drowned. His ghost added that Martin Blecher Jr. watched the entire scene without taking any action to stop it or save Thomson.

During the 2000s, themes such as masculinity, love, creativity, and nature were taken up in several books of poetry referencing Thomson. Troy Jollimore's 2006 collection of poems, *Tom Thomson in Purgatory*, is a winner of the (U.S.) National Book Critics Circle Award. It consists of two cycles of poems, of approximately equal length, one of which uses Tom Thomson as a very loose symbol for a creator's struggle with creativity, love, and a sense of purpose.

Kevin Irie's *Viewing Tom Thomson: A Minority Report* (2012) works much more closely with Thomson's art and life. Irie uses various Thomson paintings as lenses through which to consider how relevant a white, single, male artist working in the "north" one hundred years ago is in contemporary, multicultural, and globalized Canada, where much of the population lives in urban centres. In both these works, Thomson is positioned in a somewhat tragic role, struggling against impersonal, inexorable forces larger than the individual human.

I draw attention to these works not because they contribute significantly to our understanding of Thomson in any new, historical way, but because they signify how widespread Tom Thomson has become as a cultural symbol. In 2008, Sherrill Grace devoted an entire scholarly work not to discerning the facts of Thomson's life or death, but to understanding how Thomson has been "invented" in storytelling. Without a doubt, Thomson's name and the images he produced have become national shorthand for tragedy, brilliance, and struggle for integrity. Elements of his life, drawn sometimes from the mythological and less frequently from the factual, have permeated the common Canadian cultural vernacular during almost a century of storytelling.

After more than a decade away from writing about Thomson, during the 1980s and 1990s Joan Murray, the former curator of Canadian collections for the AGO, produced a flurry of materials concerned with Thomson's life and art. Between 1986 and 2002, she wrote five books devoted to Tom Thomson. Several, such as *Tom Thomson: Trees* (1999) and *Flowers: J.E.H. MacDonald, Tom Thomson and the Group of Seven* (2002) were image-heavy publications focused on describing Thomson's painting methods and interests.

Three of Murray's books addressed Thomson's death as a critical component of understanding his creative output. They were *The Best of Tom Thomson* (1986), *Tom Thomson: The Last Spring* (1994), and *Tom Thomson: Design for a Canadian Hero* (1998). During this period, Murray also wrote several books, such as *Northern Lights: Masterpieces from Tom Thomson and the Group of Seven* (1994) that addressed Thomson's work alongside that of his peers in the Group of Seven.

In *The Best of Tom Thomson*, Murray offered a confusing mix of elements drawn from various accounts of Thomson's death, seasoned with some new claims. She gave almost a page to Daphne Crombie's report that Thomson was murdered on the night between July 7 and 8. She suggested it was problematic, though, because of Robinson's statement that at the inquest Fraser had reported having seen Thomson on the morning of July 8, after the "party" at which Crombie suggests Thomson died. Murray also stated that Robinson claimed he thought he had seen Thomson and Fraser that morning, although they were in a canoe out on the lake. A few pages later, however, she contradicts herself, suggesting Crombie's story "fits the known facts." Inexplicably, she concluded that murder offered the most plausible explanation to the many unresolved questions about Thomson's death.

By the 1980s, much of Murray's thinking about Thomson's art had come to focus on the idea that during spring 1917 Thomson was pursuing a unique documentary realism, recording the changing seasons in Algonquin Park by making a painting every day for about two months. Murray assured her readers that the "story [of Thomson's plan] is often dismissed as apocryphal, but it is not." In support of her claim, she cited Robinson's 1930 letter to Davies, where the tale was first reported.

Understanding whether Robinson's testimony should be believed would be helped by resolving what works Thomson produced during the spring of 1917. This is not an easy task, however. Researchers can't even be sure how many works they might be seeking. In 1917, no inventory of works Thomson had left behind at Canoe Lake or produced since arriving there was made. During the 1930s, Robinson suggested Thomson had produced about sixty-two works. In the 1950s, he indicated about ninety. No systematic record of how many paintings were retrieved from Canoe Lake was produced, nor do we have a record regarding what works Thomson distributed to Dr. MacCallum or other friends that spring. Most of the works remaining in Thomson's Toronto shack were stamped with a distinctive mark after his death, but this leaves a multitude of undated, often unsigned works produced over five years.

In 1994, Murray's second book on Thomson focused on the last months of his life. *The Last Spring* provides a difficult to untangle mix of fact, rumour, and hearsay testimony. Though tightly intertwined, the threads that can be identified help us once again grasp which Thomson stories were circulating, and which ones Murray believed had credibility.

In *The Best of Tom Thomson*, Murray offered that Thomson rarely spoke about his painting "except to disparage it." In *The Last Spring*, she echoed this perception. Murray portrayed Thomson as an unhappy man who saw few prospects. She suggested "the myth that developed after his death masks the personality of a difficult, complex man who was unhappy with his situation ... he had no home, no wife, poor prospects." As support for this position, she noted that Davies describes Thomson as saying, "Here's some of my junk." She pointed out that he had told MacCallum, "I am only a bum artist anyway."

This portrayal does not entirely align with Murray's discussion of Thomson's apparent excitement over the work he was producing that spring. Once again, Murray depended on Mark Robinson's testimony from the early 1930s. She described Thomson rushing into Robinson's cabin and asking to hang his "records": a "canvas" a day for sixty-two days. "The warden said he could," she added.

In *The Last Spring*, Murray positioned Thomson's works produced during 1917 as some of his most promising and insightful paintings. She observed that "the work Thomson painted during the last spring of his life, his day-by-day record of the changing weather of the park, looks like an unadorned report."

In the impulse to document the world as it was, Murray suggested that Thomson was making associations between his art and the activities of a botanist, Dr. William Brodie. Murray did not make a convincing connection between the two men, though. She never discussed any correspondence or meetings between the two men, and no record of Thomson referring to Brodie's work was identified. Murray even appeared to be unclear what the relationship might have been between Thomson and Brodie. In *The Last Spring*, Murray identified Brodie as Thomson's "uncle." In *Design for a Canadian Hero*, Murray identified Brodie as Tom Thomson's "cousin." At another point in the book, she offered the nonsensical explanation that Brodie was "the son of [Thomson's] grandfather's old friend James, and thus his grandmother's first cousin (though the family always called him 'uncle')."

Despite the tenuous connection, Murray insisted that Thomson's "use of the word 'records' was also important. He meant the word in its dictionary sense: he felt he had created documents of the scene before him." The difficulty with this assertion, of course, is that it is Mark Robinson who used the word "record." We have no evidence that Thomson referred to his sketches this way.

In fact, the idea that Thomson was trying to provide some kind of "record," an exact depiction of scenes, does not at all fit with how Thomson and his peers approached their work. In their paintings, they often relocated, eliminated, or introduced objects to achieve what they believed to be effective design. Additionally, given his rough application of thick, impasto paint, and quick painting style, it is hard to conceive of Thomson's paintings as more than a quick impression of a scene. They were certainly not intended to provide any kind of authoritative, accurate view. He certainly would not have made this claim for the works on canvas that he developed in his Toronto shack each winter, given his willingness to abstract elements from the sketches.

Turning to Thomson's death, Murray gave serious consideration to two methods by which Thomson might have met his end. She stated that Thomson was in a fight with Shannon Fraser the night of July 7, where "he expressed anger over money he'd lent." According to Murray, Shannon Fraser believed Winnie was coming to Canoe Lake to confront Thomson about marriage. Of course, Murray could not have heard this testimony from Fraser himself. He was long dead by the time Murray was studying Thomson. Judging by Murray's source citations, her information concerning Fraser's perspective was gained from Charles Plewman's 1972 testimony. As for the fight, Plewman mentioned nothing about a drinking party, or more important, any fight between Thomson and Fraser. This portion of Murray's tale could only be derived from William Little's 1970 book or Daphne Crombie's 1977 testimony.

Further developing Fraser's role as an antagonist in Thomson's final hours, Murray turned to the letters Winnie Trainor wrote to members of the Thomson family. Murray described how "Fraser's insinuation that Thomson didn't want to marry her made Trainor so angry she went to Thomson's family. She told his sister that Thomson hadn't liked Fraser as he 'hadn't a good principle.'" This is a claim that does not accord well with other information available about Thomson's relationship with the Frasers. If Thomson had such dislike of Shannon Fraser, why he would continue to live at Mowat Lodge or help with tasks around the lodge is hard to understand.

Murray provided her most damning indictment of Shannon Fraser, though, when she repeated the claims Daphne Crombie had shared with Ron Pittaway in 1977. Without judgment, Murray simply repeated the story, likely gathered from listening to the audio record produced by Pittaway (she includes a transcript of the full interview in *The Last Spring*). For her part, Murray offered that when she interviewed Crombie during 1971, she found the woman to be "a careful witness." Murray seemed to overlook, however, that Crombie could only be a careful witness to Annie Fraser's confession.

In 1998, Joan Murray authored another Thomson book, *Tom Thomson: Design for a Canadian Hero*. The text restated many of the ideas about Thomson's death that she had offered only four years earlier in *The Last Spring*.

Somewhat surprisingly, Murray again attempted to buttress Daphne Crombie's credibility. Returning to her 1971 interview with Crombie, Murray claimed, "She did not seek notoriety for her version of Thomson's death. Indeed, she did not mention one word about it...." Murray implied that — at least in 1971 — she did not concern herself with such stories during her research. Seeking to explain why Crombie did not mention Annie Fraser's confession to her, Murray stated that "as a serious art scholar, I did not ask." We must surmise, of course, if Crombie's story is to be believed, that she felt in 1971 that a "serious art scholar" wouldn't be interested in how Tom Thomson had died. It is useful to keep in mind, then, how Crombie opened her 1977 interview with Pittaway: by asking, "What am I saying that would be worthwhile?" The murder story she had been secreting away for sixty years seems in 1977 to be pretty much the only thing that she could conceive of to share with a historian about Tom Thomson. That it didn't enter her mind in 1971, only six years earlier, that a Thomson researcher might be interested in Annie Fraser's confession about helping to eliminate Tom

Thomson's corpse raises a number of vexing questions about Murray's logic and her trust in Crombie's story.

In 1996, S. Bernard Shaw wrote *Canoe Lake: Tom Thomson and Other Stories*, in which he attempted to place Thomson's time at Canoe Lake within the context of the development of the Ontario lumber industry and Algonquin Park during the late nineteenth and early twentieth centuries. Shaw's work provided a generally well-measured survey of materials written about the Thomson case, and offered his own, rather far-fetched speculations regarding how Thomson might have died.

Shaw's work, like much before it, used untrustworthy stories that had become entwined with historical facts. Shaw repeated the story of how Thomson had unsuccessfully tried to enlist, and related that Thomson, Fraser, Blecher, and some of the guides attended a drinking party the night of July 7. At the party, Shaw stated, Fraser quickly became "bellicose." Blecher, who Shaw suggested was one of Thomson's rare enemies, was harassed about being a draft dodger. Lifting directly from William Little's creative account, Shaw stated that Blecher had left the party, threatening Thomson, "Don't get in my way if you know what's good for you." Shaw repeated Mark Robinson's 1950s testimony of how, the next morning, he saw Thomson and Fraser fishing, was spotted by the two men, and Thomson had said, "Howdy" to him.

Noting stories that a fight might have followed disagreement about the war, Shaw speculated that an additional source of conflict between Thomson and Blecher might have been Winnie Trainor. He pointed out that the Blecher and Trainor cottages were next to each other, and that as a single woman in a community where there were few women eligible for marriage to be found, Trainor would have strong attraction.

Although it suffered from some unfortunate shortcomings in its use of sources, Shaw's work admirably subjected some evidence to critical assessment. Shaw highlighted several reasons for approaching Mark Robinson's testimony with skepticism, observing that Robinson's accounts "vary in detail over ... 38 years." However, Shaw suggested the differences are not that important, as the "substance remains constant." Waffling over what to make of Robinson's testimony, he observed that by the 1950s Robinson would boldly proclaim his belief that Thomson had been murdered and that his body had not been removed from Canoe Lake. In 1917, however, no one (not even Robinson himself) recorded Robinson making any effort to speak against Dr. Howland's or Dr. Ranney's findings of "accidental drowning."

Shaw also asked what would seem to be an obvious, but far too rarely posed question regarding the inspection of Thomson's corpse. How could an experienced doctor, along with a soldier only just recently returned from service on the front lines of the war in Europe (where we would expect he would have become unsettlingly familiar with seeing bullet wounds and decomposing corpses), completely overlook a bullet wound in the side of a man's head, or mistake it as a "bruise"?

Shaw's analysis is weaker when it comes to considering how the inquest was conducted. Like William Little, he suggested that organizing the inquest in the Blechers' cottage served to "inhibit" testimony, particularly regarding antipathy between Thomson and Martin Blecher Jr. This assertion raises the question of what, exactly, inquest attendees might have discussed that night if they were afraid to give voice to their sentiments and suspicions. Shaw suggested that the inquest lasted from approximately 10:00 p.m. to 1:00 a.m. Over three hours, even the most reticent in attendance would have had time to at least hint at misgivings they might have had about the death of someone so many claimed as their dear, respected friend.

Addressing the exhumation of Thomson's remains from Mowat Cemetery and their transfer to a burial site in Leith, Shaw's account wobbled between insight and imagination. He related the story of how F.W. Churchill, the undertaker, had refused Shannon Fraser's offer to help with the digging. He also shared that Fraser felt that the weight of the filled casket was not distributed as it should have been with a body inside. Shaw stated that Fraser's concerns kept him awake at night. This last claim suggests Shaw at least occasionally strayed into writing fiction. Although many authors concerned with Thomson's death have claimed to represent Fraser's statements, it must be stated again that Fraser never actually recorded his recollections of any of the events in question, except for a few telegrams and letters written in 1917. Compounding the problem of manufacturing testimony, none of the works that claim to represent Fraser's insights suggest that Fraser lost any sleep over his concerns around Thomson's exhumation.

Describing the 1956 exhumation of the remains at Mowat Cemetery, Shaw related William Little's version of events with little attempt at criticism or analysis. Instead, he introduced a list of rather far-fetched scenarios that might serve to reconcile how the remains of an Aboriginal man might be found in what was believed to Thomson's original, and supposedly empty, grave.

The ideas include the possibility that the body found in Canoe Lake was actually that of an Aboriginal, not Tom Thomson. Shaw also suggested that the body discovered in Mowat Cemetery in 1956 could actually have come from a previously existing unmarked grave. He offered that the 1956 dig mistakenly exhumed one of the two existing, marked Mowat Cemetery burials. Stretching believability even further, he stated that before being investigated by scientists in Toronto, the bones exhumed from Mowat Cemetery in 1956 had been switched with some other remains.

Shaw also proposed that Thomson's death might be explained by a rare medical condition known as micturition syncope, which causes a man to faint while urinating. Shaw's speculation regarding this condition's role in Thomson's death is based on the death of a British man, Robert Mitchell, who apparently suffered it. In 1991, Mitchell died by drowning after fainting while urinating off of his boat. As Shaw admitted, no one recorded observations such as the buttons on Thomson's fly being open, providing the theory with no supporting evidence.

Almost a century after Thomson's death, Shaw's theories are nearly impossible to substantiate, even if we were positively in possession of Thomson's remains. They certainly didn't build upon any similar, earlier proposals. In their far-fetched conception, they point perhaps rather to the entertainment value that had accrued around Thomson's death.

By the 1990s, Thomson's demise had come to be approached in much the same way as other famous deaths: a sinister crime covered up as a tragic accident. However, these books may also point to exhaustion of interpretation around Thomson's death. By the mid-1990s, no significant new testimony had been introduced into discussion of the case for twenty years. Nonetheless, the same period had seen more works published on the topic than had appeared since Thomson's death. The only area that seemed to be left for authors new to the topic was to offer wild, novel speculation.

Just as Roy MacGregor and Joan Murray had made Tom Thomson a focus within their published works, art critic and historian David Silcox published a second work on Thomson, *Tom Thomson: An Introduction to His Life and Art*, in 2002. As he had twenty-five years earlier, Silcox dismissed the "endless speculation" about how Thomson died, "none of which" he assessed, "had added anything to our appreciation of [Thomson] as an artist." It is particularly baffling, then, why Silcox felt the need to narrate, however briefly, the story of Thomson's death in both of his books.

Silcox's assessment was consistently flawed. In 2002, Silcox repeated the theory he had first offered in 1977's *The Silence and the Storm*. He noted that one "story is that [Thomson's] feet were tangled in wire." Intending to correct the record, Silcox states, "In fact Thomson had carefully wrapped copper fishing line around one ankle, which was either sprained or arthritic." Silcox's confident statement of "fact" is even more curious than when he offered similar claims in 1977. There are no documented statements of Thomson being arthritic. As discussed earlier, the claim that Thomson had suffered a sprained ankle had a highly dubious history. If Silcox intended his claim to be accepted as factual, it certainly deserved more supporting evidence.

Silcox also made a questionable decision when he described Thomson's corpse as having "sustained a four-inch cut on his right temple," and stated that "his right ear had bled." It is nearly impossible to conceive how he could not have been aware that multiple contradictory descriptions of Thomson's corpse existed, and that the one he described departed considerably from the majority of claims, let alone the primary evidence.

Given his feeble claims, it is rather surprising that Silcox adopts a particularly aggressive tone in assessing the work of his peers. For instance, he suggests that there was little controversy concerning Thomson's death until about 1930, when "Blodwen Davies whipped up speculation with the enthusiasm of a yellow journalist." Far from maintaining a neutral tone, Silcox perhaps unwittingly raises the misogynistic spectre of female mental illness when he refers to Davies's work as generating "hysteria" about the circumstances surrounding Thomson's death. Silcox's own research and analytic skills certainly don't suggest superiority to Davies's efforts.

In 2015, Silcox produced a short work on Thomson for the Art Canada Institute. In this work he claims that the "simplest explanation is therefore likely the correct one": that Thomson stood up in his canoe, fell, and was knocked unconscious into the water, where he drowned. Perhaps marking a break with his long-standing position, Silcox makes no mention of Thomson's fall being caused by a sprained ankle.

The important place Tom Thomson has taken in the twenty-first-century Canadian psyche is indicated in part by the recent proliferation of simple, short biographies of Thomson. These works serve to acquaint people with some of the more exciting, mysterious, and tragic elements in the life of a man whose name consistently is mentioned in lists of famous Canadians.

Three works illustrate this trend handily: Jim Poling Sr.'s *Tom Thomson: The Life and Mysterious Death of the Famous Canadian Painter* (2003), Neil Lehto's *Algonquin Elegy: Tom Thomson's Last Spring* (2005), and Wayne Larsen's *Tom Thomson: Artist of the North* (2011). All of these books synthesize provocative elements from previous works about Thomson, and rehash oft-repeated but weakly supported stories that have become part of the Thomson mythology. These works also depend on the interjection of elements that are either purposely fictional or grounded in lamentably poor research.

Poling's work repeated common myths: Thomson's support for the war effort and failed enlistment attempts, the party on the night of July 7 where Thomson fought with Blecher and with Fraser, the attempt to land the elusive trout, and the fishing line wrapped around one of Thomson's legs when his body was found.

He also made some tweaks to the story, though for what reason or by what evidence is impossible to know. For instance, Poling suggested that Thomson's corpse was bruised on the left temple but had blood in the right ear. Aside from the question of why the right ear would be bleeding when the left temple was bruised, this claim does not fit with any of the first-hand accounts of 1917.

Perhaps wisely, Poling concluded his tale with the observation that knowing exactly what happened to Tom Thomson, both how his life ended and where his remains are buried, is not critical to understanding the man's contributions to Canadian art. This may be true. It may also be an attempt to rationalize away the difficulty of separating facts from fictions about Thomson's death.

Similar to Poling's work, Wayne Larsen's *Artist of the North* filled gaps in our knowledge about Thomson's life with imagined scenarios and conversations. He repeated popular myths as well, such as the claim that Thomson was working on a series of paintings to document the changing seasons in 1917. He also told the story of how Thomson asked Robinson's permission to hang his paintings in the Joe Lake ranger's hut. Larsen developed the tale even further, departing from Robinson's testimony by describing how Thomson actually did hang "several dozen" sketches in the cabin. Larsen also departed from any previous accounts when he claimed that Thomson had asked Shannon Fraser to repay a debt on the morning of Sunday, July 8.

Much like MacGregor's *Canoe Lake*, Neil Lehto's self-published *Algonquin Elegy* tells the story of Thomson's death within the frame of a fictional story. The approach provides significant storytelling freedom. Unfortunately, it also allows the author to avoid having to clearly indicate what information is derived from evidence and what is fictionalized. Unable to know the difference, Lehto's readers are left having to assume that all assertions could be fictional. The wisdom of such an assumption is buttressed by Lehto's indication that he was working from a very limited selection of the primary documents related to Thomson's death.

These few, select samples of creative storytelling regarding Thomson's death reveal how works such as those by Poling, Larsen, and Lehto might serve to complicate, rather than accurately reflect, thinking about Thomson's death. As storytelling, they provide fine entertainment and a generally acceptable level of "truth" about Thomson. As history writing, they are sorely lacking in rigour. By repeating the mistakes or fictions of previous authors, these works and others like them serve to further cement incorrect and flawed elements into the mythology surrounding Thomson, and make the separation of fact from fiction regarding Thomson's life increasingly difficult.

In a similar vein, two recent digital initiatives mix creativity with reference to historical materials, while taking advantage of new storytelling technologies.

In 2011, an Ottawa man (who has not revealed his name publicly but apparently appeared at a few public events) created a Twitter account under the name Tom Thomson. With this alias, the man has annually posted a flurry of tweets communicating what he represents as Thomson's thinking during the last year of his life. The man has also created a parallel blog, which offers him opportunities to post longer messages. Some of the content used by the Thomson Twitter account's creator is clearly drawn from primary materials, such as Thomson's letters, while some is likely the man's creative interpretation of what Thomson might have been thinking. The challenge for the casual consumer is that no distinction between the two is made, thus collapsing fact and fiction into each other as a seamless, undifferentiated continuity.

Owen Sound's Tom Thomson Art Gallery has undertaken a similar project. Appearing online in the summer of 2015, the blog *Betwixt and Between: The Untold Tom Thomson Story* tells another semi-fictionalized account of Thomson's life. By late 2015, content posted on the blog included historical images and quotations from archival documents related to Thomson's life, as well as references to marginally related historical events, fictional statements, and contemporary creative pieces presented as historical artifacts. The gallery is also planning a touring exhibition component.

Over time, this work may change direction and focus, but within the first six months of its existence, it focused on exploiting the capacity of digital media to tell history. As gallery director Virginia Eichhorn described the project, "People are going to have an opportunity to have an immersive experience with Tom Thomson through a possible story from his life."

As can be observed with previous attempts to mix fiction and fact in exploring Thomson's life, telling history this way dismisses the risks inherent in giving priority to telling "a good story." Referencing real historical facts and artifacts while interjecting mythical elements and fictional content can generate interest in Thomson's story, but it also marginalizes the more mundane elements of his life that are actually confirmed by evidence. When the facts of the man's life are already so muddled, the interjection of additional fictional elements serves to even further complicate resolving the historical truth about what happened to Tom Thomson.

As the one-hundredth anniversary of Tom Thomson's death nears, storytelling about the events that took place during the summer of 1917 shows an unprecedented variety of approaches. Some of these efforts have been more serious, and more successful, than others. Some have aimed to entertain or to merely use popular versions of the Thomson story as a backdrop for the playing out of other concerns. Some have sought to play upon, rather than resolve, the mysteries as a means to entertain.

Considered apart from the relative quality of these works, the growth of interest in Thomson's death establishes without a doubt that the man's presence — as symbol, as story, as model, and as lesson — has become cemented into Canada's national consciousness. From children's stories to songs, from poetry books to parlour games, from fiction to academic history, Thomson's death has moved from something regarded as a fringe concern of conspiracy theorists to a historical reality deserving analysis.

For every step forward that these works have contributed to understanding the end of Thomson's life, unfortunately, it seems that misinformation and poorly grounded speculation has pushed our understanding two steps back.

Having considered the plentitude of approaches to Thomson's death told over the last century, then, let us consider the question at the heart of this study: How *did* Tom Thomson die?

PART THREE

THE MANY DEATHS OF TOM THOMSON

10

THE MURDER OF TOM THOMSON

Of course, foul play was suspected, and Lauren Harris, among others, was of the opinion that Thomson was murdered.
— DAVID SILCOX, *TOM THOMSON: AN INTRODUCTION TO HIS LIFE AND ART*, 2002

CANOE LAKE WAS CALM when Thomson went missing, and he knew the region well. He was believed to be an expert canoeist and swimmer who had a record of being able to handle himself and heavy packs on lengthy trips in far rougher waters. Several of Thomson's friends asserted that he was a heavy drinker and an opinionated man. They suggested that he had perhaps crossed someone in Algonquin Park. Others speculated that his high morals had led him to confront poachers or naysayers about Canada's war efforts. Some quietly whispered suggestions that a love triangle — over a local woman, or perhaps even a "half-breed" — had led to a fatal conflict.

The possibility that Tom Thomson was murdered has been considered ever since he disappeared in 1917. In the absence of any evidence, the idea devolved into idle lore repeated around campfires. As time passed, and as Canoe Lake came to be dominated by campers and canoe-trippers looking for adventure deeper in the park, the desire of locals to protect the reputation of the place gave way to the morbid curiousity of outsiders. Fears of German saboteurs, lovers' quarrels, and sordid drunken fights enlivened what otherwise might seem the rather mundane history of a protected rural community devoted to camping and fishing.

As discussed in part 2, the idea that Tom Thomson was murdered came to dominate popular thinking about Thomson's death during the late 1960s. With the evolution of testimony and storytelling about the events in question established, closer analysis of the evidence used to support the murder theory is possible.

The suggestion that Tom Thomson might have been murdered appeared in newspaper reports published even before his body was discovered. These articles didn't give the theory particularly deep consideration; they merely listed it among the possible explanations for why a man might go missing.

Other documents produced in 1917 don't give the idea much credence, either. Perhaps the most detailed consideration of murder is the December 1917 letter George Thomson sent to Dr. MacCallum. In the letter, George questioned why Shannon Fraser had suggested that Tom committed suicide. In the absence of evidence supporting the suicide theory, he intimated that Fraser might be attempting to provide a plausible alternative to murder for reasons he doesn't state. However, considering the facts he was aware of, George concluded that the most likely explanation for Tom's death was that it was a tragic accident, not murder.

No one living at Canoe Lake in the summer or fall of 1917 left any record of seriously considering that Tom Thomson had been murdered. The closest suggestion can be found in Winnie Trainor's September 1917 letter to T.J. Harkness. Trainor suggests that there was "bad blood" between Thomson and Shannon Fraser. Perhaps hesitant to boldly assert in writing that she believed Fraser was capable (if not guilty) of homicide, she stated that she had information she could only communicate in person. If she did believe Thomson had been murdered, it was not a suspicion that she ever raised again. It is worth noting, however, that Trainor suggested on more than one occasion that she had stories to tell about Thomson that she could not put in writing.

The lack of discussion of murder in 1917, and even in the years immediately following Thomson's death, does not mean that murder was not possible. It does suggest, however, that whether in public forums or in private reflections, no one who was close to Thomson, or for that matter any of the residents of Canoe Lake, thought the idea merited much thought as a reasonable explanation.

Despite the innocent explanations that dominated the discussion during the decade after Thomson's death, the prospect of murder was seriously raised in the 1930s.

Mark Robinson, in his early correspondence with Blodwen Davies, suggested that interviews with Shannon Fraser, as well as Bessie and Martin Blecher Jr., might offer useful information — provided they could be convinced to tell the truth. What Robinson believed the true story to be, and how the true story differed from the version or versions regarded as truthful, he does not say.

Robinson's suggestion could be interpreted in one of two ways: either he knew an alternate story that he was unwilling to tell to Davies, or he suspected Fraser and/or the Blechers of knowing something more about Thomson's death than he knew. If Robinson knew more, particularly if he had any kind of evidence indicating foul play, what we know of his personality (if not the responsibilities attached to his job) suggests that he would have taken some kind of action to prosecute the murderers; as we know, he did not. At the time, he did not record in his diary any suspicions or evidence contrary to the official findings. The only notation he made was that some person or persons were unsatisfied with how the coroner had gathered evidence at Canoe Lake. On this basis, the most reasonable conclusion we can reach is that Robinson could not find any evidence to support his suspicions regarding Fraser's and the Blechers' knowledge about Thomson's death.

Robinson was certainly hostile to Martin Blecher Jr. Only a month after Robinson's return to Canoe Lake following two years of military service in Europe, he noted in his daily diary that he suspected Blecher of being a German spy. He did not record what his grounds for this belief might have been.

Beyond Robinson's unsupported suspicions, what kind of evidence has been used to advance the theory that Tom Thomson was murdered? Much has been made of his claim that Thomson's body showed bruising and bleeding. The apparent absence of water in his lungs seemed to suggest a sudden death, perhaps even one that occurred before the body entered the water. Most suspicious, though, is the fishing line that Mark Robinson reported having found wrapped around Thomson's ankle; an oddity best explained by someone else having placed it there. Many of the murder theorists have also based their arguments on the party that Thomson is believed to have attended on the night of Sunday, July 7. At this party, it is suggested, Thomson got into a fight with either Fraser or Blecher (or maybe both), sustaining an injury that would prove fatal, or that would lead to a fatal confrontation the next day.

The idea that Thomson and Blecher might have had a fatal exchange has been supported by suggestions that the two men had a long-simmering dislike for each other, for reasons that might have included a difference of position on the war in Europe, affections for Winnie Trainor, or a simple clash of personalities. Fuelled by alcohol, which was said to make both men grouchy and violent, and forced into close contact in the small community, it seemed destined that the two men would come to blows.

Furthermore, suspicions about Blecher also play into most versions of the murder theory with regard to who first saw Thomson's canoe floating in the lake. Most accounts have the Blechers seeing the canoe only a few hours after Thomson departed, but not immediately investigating their find or reporting it to Robinson. Their lack of initiative seems suspicious. Some accounts do have the Blechers taking action, bringing the canoe to their own boathouse but not reporting the find. This response seems even more sinister when we know Thomson, the canoe's owner, would later be found dead in the lake.

These factors are not the only elements that have been used to argue that Tom Thomson was murdered, but they are some of the most common references drawn upon by murder theorists. Careful consideration of the evidence related to each of these areas of suspicion should help to clarify the viability of the murder theories.

Much of the speculation that Thomson was murdered hinges on claims about signs of violence having been found on Thomson's corpse.

What do we know about the condition of Thomson's corpse? Few observations were recorded at the time his body was found and examined. Mark Robinson included some notes in his diary the evening after the body was examined, and Shannon Fraser made some brief comments in a letter to Thomson's father. These are the only unadulterated, first-person accounts we have describing the condition of Thomson's corpse when it was found. While Robinson's notes seem to be trustworthy, Fraser's testimony must be carefully weighed, as he doesn't specify whether he had actually looked at Thomson's corpse, or was merely retelling what he had been told by others.

We also have two other accounts, although these exist as copied versions of what is claimed to be first-hand testimony. In 1931, the Crown attorney's office supplied Blodwen Davies with a copy of the examining doctor's affidavit regarding the condition of Thomson's corpse. The same year, George Thomson wrote Davies and included a transcript of what he claimed was the coroner's handwritten affidavit. These latter two accounts differ in two important ways. We must take care in loading the differences with too much importance, though, as they may have been introduced during copying. If this is the case, the differences will simply muddle our understanding.

All four of the documents record that Tom Thomson's body was discovered floating in Canoe Lake on the morning of Monday, July 16, eight days after he had gone missing. On July 17, either Mark Robinson or G.W. Bartlett, the Algonquin Park superintendant, requested that Dr. G. Howland, who was holidaying at Canoe Lake, examine the corpse. The coroner had been expected to arrive on the train the day before but had not. An undertaker and his assistant had arrived, however, and were waiting to work on Thomson's clearly decomposing corpse.

The day Thomson's body was examined, Mark Robinson noted a bruise about four inches long on the left temple, "evidently caused by falling on a Rock." He stated that "otherwise [there are] no marks of Violence on Body."

The next day, Shannon Fraser wrote Thomson's father that the doctor had found a bruise over Tom's eye, and "thinks he fell and was hurt." Fraser does not note which eye the bruise was found over.

The copy of Dr. Howland's affidavit supplied to Blodwen Davies in 1931 states: "Bruise on right temple 4 inches long. No other external marks. Air issuing from lungs, some bleeding from right ear."

This version of Howland's account differs in several ways from the version of Dr. Ranney's notes that George Thomson claimed to have. George's version includes notations regarding the clothes Tom's corpse was wearing as well as additional details regarding the condition of the body. This version states:

> Body clothed in grey lumberman's shirt, khaki trowsers [sic] and canvas shoes. Head shows marked swelling of face, decomposition has set in, air issuing from mouth. Head has a bruise over left temple as if produced by falling on rock. Examination of body shows no bruises, body greatly swollen, blisters on limbs, putrefaction setting in on surface. There are no signs of any external force having caused death, and there is no doubt but that death occurred from drowning.

Use of the present tense in the notes suggests that they may not be Dr. Ranney's comments but rather Dr. Howland's observations. Regardless, their most important characteristic is that, like Robinson's statement, they identified Thomson's temple as being bruised on the left side, not the right, as the copy of the Crown attorney's affidavit stated.

The question of whether the bruise was on the left or right side of Thomson's temple has certainly vexed commentators. A number of writers have repeated the claim Blodwen Davies made in her 1935 text, that Thomson's right temple was bruised. These writers include William Little, David Silcox (1977, 2002), Joan Murray (1994), and Neil Lehto.

The *Death on a Painted Lake* project's discovery of Davies's 1931 request for the attorney general to approve exhumation of Thomson's grave throws Davies's 1935 statement into doubt. In her July 1931 request, she identified Thomson's left temple as being bruised, not his right.

What prompted Davies to switch location of the bruise from left to right? In May 1931, she had received Dr. Ranney's comments about the case, and in June, the transcription of Dr. Howland's comments from the North Bay Crown attorney's office. Both of these accounts listed the wound as being on Thomson's right temple. It would appear that based on these two documents, Davies changed her assessment of which side of Thomson's head had sustained a blow.

To establish definitively which side of Thomson's head the mark was on is impossible. The Crown attorney may have erred in transcribing Howland's account. Someone may have erred in transcribing the account for George Thomson. Robinson may have erred in recording which side the bruise was on, or may have recorded either from the perspective of Thomson (Tom's left side) or his own position to Thomson's body.

The challenge of ascertaining which side the bruise was on may have helped to elevate the "bruise story" to a level of prominence that it does not merit. In 1956, Dixon, one of the undertakers who prepared Thomson's body for its first burial, wrote his comments on the condition of the corpse. He mentioned that there were no signs of violence on the body at all. This is in keeping with the accounts of Robinson, Fraser, and Howland. Dixon attributed the only marks he saw on the body to the discolouration that occurs as a human body decomposes. Most of the first-hand accounts regarding Thomson's corpse suggest putrefaction was advanced. Some mention that Thomson's corpse was swollen to twice its size, and that his flesh was blistering and peeling away. We can safely assume that Thomson's corpse, having spent over a week underwater, would display at least discolouration of the flesh.

In observations prepared in 2007 for the *Death on a Painted Lake* site, Ontario's chief forensic pathologist, Dr. Michael Pollanen, considered the first-hand accounts regarding the condition of Thomson's corpse. As had Dixon in 1956, Pollanen concluded that with the kind of decomposition noted in the first-hand accounts, any "bruising" could just as easily be attributed to post-mortem decay as it could be to peri-mortem (before-death) force. Pollanen also offered some additional valuable insights into the claim that Thomson's ear was "bleeding." He noted that decomposition is by far the most plausible explanation for the observation. As he stated in his report on the site, "The state of decomposition was probably advanced enough that the 'bruise on the right temple' and the 'bleeding from the right ear' may not be injuries at all."

If Pollanen's assessment — based on his modern experience and advanced knowledge of the field of forensics — is to be believed, we cannot say with any confidence that Thomson's body showed any sign of having been subject to violence while he was alive. Pollanen's and Dixon's findings certainly indicate that we should regard Robinson's and Howland's interpretations of what they found with suspicion. Their inexperience with forensics in general, and drowning victims in particular, might have led them to flawed conclusions regarding how Thomson's corpse came to be in the condition they found it in.

Suggestions that Thomson's corpse showed signs of trauma are not the only evidence used to support the claim that Thomson was murdered. Speculation regarding Thomson's cause of death has also involved fishing line said to have been found wrapped around his ankle.

This story deserves careful attention. No records from 1917 state that fishing line was found around Thomson's ankle. Mark Robinson's diary didn't mention this, and neither did the accounts Shannon Fraser sent to Dr. MacCallum, T.J. Harkness, George Thomson, or John Thomson (Tom's father). Dr. Howland's testimony did not mention fishing line, and neither did the account Dr. Ranney provided to Blodwen Davies in 1930 (which he claimed was based on his 1917 notes). In fact, the first time anyone raised the prospect that fishing line was found around Tom Thomson's ankle was more than a decade after Thomson's death.

In March 1930, Mark Robinson provided the first description of Thomson's corpse that contained a reference to suspicious fishing line. He told Blodwen Davies that there were "no marks on the body except a slight bruise over the left eye." He added, in a tone suggesting the claim was widely known (and departing from the account in his daily diary), that Thomson's "fishing line was wound several times around his left ankle and broken." In a follow-up communication with Davies, Robinson added that the fishing line was not Thomson's "regular fishing line."

In her 1930 biography of Thomson, Davies made no mention of the suspicious fishing line. She did refer to it in her 1931 request that the attorney general order exhumation of Thomson's grave. She did not, however, include this seemingly important detail in her 1935 book. Instead, in 1935, she asked whether Thomson's body had taken eight days to surface, alluding to the idea that it must have been anchored or that it had sunk more than once. She may have believed that fishing line was wrapped around one ankle of Thomson's body in order to tie it to something, which would explain why she did not refer to Robinson's intimation of the fishing line as anything suspicious.

In the 1940s, despite having interviewed Mark Robinson and others at Canoe Lake, Audrey Saunders did not make any mention of fishing line being wrapped around Thomson's ankle, either. In *Algonquin Story*, she noted that the body was towed from where it had been discovered to the shore of Big Wapomeo Island. Towing the body would very likely have been achieved using rope or fishing line, once again providing a reasonable, straightforward explanation for fishing line being observed around Thomson's ankle.

In the 1950s, Robinson expanded on his testimony, providing several new observations regarding the fishing line. Robinson noted that Rowe and Dickson had towed Thomson's body to shore using a rope, duly anchoring it to a tree there. Turning to his observations regarding Thomson's corpse, Robinson recalled that the body had "fishing line wrapped 16 or 17 times" around its left ankle. Robinson had never before provided such detail regarding his discovery, but he attested to its truth when he stated that he had the "exact number" recorded in his notebook and diary.

No one among Robinson's Canoe Lake audience was likely to challenge his memory, or to demand that he show them his diary entries recording those events. His status as witness, and suggestion of evidence, conveyed the strength of his testimony. We know, however, that Robinson's diary makes no mention of how many times fishing line was wrapped around Thomson's ankle. It makes no mention, in fact, of *any* fishing line or rope being found wrapped around Thomson's ankle at all.

How can we make sense of Robinson's testimony, then? One clue might be the comment Robinson makes about Dixon asking him to use his knife to remove the "strings" around Thomson's ankle. It would be logical to assume that Robinson was referring to Roy Dixon, one of the undertakers tasked with preparing Thomson's body for burial. Only a few years after Robinson's final account was recorded, Roy Dixon wrote the *Toronto Star* that Thomson's body showed no evidence of foul play. What would make sense would be for Dixon to have supervised the body's removal from the water, and to have recognized that "string" had been used to keep the body anchored to shore.

Another explanation for the fishing-line story is that Robinson simply found that inclusion of some suspicious circumstantial evidence, such as fishing line found around Thomson's ankle, provided him with a more interesting story to tell. Perhaps he felt that he needed evidence to support his otherwise unfounded suspicions that Thomson had not died by accident or suicide. Whatever Robinson's motives, evidence suggests that his characterization of the fishing line as being suspicious is highly suspect, and that its presence around Thomson's ankle as evidence of murder must be regarded as a slim possibility.

Despite its rather sketchy origins, Robinson's suggestion regarding fishing line slowly gained traction. In 1955, R.P. Little repeated Robinson's claim, adding that Thomson's body was discovered with *copper* fishing line around one ankle.

In the late 1960s, there was speculation that the fishing-line story was simply a case of misapprehension. Thomson family members reported that George Thomson had heard Tom had sprained his ankle and used fishing line to wrap or splint it.

During the early 1970s, William Little and Roy MacGregor again drew attention to the reported presence of suspect fishing line. Both suggested that the line's presence signified something not fully accounted for, and offered that when considered with other evidence, should be regarded as a sign of Thomson having been a victim of foul play. However, in 1977, and again in 2002, David Silcox countered Robinson's story that the fishing line suggested foul play, repeating the claim that Thomson had wrapped fishing line around his ankle intentionally to splint a sprain. But again, all these accounts assume the reports of the fishing line are reliable.

It is very curious that, in their 1917 notes about the condition of the corpse, neither Howland nor Robinson made mention of fishing line around Thomson's ankle. Both men explicitly stated that there was no evidence of violence aside from a bruise and a bleeding ear. Neither man suggested at the time that he had any suspicions regarding Thomson's death. That the presence of fishing line around Thomson's ankle was first mentioned thirteen years after Thomson's death, and only ever attested to by one person, Mark Robinson, who had not mentioned it in previous accounts, strongly suggests that this element of his testimony is suspicious. If any fishing line was present at all, the most plausible explanation provided in the primary accounts is that it was line used to tow Thomson's body to shore and to anchor the body until removal from the water. That the story about fishing line on Thomson's ankle only really emerged in discussion during the 1970s, as part of popular speculation that Thomson was murdered, further suggests that it should be given little credence in understanding how Tom Thomson died.

Setting aside questions about fishing line and wounds on Thomson's corpse, the circumstances surrounding his disappearance might still support the conclusion that Tom was murdered.

For instance, the notorious drinking party and fight (or fights) that occurred on the night of Sunday, July 7, are included as critical elements in most of the murder theories. Some have claimed Thomson and Martin Blecher Jr. fought for a number of different reasons, from the war to love. Others have suggested Thomson and Shannon Fraser fought, perhaps over money that Fraser owed Thomson. Some have even suggested Thomson fought with both men that night. As indicated in part 2, the story about the party and fights rests on unstable foundations.

Evidence from 1917 offers no indications of any party taking place, or of any kind of physical altercation. As already established, it is highly doubtful that any marks found on Thomson's corpse clearly indicated that he had been in a fight at least twelve hours before he died. No evidence from 1917 exists of anyone testifying to even a verbal conflict, threats, or raised voices.

There may have been suspicions that alcohol was involved in Thomson's death. Within days of Thomson's body being discovered, Mark Robinson noted in his daily diary that he had been ordered to block any further shipments of alcohol to Shannon Fraser. Ironically, he was not instructed to block similar shipments from coming in for Martin Blecher.

Robinson was also ordered to have a map and lease drawn up for the land Fraser was occupying. If Park Superintendent Bartlett suspected Fraser might have been involved in Thomson's death, ordering these actions would make sense as a means of exerting some control over the Canoe Lake community. On the other hand, if Bartlett's decisions were based on information he was receiving from Robinson — who was, after all, Bartlett's eyes and ears around Canoe Lake — then his decisions should likely be regarded as reflecting Robinson's anxieties and suspicions.

This suggestion becomes important when we consider the party story's origins. The drinking party was first introduced into discussions of Thomson's death by William Little in 1970. This fact requires pause to appreciate. The first recorded reference to a drinking party and fight involving Tom Thomson on the night before his death dates from more than fifty years after Thomson's body was discovered! The large gap between the events in question and appearance of testimony about them should raise suspicions.

That none of the men who had supplied testimony about Thomson's death in 1917 would mention such a critical event that they themselves had been involved in is perplexing. If Thomson had died as a result of injuries sustained in a fight, wouldn't one of the men who was not under suspicion, but present at the inquest have raised his concerns? Would one of them have not at least mentioned the event to Mark Robinson, who would very likely have noted it in his diary? If the fight was introduced as a concern at the inquest, did Dr. Ranney perhaps dismiss it as unimportant? Is it reasonable to conclude that a coroner would dismiss plausible evidence that a homicide might have occurred, even if that homicide might be difficult to prove? None of these questions can be given satisfactory answers.

The proposition made by the likes of Blodwen Davies, William Little, Roy MacGregor, and S. Bernard Shaw, that the inquest attendees were somehow intimated by being in the Blechers' house and in the presence of an authority figure such as the coroner, are flimsy. Robinson gives the impression that he was not shy about claiming his authority (such as when he suggested that the undertaker he discovered at Canoe Lake station should have consulted park authorities before exhuming a casket). He also had time alone with Dr. Ranney to raise his concerns after the inquest and the next morning. According to Robinson's own testimony, Ranney seems to have respected his authority. He was, after all, able to recommend to the doctor persons who should be included at the inquest.

The idea that several of the men at the inquest (Blecher Jr., Fraser, Rowe, and perhaps others) attended a drinking party the night before Thomson died, and that none of them referred to the event at the inquest, is difficult to accept. The inquest aside, that rumours about the fight — if it did occur — did not appear until more than five decades had passed is incomprehensible. The most sensible explanation is that this event is the product of gossip and the desire to tell a compelling story. It certainly has no basis in evidence.

The believability of the story is undermined by its distance from the events in question. It is also hard to believe because circumstantial evidence contradicts the story's foundational premises.

Proposals of a fight between Fraser and Thomson usually rest upon the claim that Fraser owed Thomson money. In August 1917, Winnie Trainor reported to the executor of Tom's estate that Fraser had repaid the money he owed Tom. This does not rule out that Fraser and Thomson might have fought about something else, but if so, it leaves open the question of what the fight concerned.

In 2010, Roy MacGregor suggested that Hugh Trainor might have convinced Fraser to discipline Tom over his treatment of Winnie. He speculated that this fight took place on the night of Monday, July 8, after Thomson is almost universally agreed to have disappeared. MacGregor's theory flies in the face of Winnie Trainor's own statements. If Winnie Trainor is to be believed, she and Mark Robinson had little respect for Fraser. According to Winnie, her father "detested" Shannon Fraser. That Hugh Trainor would entrust such a sensitive task to someone he held in such low regard is doubtful.

Much has been claimed about Tom Thomson and Martin Blecher Jr. being hostile to each other. This may be true. There is not any solid evidence to support the belief, however. No evidence produced prior to the 1970s explicitly identifies Thomson and Blecher being in conflict. Rumours regarding arguments between Thomson and another Canoe Lake man circulated as early as 1917, but nowhere is the identity of the man clearly indicated.

Contrary to stories about animosity between Thomson and Blecher, there is evidence suggesting that Thomson and Blecher chose to interact socially in a friendly fashion at least once. In August 1914, park ranger Bud Callighen noted in his daily diary that Thomson, Bessie, and Martin Blecher Jr., accompanied by other Blecher relations, stopped by his ranger's cabin on their way back from Cache Lake. In fairness, that was three years before Thomson's death, and it is only one occasion. Callighen's single notation of Thomson's positive relationship with the Blecher family, however, is more primary evidence than we have of Thomson and Blecher being in conflict.

Suspicions regarding Martin Blecher Jr.'s involvement in Tom Thomson's death may have been, as the literary scholar Peter Webb has suggested, largely a product of anti-German hostility. In spring 1917, Mark Robinson indicated his belief that Blecher was a German spy, for instance. That he might seek to associate a mysterious death with the man makes sense in light this suspicion, and may have served to influence gossip for a long time after Thomson's death. Aside from gossip and groundless impressions, however, no evidence indicates that Thomson and Blecher had anything other than neighbourly interactions.

If Thomson died on the night of Saturday, July 7, it would be very difficult to explain Robinson's testimony that he saw Thomson the next morning. Robinson's testimony even calls into question the trustworthiness of the fight story, and the bruise the fight supposedly led to, as Robinson did not note seeing any wounds on Thomson only hours before he is supposed to have died.

If Fraser was involved in a fight with Thomson, he may have had reason to lie or keep silent about Thomson's injuries. As others also claimed to have seen Thomson that morning without cause to note anything out of the ordinary in his appearance or behaviour, evidence suggests Thomson was likely alive on Sunday morning, and does not appear to have borne any significant bruising or other wounds that would have had to develop very soon thereafter in order to show up on his body before he died.

Even if Thomson and Blecher were cordial with one another, the response of Bessie and Martin Blecher Jr. to seeing Thomson's upturned canoe in the lake raises questions.

On July 10, 1917, Mark Robinson and Shannon Fraser wrote accounts of the alarming discovery of Thomson's canoe. Both accounts stated that the canoe was found upside down. Robinson's diary records that the canoe had been spotted by Martin Jr. and Bessie Blecher about 3:05 p.m. on July 8, as they were crossing the lake en route to Tea Lake Dam. They assumed it was a canoe they had heard had slipped its moorings, and intended to pick it up when returning. Robinson also noted that about 9:15 a.m. on the morning of July 10, Shannon Fraser informed him of the Blechers' sighting.

Murder theorists often draw attention to the idea that the Blechers did not investigate an overturned canoe, or report seeing Thomson's canoe adrift on the lake. The average responsible person, it is offered, would not simply carry on and fetch the canoe later.

Later testimony provided by Mark Robinson — although confused — does suggest suspicious behaviour on Blecher's part. In March 1930, Robinson informed Blodwen Davies that the discovery of Thomson's canoe had been reported on the morning of July 9. He also claimed this was when the canoe was retrieved from the lake. He noted that he was not aware before the inquest on the evening of July 17 that Martin Blecher Jr. and his sister had been the first persons to spot it. Clearly, Robinson is mistaken in much of this testimony. He noted in his 1917 daily diary that Shannon Fraser reported the Blechers' discovery of Thomson's canoe to him on July 10. He added that he and Fraser immediately visited the Blechers to inquire about the discovery.

In September 1930, Robinson provided Davies additional information, stating that the Blechers had helped to search the lake for Thomson but did not assist with the search in the woods.

In 1955, R.P. Little introduced an entirely new story of how Thomson's canoe was discovered. He reported that after Martin Blecher Jr. and his sister, had spotted the canoe, they retrieved it and brought it back to their boathouse, where it was spotted by another Canoe Lake resident, Charlie Scrim, on the morning of July 10.

A year later, Rose Thomas told Ottelyn Addison that Martin Blecher Jr. had towed Thomson's overturned canoe to Shannon Fraser's. The following morning, July 9, Fraser came to the train station hoping to send a telegram to Owen Sound (where Thomson's parents lived), as he feared Tom had drowned.

In 1970, William Little introduced yet another variation on the story, reporting that Charlie Scrim was actually the person who had found Thomson's canoe. According to Little, the Blechers mentioned their sighting to Shannon Fraser on the morning of July 9. The following day, Shannon relayed their comment to Scrim, who immediately went out in search of the canoe. It was Scrim, Little asserts, who reported his find to Robinson.

From these contending reports, what can be stated with confidence? The majority of testimony suggests that the Blechers did not take Thomson's canoe and store it in their boathouse. That they misidentified the canoe as one that had gone missing from its moorings is impossible to prove (or disprove). That their misidentification should be interpreted as suspicious behaviour really requires more evidence. Some consideration should also be given as to why the Blechers did not retrieve the canoe on their return trip, if that is what transpired. That no one else travelling the lake or on the shore spotted the canoe for more than thirty hours after the Blechers' sighting suggests that it might not have been easily visible.

It is also useful to consider whether Rose Thomas's 1956 testimony contains any truth. Is it plausible that the Blechers retrieved the canoe and towed it to the Mowat Lodge dock? If they identified the canoe as Thomson's, they would know that was where he was staying. If Thomson's having drowned was not considered, could they have merely assumed that his canoe had somehow slipped away from the dock and overturned? If so, is the delay in communicating discovery of the canoe attributable to Fraser's actions rather than the Blechers'?

The reasonableness of this question is supported by the version of the story recorded by Mark Robinson in his 1917 diary and R.P. Little during the 1950s. In this version, discovery of the canoe is reported to Mark Robinson by Charlie Scrim, not Fraser or Blecher.

Although the facts behind this particular element of the story remain difficult to ascertain, most versions suggest that both the Blechers and Shannon Fraser concluded that Thomson's overturned canoe did not need to be reported to Mark Robinson. That the Blechers did not seem overly anxious regarding the canoe (whomever they believed it belonged to) was the same response that Shannon Fraser gave the situation when he became aware of it. Robinson, too, notes in his daily diary on July 10 that "after hearing different evidence we returned expecting to hear of Mr. Thomson returning soon." Certainly, there is very little in this element of the story to point to the Blechers as being singularly guilty, or even engaging in behaviour that was regarded as suspicious at the time.

A final, somewhat curious element murder theorists have turned to as having some significance is the claim that Thomson's watch stopped at 12:14.

In 1931, Blodwen Davies told the attorney general that Thomson's watch stopped after one o'clock. She never published this claim, though, and her submission remained lost in the attorney general's files until 2008. In 1934, however, George Thomson told Davies that he had Tom's watch, and that it had stopped at 12:14. This letter was included in the Davies material deposited with the national archives. Some have used the last time recorded on the watch as an indicator of the general time Thomson's body, and therefore his watch, must have entered Canoe Lake. Most have assumed that Thomson died in the early afternoon, shortly after the time Fraser reported that he had departed from the Mowat Lodge dock.

Roy MacGregor has suggested that perhaps Thomson did not die in the afternoon, but after midnight on Monday, July 9. He speculates that Thomson might have returned to Canoe Lake late Sunday, July 8, and been the victim of some kind of attack that led to his body entering the water about midnight.

No author has considered that Thomson's watch might not have been on his person when he drowned. Thomson likely had a pocket watch.

Wristwatches had yet to become widely popular. On his first visit to Canoe Lake, George packaged most of his brother's belongings for return to Owen Sound. He retrieved the casket on his second. Is it not plausible that Tom's watch might have been with the belongings left in his room at Mowat Lodge? Would he have had cause to carry his pocket watch with him if he intended to leave Mowat Lodge on an afternoon canoe trip?

Additionally, would George have kept a watch that had been under the surface of Canoe Lake for over a week? The mechanism would surely have been wrecked, and unlike his brother's paintings, art supplies, or letters, a broken watch would seem to offer little comfort to his family. If the watch was not wrecked, however, it might have seemed to have more value as a memorial token of his brother.

On the other hand, if George had merely packaged up his brother's watch, why would he give any indication that the time at which the watch stopped might have been significant? If Davies had raised this question, would it not have been more sensible for him to explain that the watch had never been in the water? These are difficult questions for which to provide satisfactory answers.

Like so many other aspects of this case, the watch evidence is circumstantial. We cannot be sure of what it really means with regard to Tom Thomson's death. We must at least take into account that a reasonable alternative offers the strong likelihood that Thomson's watch was not on his person at the time of his death. This position suggests that any murder claims based on use of Thomson's watch as evidence depend on weak evidence.

Most of the theories that Tom Thomson was murdered rest on evidence that, upon close consideration, is found sorely wanting for credibility.

Suggestions that Thomson's body showed signs of trauma — such as bruising and bleeding — are most logically explained as the overreaction of observers with little experience with drowning victims, some of whom were traumatized by the sight of their friend's decomposing corpse.

That none of the observers recorded any indication that the body showed signs of suspicious treatment — such as fishing line wound around Thomson's ankle — points to the fact that these stories are anything but trustworthy.

These claims may have arisen from the desire of Mark Robinson and others to tell an interesting story. Perhaps Robinson's memory of the fishing line quite understandably and innocently became confused over time. That both stories were first introduced in 1930, and considerably evolved thereafter, also points to a significant limitation in accepting them as offered. They are certainly not reliable claims upon which to base a murder investigation.

The drunken, violent party theory also suffers from being introduced at a much later point and subsequently evolving. It is impossible to believe that this kind of event — one that could be so easily identified as important in the context of Thomson's death — would be treated with complete silence for more than fifty years by those around Canoe Lake. If the story was true, it is especially hard to conceive how several men who had been at the party and witnessed the potentially fatal altercation would not have raised the issue at the inquest. It is also implausible that the coroner would dismiss, without inquiry, revelations that a dead man had experienced a head trauma in a fight the night before he died, or that he had been threatened with violence by a man who was seemingly so roundly disliked in the community. That William Little was the first to mention the event decades after it was supposed to have occured, and to report it with details such as direct quotations of conversation, points to his having concocted the story.

Little is not alone in weaving fictional elements into supposedly factual accounts of Thomson's death. Roy MacGregor and Neil Lehto, for instance, have both used fictional elements in telling Thomson's story without clearly separating what reflects factual evidence. Others have used Thomson's story in completely fictional tales. While this approach can certainly enhance the pleasure to be found in the story, it serves to complicate accurate understanding of the historical events.

Much of the information presented as evidence that Thomson was murdered springs from semi-fictional accounts of his death. If we approach Thomson's demise from the perspective of what the available historical evidence indicates, however, we can reasonably and confidently conclude that Tom Thomson was not murdered.

11

THE SUICIDE OF TOM THOMSON

*The myth that developed after [Tom Thomson's] death masks the
personality of a difficult, complex man who was unhappy with his
situation ... he had no home, no wife, poor prospects.*

— JOAN MURRAY, *TOM THOMSON: THE LAST SPRING,* 1994

THE POSSIBILITY THAT Tom Thomson might have voluntarily chosen to
end his life was raised almost immediately upon discovery of his body in
Canoe Lake. It appears to have begun as gossip circulating around Canoe
Lake, and though at the time firmly refuted by members of the Thomson
family, it is a theory that has gained popularity since the 1970s.

The romantic stereotype of a disaffected artist, tormented by his vision
and his desire to create, frustrated by the necessity to earn a living and
overcome philistine resistance, is a trope that many find familiar. In
Thomson's case, it has been proposed that along with his art, several
other concerns might have driven him to self-destruction. Could he have
been so depressed regarding his artistic career or his failed attempts to
enlist that he would be driven to suicidal thoughts? Did suicide seem to
be the only escape route available to avoid marrying or becoming a father?

As with the murder theories, only by giving close attention to the
historical evidence can we see whether suicide provides an adequate explanation for Tom Thomson's death.

* * *

In September 1917, one of Thomson's artist friends, J.W. Beatty, visited Canoe Lake to direct the building of a cairn memorializing Tom. As recounted by George Thomson in a letter to Dr. MacCallum, Beatty heard from Shannon Fraser that Tom had committed suicide. Someone had also reported to George that this was what the Frasers suggested to the coroner at the inquest into Tom's demise. George flatly rejected the idea as the least plausible of explanations for his brother's death. Infuriated at the idea that Fraser, who proclaimed his close friendship with Tom, would spread such gossip, George wrote an angry letter to Shannon asking for an explanation. Shannon — or more likely Annie Fraser writing in Shannon's name — explained that they had said nothing of the sort at the inquest or elsewhere. The Frasers' letter suggested that before George make further accusations of this sort that he get his facts straight, and inform the Frasers who was spreading malicious gossip about them.

Gossip about Thomson's frame of mind was circulating among some of his friends very soon after discovery of his body. On July 19, the day Thomson's coffin was en route to Owen Sound, former Thomson studio mate (and future member of the Group of Seven) Franklin Carmichael speculated about whether Thomson might have committed suicide. Writing to Arthur Lismer, he offered his opinion that "the idea of Tom himself being responsible for it (which seems to have entered into some of the discussions) hardly strikes me as being probable. It is hardly fair to presume on his eccentricities to that extent." Of course, Carmichael, or for that matter George, had not seen or spoken to Tom for months. It is possible that his mood had deteriorated since the winter.

If Tom's state of mind had turned self-destructive, it is reasonable to expect that either his letters or behaviour might provide some kind of indication. Considering the tone and content of Thomson's letters of summer 1917, there is little evidence that he was melancholy, let alone entertaining suicidal thoughts. He told his father that he expected to be able to afford to paint for another year, which would seem to indicate some sense of security. If he was putting an optimistic gloss on his situation for his father, his correspondence with others provides no contrary indications.

He makes no pleas for money to Dr. MacCallum, and does not seem to have been in a rush to sell the artworks he was accumulating.

Thomson was making plans for the second half of the summer season. By June, he reported he had made commitments to guide fishing parties in July and August. Thomson suggested to his family that he was debating making a trip to western Canada to see the Rocky Mountains, which two years earlier his painting friend and mentor A.Y. Jackson had found so inspirational. The day before he died he had promised to send his patron in Toronto some of the artwork he had produced around Canoe Lake during the spring. None of these letters he produced during the spring of 1917 communicate a sense of urgency, resignation, ennui, or despondency.

Long after the fact, people who had been around Canoe Lake affirmed that Thomson had, in the words of R.P. Little, "seemed in excellent spirits that spring." Looking at his artwork, Harold Town and Joan Murray have suggested that he seemed to be at the peak of his creativity, driving confidently and deftly toward a true breakthrough in his painting.

Within the last decade, it has been suggested by Roy MacGregor and Neil Lehto that Thomson might have suffered from a mental illness such as bipolar disorder. The words and ideas Thomson left, particularly during his last days, do not suggest that he was thinking out of the ordinary in any way. He does not seem to have been subject to illusions of grandeur or unusual power. Nor does he give the impression that he is preparing to say goodbye to anyone, lamenting his life, or fearing for his future. Of course, severely depressed persons are not required to telegraph their feelings to anyone. That someone so desperate provided nothing that might be used as support for such a diagnosis suggests that Thomson's frame of mind was not unusually depressed, though. At this point, retroactively diagnosing Thomson is, at best, a guessing game.

If the best evidence we have seems to suggest that Thomson was not depressed, what other factors might have led him to consider suicide? Since the 1970s, some have suggested that Thomson killed himself to avoid being forced into marrying Winnie Trainor. The evidence for this is also flimsy, though.

Thomson left no mention of being attracted to Trainor or that he was considering marrying her. Likewise, Trainor never left a claim that she was attracted to Thomson or engaged to the man.

The suggestion that Thomson and Trainor were engaged was first made by Mark Robinson to Blodwen Davies in 1930. It is important to note that Robinson told Davies this was not something he knew first-hand, but that he had heard from someone else who claimed to have heard it from Trainor. A similar rumour was communicated to Eric Brown, the National Gallery director, by a Huntsville man in 1933, although this man may also have been Robinson's source (if Robinson's account can be believed).

During the 1950s, Dr. Noble Sharpe indicated that Trainor had told him by telephone that she and Thomson were engaged. In 1970, he included this claim in his *Canadian Society of Forensic Science Journal* article. The same year, William Little stated in *The Tom Thomson Mystery* that Trainor's nephew had documents that offered proof of Thomson and Trainor's engagement. The documents have never been produced, however, despite requests by several sympathetic investigators.

Claims that Trainor and Thomson had a romantic relationship were invigorated in 1970, when the National Gallery of Canada published a pamphlet containing a series of photographs taken by Thomson. Two of the photos featured a woman, identified by a Thomson family member as being Winnie Trainor. In the photos, the woman sports several rings on the fourth finger of her left hand, a spot traditionally reserved for wedding bands.

Identification of the woman in the photos as Trainor, however, suffers from a critical leap of logic. As Thomson did not have a camera with him in 1917, the photos would all have to date from 1916 or earlier. The images taken outside of the Toronto region may, in fact, record events on a single trip north. Most of the images can be identified as trips Thomson took in 1912 or 1913 (one image is of a friend who moved to Denver late in 1913). Even a generously late dating of the two photos to 1916 would suggest Trainor and Thomson had been formally engaged for over a year. That the engagement would not have been reported in Trainor's or Thomson's hometown newspapers, that no mention of their engagement would have been made in letters either person wrote for over a year (even to each other), or that Thomson or Trainor would not mention this in their correspondence with Tom's family defies imagination.

Aside from the dating of the photos, identification of the woman in the photos as Trainor is disputed. In 2010, Roy MacGregor claimed the images were not of Trainor. Following the dating scheme suggested above, there seem to be grounds to doubt the identification. In this case, the presence of rings on the unidentified woman's finger might very well indicate that she is engaged or married, but not to Thomson. If the photos are not of Trainor, then even this flimsy evidence of her engagement to Thomson is voided, and the engagement tale is left entirely contingent on hearsay and gossip.

In the absence of any evidence of an engagement, the possibility that Thomson and Trainor were romantically involved might still be entertained. As has been suggested, perhaps Thomson enjoyed spending time with Trainor but was not interested in marriage.

The first suggestion that some kind of disagreement about marriage plans might have caused Thomson to seek an escape was made by Charles Plewman in 1972. Plewman claimed to have known from Shannon Fraser that Winnie was coming to Canoe Lake to press Thomson on whether he would marry her or not.

In 1973, Roy MacGregor repeated Plewman's claim. He buttressed the idea with the suggestion that Thomson had booked a honeymoon getaway at nearby Billy Bear resort. On what evidence MacGregor based his assertion is murky. As Billy Bear staff informed me in 2007, and as MacGregor notes in *Northern Light*, Billy Bear's reservation records for this period have not been preserved. Unfortunately, MacGregor did not indicate what his source regarding the booking was. A previous source does make a similar claim as MacGregor, however: William Little in *The Tom Thomson Mystery*. Might MacGregor merely be reporting Little's unsubstantiated claim as fact?

Despite the thin evidence supporting the rumour that Thomson and Trainor were engaged, the idea that they were a couple "with intentions" has been reported as fact in most accounts since the 1970s. MacGregor's 2010 book uses this suggestion as the foundation for its claims.

It seems that understanding of Thomson and Trainor's relationship has become confused over the last century. As early as August 1917, Thomson family members suggested that perhaps Trainor's affections for Thomson were not requited. Perhaps Trainor believed Thomson had made a commitment to her, whether he had formally proposed or not. Perhaps she felt a strong affection for Thomson and strongly hoped or believed that one day he would be won over, leading eventually to marriage. Perhaps, in the absence of anyone to contradict her after Thomson's death, Trainor introduced the idea of a tragically lost fiancé as a means of staving off uncomfortable questions regarding why she never married. The truth is unlikely to ever be definitively established. Reports that Trainor claimed to have been engaged might be conditionally accepted. However, the absence of any solid evidence supporting these hearsay claims does not provide much substance to the idea that Thomson committed suicide to avoid being forced into marriage.

MacGregor has long maintained that perhaps Thomson was afraid of something more than marriage. The prospect that Trainor may have been pregnant with Thomson's child is a key factor in much of the speculation regarding an expedited marriage contract; if proved, it would be explosive.

The pregnancy claim has developed with somewhat different arguments than those based around a simple difference of affections between Thomson and Trainor, and so merits distinct consideration.

In 1977, Roy MacGregor claimed that he had discovered a 1917 announcement published in the *Huntsville Forester* indicating that Winnie Trainor was intending to spend the winter in Philadelphia. He suspected that she had left to hide a pregnancy and give birth to Thomson's child. He elaborated on the idea in his 1980 historical fiction novel *Shorelines*.

MacGregor's suggestion that Trainor was pregnant is plausible, although dependent on purely circumstantial evidence. As he observes in 2010, in the intervening thirty years since discovering the brief note regarding Winnie's trip, he has not been able to find any further evidence of Trainor's activities during the winter of 1917–18, or to support his idea that she might have given birth to a child.

In the late 2000s, Neil Lehto suggested on his *Algonquin Elegy* website that a "sensitive line of inquiry" might provide useful evidence that Trainor was pregnant. He draws attention to Mark Robinson's daily diary entry for July 17, 1917: "Miss Trainor and Miss terry went out on the evening train." Interpreting the name "Miss terry" as code for "mystery," Lehto stated his belief that "Mark Robinson wanted us to know he believed Winnie Trainor was, indeed, pregnant with Tom Thomson's child and that the inquest heard evidence of Winnie's letter pleading for their marriage." He further speculated that if this was what transpired, the coroner was too quick to dismiss the possibility that Thomson might have committed suicide. He suggested that the Trainor family sought to send Winnie out of Canoe Lake before the coroner could discover that she was pregnant.

Lehto's reading of Robinson's diary entry as something like a plot twist in an Agatha Christie mystery novel is far-fetched. Robinson's notation is simple to explain. In a margin note within her August 1917 letter to T.J. Harkness, Trainor stated that the unwed daughter of a Huntsville neighbour, Dr. Terry, had accompanied her to Canoe Lake for Tom's funeral. It is reasonable to expect that Lehto's mysterious "Miss Terry" would have accompanied Trainor back to Huntsville on the train that evening. Far from the "sensitive inquiry" he himself called for, Lehto's discovery of an encoded message in Robinson's diary is yet another example of how theories about Thomson's death are often justified using outlandish and ill-informed speculation.

The prospect that Winnie Trainor was pressuring Thomson to marry her on the basis that she was pregnant is difficult to accept if no reliable evidence supporting her pregnancy has been produced. This is not to say that a pregnancy might very well have been hidden as much as possible, but it is also reasonable to expect it would have resulted in more evidence — circumstantial or not — than has been discovered. That gossip regarding Trainor's pregnancy would not have surfaced until fifty years after Thomson's death — particularly in the rumour-rich environments of Canoe Lake and Huntsville — exceeds credulity.

Could the circumstantial evidence that exists be explained in some other way than that Trainor was pregnant with Thomson's child? Certainly. What is entirely plausible and simpler to believe is that Trainor's travel might be an entirely reasonable response under the circumstances of the tragic death of a loved one. If it is accepted that Thomson's death represented Trainor's tragic and unexpected loss of the man she had deep affections for — that she even perhaps harboured desires to marry — she might have sought to escape from the places offering reminders of him. If she was in mourning, her family may have also sought to move her out of the local community for a time, particularly if she showed signs of mental instability, as the Thomson family suggested during the fall of 1917.

In the interests of argument, we can consider that Thomson might have experienced some kind of depression or anxiety that led him to be suicidal on the morning of Sunday, July 8. It is possible that there were few advanced signs of his condition, or whatever triggered his strong emotional response. Even allowing for all of this, the few final accounts of Thomson's demeanour on that last morning don't provide any indications that he was behaving any differently than usual.

Several first-hand accounts list the provisions that Thomson took with him, or that were found in his canoe. They all suggest that he took enough food to last him a day or more. They indicate that his provisions were wrapped in his canoe in such a way as to keep them safe and dry. If Thomson intended to commit suicide that afternoon, is it plausible that he would stock up on provisions, carefully pack them away in his canoe, and within an hour kill himself almost within sight of the dock he departed from?

If Thomson intended to commit suicide that day, no one who reported seeing him that morning interpreted his statements or behaviour to indicate anything out of the ordinary. Until the 1970s, accounts of Thomson's last morning suggest that he was actually in good humour, visiting with people and perhaps planning to play a practical joke on a friend. These accounts are difficult to reconcile with the behaviour of a man who was about to commit suicide.

Of course, it is possible that Thomson might have been engaging in a rather involved ruse to disguise his plans. Perhaps he was merely acting in order to avoid alarming his friends. Perhaps he was happy that morning, and his decision to commit suicide was spontaneous. Both of these possibilities belong on the margins of consideration, though. There is little evidence to support them, if any might exist. There is, however, much evidence against them.

Supporters of the suicide theory have been challenged to explain reports regarding the condition of Thomson's corpse, as well as the circumstances in which it was found. Their attempt to explain how Thomson's body might have come to be bruised, bleeding, and tied up with fishing line has produced some rather convoluted speculation.

Some have suggested that Thomson's head struck a submerged log when he dove into Canoe Lake to kill himself. The same has been suggested to explain the bleeding from his ear. That Thomson's body had fishing line around one ankle poses a real complication to the suicide theory. Perhaps he might have attached the other end of the line to a weight in order to drown himself? If so, the line would likely have been anchored more securely to his body than to be wound around his ankle a few times. That the only person to suggest such a disposition of the line was Mark Robinson, in his third testimony, told more than thirty-five years after Thomson's death, suggests weak probability for the truth of his claim.

As has been explored elsewhere in this book, most of the observations regarding the condition Thomson's corpse was found in can be attributed to flawed explanations of naturally occuring decomposition and questionable suggestions made long after the events in question. Certainly, as explored in the previous chapter, the fishing-line story should be disregarded as any sign of suspicious actions. Without any of these observations to guide our analysis, we are compelled to work from the position that Thomson's body bore no signs of violence and no signs of manipulation. In the absence of any signs of damage or intervention, the prospect that Thomson tried to commit suicide by any method other than leaping into the water is quite low.

With no reliable signs of damage to his body, or signs that his will to live was somehow diminished, the suicide strategy Tom Thomson seems to have opted for makes the entire theory highly suspect. Leaping into the waters of Canoe Lake on a Sunday afternoon in July would be a rather risky gamble for a man who was seeking to kill himself. The chances of being seen were high. The likelihood of death from self-imposed drowning was low. If little water was found in Thomson's lungs, it is implausible that he inhaled water to kill himself. If he sought to knock himself unconscious, he ran the risk that he would not fall into the water but back into his canoe, or fall into the water with nothing more accomplished than giving himself a nasty bump on the head.

As a man with abundant access to guns, knives, and ropes, and having seen what trains, wild animals, and various aspects of the lumber operations in the region could do to a human body, it is inconceivable that Thomson would choose to try to kill himself by leaping into Canoe Lake. If he seriously sought death, proponents of the suicide theory are suggesting that Thomson attempted to kill himself using what was likely one of the least effective, most untrustworthy methods available. This realization alone seriously diminishes the plausibility of the idea that Tom Thomson successfully attempted suicide.

Given that all evidence points to Thomson being quite hopeful about his prospects, in good humour, and without significant stress, the suicide theory should be seen more as a product of suspicious thinking and imagination than a careful analysis of historical evidence and logic.

12

THE BODY OF TOM THOMSON

What happened to [Tom Thomson's] body? He lies, still, at Canoe Lake. The undertaker, Churchill, had no desire to do the job in the first place, and didn't.

— ROY MACGREGOR, *NORTHERN LIGHT: THE ENDURING MYSTERY OF TOM THOMSON AND THE WOMAN WHO LOVED HIM,* 2010

BY THE 1950s, rumours suggesting that Tom Thomson had not died by accident and that his body might remain buried in Algonquin Park had taken hold. When human remains were discovered close to the location where Thomson was originally buried, these rumours took on a semblance of fact. As with other speculation regarding Thomson's death, interpreters of the importance of the remains discovered in 1956 have taken great liberties with facts and logic.

The historical account of Thomson's burials indicates that although his remains were initially buried at Mowat Cemetery, they were exhumed sometime on the night of July 18 or during the early morning of July 19. The remains were then shipped out to Owen Sound on the July 19 night train. Primary accounts of the exhumation include Robinson's very brief account from his diary, as well as a few letters between family members. Unfortunately, these accounts are often short and rather ambiguous regarding who did what and when.

We can tentatively reconstruct what occurred using accounts written between July and September 1917 by those involved. Winnie Trainor headed toward Canoe Lake from her home in Huntsville, Ontario, likely as soon as she learned of Thomson's death. She later told T.J. Harkness, Tom Thomson's brother-in-law and executor of his estate, that before she arrived at Canoe Lake she had tried to get changes made to the arrangements that were being made there. On July 18, she was billed for a call to the Thomson family in Owen Sound and four calls to R.H. Flavelle, an undertaker in Kearney, Ontario. The undertaker's bill, submitted to Harkness, also includes costs for calls to Owen Sound and Canoe Lake. In September 1917, Tom's sister Margaret reported to Dr. MacCallum that George Thomson (Tom and Margaret's brother) had sent a telegram to Canoe Lake with the family's instructions regarding what to do with Tom's remains, and that Shannon Fraser had received the telegram but did not show it to anyone else. Trainor claimed that after arriving at Canoe Lake (very likely on July 17), and after some struggle, she was able to see the telegram from the Thomson family. She then made suggestions about what should be done, and her suggestions were refused.

Later correspondence between Flavelle and Harkness suggests Shannon Fraser made the initial burial arrangements. When Harkness indicated to Flavelle his belief that the undertaker's bill was exorbitant, Flavelle responded that he would simply direct the bill to the buyer, and promptly sent it to Fraser. The same day Thomson was buried, Mark Robinson's diary records that Shannon Fraser received a telegram communicating intentions to exhume Tom's body, but that Robinson did not know who had ordered this. Robinson's diary entry for the following day states that Tom's body was exhumed "under direction of Mr. Geo. Thomson."

The record strongly suggests that Shannon Fraser was a prominent decision-maker at Canoe Lake. This brief summary of events certainly points to confusion, crossed messages, and individual culpability for inaction with regard to the Thomson family's wishes. The difficulties caused by the limited communications available between Canoe Lake and the outside world may have contributed significantly to the confusion regarding what to do about Thomson's remains. Later descriptions of these events, however, have often suggested that darker motivations — particularly on the part of Fraser — were at play in the awkward progression of events around the two burials of Tom Thomson.

* * *

Thomson's death certainly provided lessons for those at Canoe Lake. Less than a month after Tom Thomson's death, John Colson, the father of the man operating the Algonquin Hotel, passed away in his hotel bed. Mark Robinson noted in his daily diary the precise set of actions he undertook. As soon as he was notified, he sent for a doctor (not Dr. Howland, it might be noted) who filled out a death certificate. Robinson also contacted an undertaker, Roy Dixon, the same man who had cared for Thomson's remains. Accompanied by the furniture dealer/ undertaker Flavelle, Dixon arrived on the 10:00 a.m. train the morning following Colson's death and the body was shipped out to Guelph, Ontario, on the train that evening.

Why is all of this worthy of note? Clearly, Dixon was familiar with the requirements for shipping a body by train, had the necessary resources (such as a metal-lined coffin), and the ability to prepare the corpse. He was able to meet these with less than twenty-four hours' notice. That Flavelle and Dixon were not prepared to treat Thomson's corpse in the same fashion less than a month earlier suggests that the initial poor preparations to ship Thomson's corpse by rail — such as not having a metal-lined casket available for shipping — was not their fault, but rather due to their not having received any instructions that Thomson's body was to be removed from Canoe Lake by train.

When the undertakers' services were solicited for Thomson, Shannon Fraser did not likely know the family's wishes. His pre-emptive decision to arrange burial at Canoe Lake produced a challenging conundrum. When Fraser was notified of the family's wishes, the undertakers were certainly already at Canoe Lake, if not already preparing the body for burial. Shannon Fraser was not likely eager to admit his error. Additionally, if characterizations of his financial sensibilities are anywhere near accurate, he may have feared that he would be expected to bear the costs for the error out of his own pocket. He had, after all, taken the initiative to contract the undertakers and order a casket without knowing the Thomson family's desires. It's possible he found it much easier to simply pretend that he had not found out about the family's wishes until it was too late, and hope that the problem might just "go away," with the family either covering the costs or deciding to leave Tom buried at Canoe Lake.

While chaos reigned during the arrangements for Thomson's burial, accounts of how Thomson's body was exhumed from Algonquin Park suggest the process was surprisingly efficient. Much has been made of the speed and effectiveness around Churchill's exhumation of Thomson's body. In his 1917 diary, Mark Robinson noted that Thomson's coffin was shipped out on the evening train on the day following the undertaker's arrival at Canoe Lake. In a later account, Robinson suggested that Shannon Fraser had picked up the undertaker from the cemetery only a few hours after dropping him off. Several observations should be noted, however. The latter story is Robinson's version of events, not Fraser's. According to another hearsay story offered by Frank Braught, Fraser offered quite a different account. In 1956, Braught testified that Fraser had told him the undertaker worked through the night, and that Fraser had picked him up the next morning. This would have given the undertaker an extra four or five hours of working time at least, making his progress far less suspicious and entirely reconcilable with Robinson's original observation.

Another aspect that has been overlooked is that we have a comparable event by which to gauge the undertaker's progress. In 1956, over the course of three or four hours, four men working in the soil close to Mowat Cemetery managed to dig three holes roughly equivalent to the one in which Thomson was buried. In 1917, Churchill, the undertaker, was digging on his own, in soil that had been dug only a day before. Given the 1956 results, is it really so difficult to imagine that within a few hours he could have uncovered a coffin and transferred Thomson's body — which was embalmed and likely enclosed in a shroud — into another coffin and then roughly refilled the hole?

Robinson stated that Fraser had found the coffin too light for a body, and some of the train luggage handlers reportedly had made the same comment. If we choose to trust this testimony, it raises several questions. How much experience did these men have with hoisting coffins? How much knowledge did they have of embalming techniques? What sort of practices did the undertakers carry out at Canoe Lake? Did they remove most of Thomson's internal organs? Did they bleed the body? How much weight might these practices have removed? Additionally, how much did these men expect a metal-lined casket to weigh? Might they have been anticipating something far heavier and mistaken the lack of weight offered by a simple tin lining as the absence of a body? We are never likely to know the answers to these questions. They do offer plausible, sensible reasons to doubt the far more fantastic prospect that an undertaker decided to defraud a customer by shipping an empty casket to a family awaiting return of their son's remains.

As discussed in part 2, in fall 1956 F.W. Churchill, the undertaker responsible for exhuming Thomson's body and preparing it for shipment out of the park, spoke out against suggestions that Thomson's body might not have actually been transferred out of Mowat Cemetery. He stated that he had transferred Thomson's "badly decomposed but still recognizable" remains into a metal casket that he could seal, after which he returned the empty coffin and its "rough box" container to the grave.

Also, in 1956, experts consulted by the OPP Crime Lab concluded that the remains found near Mowat Cemetery were likely those of an Aboriginal male. Between the 1950s and the 1970s, a marginal element of the conflict over identification of the remains was the question of whether Aboriginal peoples could be found in the region during the period when Thomson had died. Some would claim that none could be found nearby, while others, including Dr. Noble Sharpe, insisted that they regularly travelled through the area. As a small contribution to this debate, it is worth noting a remark contained in Mark Robinson's daily diary. On July 30, 1915, Robinson noted having to discipline two guides who had been guilty of giving liquor to an Aboriginal person from the Golden Lake Reserve who was travelling through the area Robinson was responsible for.

In early 1969, the CBC television feature dealing with Thomson's death led to an outburst of discussion similar to that caused by the discovery of the remains in Mowat in 1956. The special, produced with assistance from William Little, whose book regarding Thomson's death was just about to go to print, suggested that Thomson's remains might be those found in the park.

In his book, Little claimed that George Thomson and an undertaker received the body in Owen Sound on the early afternoon of July 19, 1917.

Ottelyn Addison, whose book about Thomson was published in 1969, claimed that George Thomson had returned to Canoe Lake on July 19 to accompany his brother's coffin to Owen Sound. Neil Lehto has pointed to a George Thomson letter on Mowat Lodge letterhead, dated July 19, as proof that George accompanied the body from Mowat to Owen Sound. Lehto asserted that George may have lied to Little about his presence in Canoe Lake to cover up that he never actually confirmed if Tom was in the coffin.

Churchill's testimony does suggest that Thomson's body was in fact removed from the park. This version of events is supported by testimony provided by the niece of two women who were childhood neighbours of the Thomson family in Owen Sound. She came forward in 1969 to report that her aunts clearly recalled their cousin visiting the Thomson family home while Tom's body was there. The cousin had told these women that Tom's father insisted on having the coffin opened, although the undertaker was reluctant to comply, and that the elder Thomson and the ladies' cousin observed Tom's body.

Margaret Thomson's July 1917 letter to her sister Minnie states that Thomson's body remained at the undertaker's, not the Thomson family home. This throws the testimony of the two ladies into doubt. Minnie's testimony, however, suggests that the Owen Sound funeral home operator would have handled the casket, and would have noted if the casket was unduly "light." He might even have transferred the body from the casket used for shipping the body by rail into something more suitable for a family service. If so, the absence of remains from the casket would have been obvious.

Despite suggestions that a number of people viewed Thomson's corpse between July 18 and 20, 1917, on its trip between Mowat Lodge and burial in Leith Cemetery, the idea that Thomson's body might remain in the park persists in popular speculation. For instance, in 1973, Roy MacGregor related a story of dubious origins that some of Thomson's friends exhumed his body themselves and relocated it within the park before Churchill arrived to take it back to Owen Sound.

MacGregor returned to the question of where Thomson's final resting place is in 2010's *Northern Light*. He clearly challenged the police lab's 1956 findings. As discussed in chapter 8, MacGregor asked forensic archaeologists to study photos of the skull found in 1956 in the place some believed to be Thomson's original burial site. These experts were encouraged to compare images of the remains to photos of Thomson's skull. Based on their conclusions that the skull matched traits of a European male rather than those that would be found in a North American Aboriginal male, a forensic artist was sought out to reveal what the person whose skull had been discovered might look like. Building up tension worthy of a television crime drama, MacGregor describes how he is informed by email to "take a Valium" before he looks at the artist's interpretation. The reader knows, of course, what to expect. The face produced by the forensic artist looks remarkably like Thomson's.

Some commentators have suggested that these findings definitively resolve many questions around the case. The similarity of the drawn visage to Thomson's face should be approached with some hesitation, however. The artist's interpretation is not as conclusive as MacGregor implies. Instead of simply being provided photos of a skull and instructed to flesh out what its owner might have looked like, the forensic artist was expressly told to depict the "John Doe" skull's owner as a Caucasian who lived in the early twentieth century (when Thomson lived), was in his early forties (the same age as Thomson), and who wore his "straight black hair medium length, parted on the left" (the same way Thomson did). Given these instructions, it would be surprising if the drawing did *not* come out bearing some resemblance to Thomson.

This criticism does not intend to discount entirely the possibility that the forensic artist produced a face that could reasonably depict what the person whose skull was discovered near Canoe Lake in 1956 looked like. It should raise significant doubt that the depiction in any way authoritatively resolves the identity of those remains. In particular, the conclusion that the remains must be Thomson's — based on the leading instructions provided to the artist interpreting the remains — suggests some careful stage direction was at play. Certainly, a result produced in a blind exercise would be much more convincing.

When asked whether any existing archaeological technologies might produce some sort of informative, if not definitive, indication of who is buried at either Mowat or Leith Cemeteries, experts have offered that little would serve the purpose better than excavation. Ground-penetrating radar would be confounded by tree roots and would not indicate much other than that soil had been disturbed. Given that the casket buried in Leith may be metal-lined, it would be impossible to "see" inside without actually opening it.

Dr. Noble Sharpe recommended that after being studied, the remains located at Canoe Lake in 1956 be reinterred. He believed that they had been returned to Corporal Rodger for that purpose. Some have claimed that they managed to grave-rob grisly souvenirs, such as toe or finger bones, from the site between the first dig in 1956 and the arrival of the OPP investigators. Establishing the provenance of any such pieces would be very difficult, and completely undermines the trustworthiness of any results that might be produced by testing them.

Even locating the remains found in 1956 poses challenges. The Centre of Forensic Sciences has reported that it does not hold any remains related to the case. Some believe that the small white cross that can now be seen a few metres north of Mowat Cemetery was placed there by Corporal Rodger to mark the location of the remains. Others claim that the cross was placed there somewhat randomly by the CBC crew in 1968 when they were filming their docudrama about Thomson's fate. Some have offered that the cross is certainly not in the right location to mark the 1956 discovery. Any attempt to excavate these remains, if they are now buried there, would first require identifying where — within the general vicinity of Mowat Cemetery — the remains are located.

Without scientific proof regarding the identity of the remains discovered beside Mowat Cemetery in 1956, or alternatively, identification of any remains that might be exhumed from Thomson's grave in the Leith Cemetery, it is impossible to definitively prove that Thomson's body was indeed moved from one site to the other, or that it remained buried beside Mowat Cemetery. However, accounts written immediately following Thomson's death, and the testimony of those who were involved, do provide strong reasons to conclude that the body was exhumed and moved from Canoe Lake to Leith. That being said, the mystery in this case may very likely have less to do with where Tom Thomson is buried and more to do with who it is that's buried at the site where Thomson may have been originally buried.

13

THE ACCIDENTAL DEATH OF TOM THOMSON

The Dr found a bruse [sic] over his eye and thinks he fell and
was hurt and this is how the accident happend [sic].
— J.S. FRASER, LETTER TO TOM THOMSON'S FATHER, JULY 18, 1917

TOM THOMSON'S DEATH was identified as accidental within a day of his body's discovery. The circumstances of his death surprised many, particularly those who believed Thomson to be an expert canoeist and swimmer familiar with Canoe Lake. However, a fatal accident seemed to be the only plausible explanation. As years passed, alternative explanations began to be more openly considered. As these ideas became fleshed out, they attracted more and more attention. By the 1970s, the prospect that Tom Thomson had died by accident was being dismissed by most commentators on the case as something only the quaintly gullible might still believe.

Given the circumstances of Thomson's death, as well as of the analysis of his corpse, it is possible that the coroner might have reached an incorrect conclusion in 1917. However, admitting the possibility of a flawed conclusion should not be interpreted as equivalent to accepting that an error was made. As with other theories regarding Thomson's death, it is important to consider the evidence that has been offered in support of the accidental drowning proposition.

* * *

On the morning of Monday, July 16, Tom Thomson's corpse was discovered floating in Canoe Lake, not far from Mowat Lodge dock where he had set out by canoe eight days earlier. The following day, after spending a night anchored in some way to an island, his body was pulled from the water. Mark Robinson identified the body as that of Thomson, after which Dr. Goldwin Howland examined it. As previously mentioned, Howland noted a bruise on Thomson's temple and that there was air in Thomson's lungs. Howland also observed that there were no marks of violence on Thomson's body. Robinson made very similar notations in his diary. On the basis of his observations, Howland concluded that the most plausible cause of Thomson's death was drowning, likely due to an accident. He wrote up a death certificate, and Thomson's body was buried the same day.

A few hours after Thomson's body had been buried the coroner, Dr. Ranney, arrived at Canoe Lake. Late that evening, Ranney heard evidence from most of the key people who could offer information regarding Thomson's death, including Mark Robinson, Shannon Fraser, Martin Blecher Jr., Dr. Howland, and guide George Rowe. Ranney concurred with Dr. Howland's conclusions. On July 19, he completed the required paperwork, such as a death certificate, the warrant to take possession of body, and the warrant to bury a body. He sent the documents to Mark Robinson. In a covering letter, Ranney noted that these documents were being supplied after the fact of burial, but they were nonetheless important to have.

Ranney's letter suggested that upon providing a mailing address, Dr. Howland would receive a fee from the government for the duties he had fulfilled at the lake. He also thanked Robinson for "your kindness," and asked Robinson to pass his gratitude along to the Blecher family for the same. He made no indication of any kind of difficulties or disagreements at Canoe Lake, or suggestions that anyone might have challenged his findings or conduct of the inquest.

In his daily diary, Mark Robinson recorded that there had been some "adverse comment" about how evidence was taken at the inquest. He did not indicate what concerns were raised or by whom. Forty years later, Robinson suggested that "one of the old guides started to remonstrate a little" about Ranney's conclusions at the inquest. The only guide present at the inquest was George Rowe, so if Robinson's testimony can be trusted, it was presumably Rowe who raised concerns.

What might George Rowe have disliked about the taking of evidence during the inquest? If a party had occurred the night before Thomson died, perhaps Rowe expected more attention to be given to any information he might have shared about the party and the possible fight that occurred there? If so, it would appear that no one else present spoke up in support of Rowe's concern. Robinson certainly makes no indication that he tried to step in to force the point. Did Rowe perhaps suspect that Thomson might have been despondent enough to commit suicide? Once again, if this was a concern that he had, no one else present gave his view enough support to compel Ranney's attention.

Robinson's diary entry provides a somewhat curious sense of the complaints. He noted that concerns were raised but did not record by whom. He did not enumerate the concerns. Most important, he did not indicate that he supported the concerns, or felt the content of the concerns were important enough to record in his diary. Given his attention to detail regarding most information he deemed worthy of recording in his diary, his notation regarding perceived shortcomings of the inquest were strangely brief. It could be suggested that perhaps Robinson was hesitant to put inflammatory or troublesome ideas down in writing, although if this is the case it is hard to fit this with his willingness to record his suspicion that Martin Blecher Jr. was a German spy, or to name guides who showed up for work intoxicated.

Working from Howland' and Robinson's notes made after examination of the body, it would appear that there was little to no evidence to support any conclusion that Thomson had died by anything other than accident. If the option to conduct a full medical autopsy was considered, neither man was qualified to do the job, nor did the situation offer the necessary conditions. A full medical autopsy did not likely seem necessary. Thomson's body did not have wounds that suggested trauma or violence. Only a short span of time had passed between Thomson being last seen and the probable time of his death. That Howland would conclude accidental death seems entirely reasonable. While explanations other than drowning, such as heart attack, brain aneurysm, or epileptic seizure were certainly possible, the true cause of Thomson's accidental death was likely deemed relatively unimportant to discover. What was obvious was that Thomson's body was clearly decomposing, and with no indication of when the coroner would arrive to investigate, was only bound to deteriorate further. It is entirely possible that Howland and Thomson's friends concluded that authoritatively identifying the cause of Thomson's accident would not change the outcome, and waiting for a full investigation seemed disrespectful to his memory.

If Thomson did have an accident, what could have befallen an experienced canoeist on a calm lake that he knew well? Any answer to this question hinges on circumstantial evidence and speculation. Do any possible answers provided this way at least meet the criteria of plausibility and credibility?

In the late 1960s, Thomson family members suggested that Tom might have been suffering from a sprained ankle when he died. If he stood in his canoe and lost his footing, or had difficulty disembarking as he came to shore, this injury could explain Thomson perhaps hitting his head and losing consciousness, falling into the water and drowning. David Silcox offers this explanation as the most plausible one available. That no one who saw Thomson during July 1917 has ever made such a claim about his ankle, and that it was first introduced more than fifty years after Thomson's death suggests the story is a concoction.

Reinforcing this interpretation is that the Thomson family members who shared it attributed the idea to Tom's brother, George, who never mentions it in any of his correspondence about Tom's death. If George had learned that Tom had a sprained ankle, he would likely have heard this on his first visit to Canoe Lake. The fact would have provided a simple explanation for how Thomson might have suffered an accident, and offered an easy counter-argument to the troubling rumours of suicide that were apparently circulating at Canoe Lake during the fall of 1917. George never raised the idea when he challenged Fraser's suspected rumour-mongering, nor did he consider it when he discussed the various theories about Tom's possible cause of death with Dr. MacCallum. In short, if George ever did claim that his brother had a sprained ankle, the claim was likely based in speculation or a desire to simply explain away a troubling mystery that after fifty years he no longer wanted to deal with.

If Tom Thomson did suffer an accident on Canoe Lake, could it have been produced by some environmental factor? It seems unbelievable that a man who had spent several summers canoeing through the park and beyond, and who knew the lake well, would encounter a fatal challenge.

The weather records of the government's Algonquin Park station indicate that the temperature average on July 8, 1917, was 16.4 degrees Celsius. The day's temperature reached a low of 15 degrees and rose to just under 18 degrees. The average high for the preceding week was in the low 20s. About a centimetre and a half of rain fell, which was little more than half of what was recorded the day before. These two days were the wettest of the preceding two weeks. Wind speed records were not maintained at the Algonquin Park station during this period.

This record indicates that no exceptional weather conditions were seen or recorded in the region during the day Tom Thomson disappeared. No tornados or water spouts were recorded, nor was any evidence that they touched down unseen recorded after the fact. No strong winds or cloud-bursts were experienced. If these were so area-specific that the Algonquin weather station would not have recorded them, it is hard to conceive that the visitors at Mowat Lodge, if not others around Canoe Lake, would not have noticed exceptional weather during the middle of a Sunday afternoon and made a speculative connection to Thomson having difficulty on the lake. That no one at the lake recorded any scenarios such as this at the time, or suggested them soon after the fact, suggests that exceptional weather conditions did not lead Thomson to have an accident.

Even though Thomson had lived around Canoe Lake for several summers, it is not outside the realm of possibility that he encountered an unforeseen, new obstacle in the water. Canoe Lake had been a focal point for lumbering operations in the area during the 1890s. Lumbermen floated logs downstream to be gathered in the relative expanse of Canoe Lake, where they were either shipped further downstream or directed into the lumber mills operating there. Most of the facilities around the lake had been built to serve the lumber industry's needs and were abandoned only about 1901. Shannon Fraser had originally come to the region in 1912 to liquidate lumber company holdings and decided to remain and open his lodge in the lumber company's former employee boarding house. The area fronting the lodge, commonly known as the chipyard, covered about a square mile. The chipyard had been created by the lumber companies dumping sawdust, wood chips, and other waste into a shallow area of the lake, which they used as a storage area for cut timber. Two photographs taken by Thomson show the chipyard as a desolate expanse covered in broken wood.

The rest of the region was not free from the by-products and waste of the lumber industry's time at Canoe Lake. The lake itself obviously contained submerged logs — known as deadheads — that might serve to overturn an inattentive canoeist's craft. After having visited Canoe Lake in 1930 and spoken to people there, Blodwen Davies noted that Thomson's final choice of a canoe route — going to the east side of Little Wapomeo Island instead of hugging the mainland shore to the west of the island — was dictated by the fact that the channel was "choked with drowned timber."

If Thomson's canoe had struck a deadhead, it's possible that it might have tipped and thrown him. He might have lost consciousness after striking his head on the canoe or a log. If he died shortly thereafter, no bruise would have had time to form. Alternatively, the effects of decomposition might have obscured it.

If Thomson fell from his canoe and struck his head, we will likely never have proof that this is what occurred. We must at least consider that it is possible and plausible. The simplicity of the theory is attractive; if nothing else, it does not require any convoluted schemes of lies and cover-ups.

An additional aspect of the circumstances of Tom Thomson's death supports the idea that he might have died by accident. Its importance is something that has been missed, largely because it has so frequently been misrepresented and questionably interpreted.

First-hand accounts from July 1917 are consistent in stating that Tom Thomson's canoe was found overturned. We have only one contemporary account of how many paddles were found in Thomson's canoe. It is surprising, given the importance he attaches to this issue later, that Robinson never chose to record any observations about missing paddles in 1917. The only account we have of how many paddles were found that is contemporaneous to the discovery of Thomson's canoe is in Shannon Fraser's July 10 letter to Dr. MacCallum. Fraser states clearly, "both paddles tied tight in the canoe." In a second letter sent to MacCallum two weeks later, he repeats the claim, writing, "the Paddles was tied up in the canoe." The tied-up paddles would serve as convenient hand grips to lift and carry the canoe, and having them lashed inside also saved having to carry the awkward items separately. That the paddles were found tied for carrying is a fairly clear indicator that Thomson was prepared to portage with his canoe.

Memories of what was found in Thomson's canoe, and what it might mean, evolved over time. In September 1930, Blodwen Davies inquired with Mark Robinson about Thomson's canoe paddles. Without elaboration, he responded, "[o]ne was found tied in his canoe for portaging." Davies did not mention this claim in her 1935 book.

In a 1955 magazine article, R.P. Little wrote that both paddles had been found inside Thomson's canoe. In the 1950s, Robinson made an odd claim. He declared that two paddles were found tied up inside Thomson's canoe, but that the "paddling paddle" was missing. This is the first time anyone had suggested that Thomson used three paddles in his canoe. Nonetheless, William Little repeated the claim in 1970.

In articles written during the 1970s, Roy MacGregor inexplicably favoured Robinson's much-revised memory, and incorporated his own creative twist. He suggested that only one paddle was found, sloppily tied into Thomson's canoe, and that Thomson's favourite paddle was missing. He introduced some creative assertions in his 2010 account of the story, suggesting that both Charlie Scrim and Mark Robinson made note of a missing paddle. He goes further, claiming that the missing paddle "was, in fact, the first evidence that cast real suspicion" about Tom's fate. Clearly, however, this is a ridiculous statement.

As time has passed, claims about the circumstances in which Thomson's canoe were found have spiralled further and further from the evidence produced at the time by witnesses. This is particularly true of accounts describing the number of paddles found and their displacement. When Thomson's canoe was turned over, no one suggested that any of his paddles were missing. Rather Fraser, the only person who thought to note the number of paddles found, indicated at the time that "both" paddles were found. Given Fraser's claim to have been on the dock with Thomson when he began his fatal trip, he would have been the best informed to observe if there was a difference between how many paddles were found in his canoe and the number he departed with. If only one paddle was found — an odd choice for portaging, which would suggest that one of Thomson's paddles had been lost — Robinson would surely have noted that in his diary entry or in his detailed list of which items Thomson was known to have departed with, which items were found in his canoe, and which items were know to be missing. It is worth noting that Robinson doesn't make any mention in his list of how many paddles were found in Thomson's canoe.

That no paddle was identified as missing by observers at the time Thomson's canoe was discovered, and that the best description we have indicates Thomson used two paddles (at least on his last trip), suggest that the missing paddle story is simply wrong. The evidence for the missing paddle is dependent on very selective use of Mark Robinson's testimony, testimony that was different each of the three times he offered it. This fact alone provides strong circumstantial evidence that there was nothing out of the ordinary in how Thomson's paddles were stowed in his canoe or how many were located with his belongings.

Although authors such as Roy MacGregor have long suggested that the accidental death finding was challenged from the moment it was offered at the inquest, these claims are patently untrue.

Much has been made of Mark Robinson's July 17 diary entry claim that some Canoe Lake residents were dissatisfied with the taking of evidence. His comment has usually been interpreted to mean that those present at the inquest felt some information had not been properly taken into account, information that might have encouraged the coroner to consider a cause of death other than accidental.

The impressions recorded at the time of Thomson's death by those who were at Canoe Lake during July 1917 all indicate acceptance of Dr. Howland's and Dr. Ranney's decision regarding how Thomson died. In a

July 1917 letter to Tom Thomson's father, Shannon Fraser reported that Dr. Howland's conclusion was that Thomson fell and was hurt. A second letter to Dr. MacCallum speculated that Thomson's death was accidental, suggesting he must have "taking [sic] a cramp or got out on shore and slip of [sic] a log or something."

Skeptics will suggest that if the murder theory is to be given its due, Fraser might have a very good reason for supporting the spread of the accident theory. In 1917, even George Thomson pondered this very thing. However, Fraser was not alone in his ready acceptance of accidental death.

In August 1917, Margaret Thomson had a long conversation with Winnie Trainor about Tom. Margaret asked Trainor directly for her thoughts on whether he might have been murdered. Winnie simply replied, "No." According to Margaret, Trainor's view was that Thomson had slipped on rocks, knocking himself into the water unconscious. As someone who knew the lake and Thomson well, her belief must be given serious consideration.

There are no direct records from 1917 indicating that anyone familiar with the case expressed doubts about Thomson having died by accidental drowning. These concerns were certainly raised later by people such as Mark Robinson. The suspicions he gave voice to in 1930, repeated by Blodwen Davies and his acquaintances from around Canoe Lake, took on a life of their own. Robinson, however, never adequately explained why his beliefs changed so much sometime between 1917 and 1930. As this work has shown, over the period of a little more than a decade, his memories of events related to Thomson's death significantly changed. Critically, suspicions should be raised by the fact that the memories Robinson called upon between 1930 and the 1950s not only increased in detail but sometimes included new claims, and were all slanted in support of his position that the official finding was flawed.

Clearly secondary accounts regarding how Tom Thomson's overturned canoe was discovered and the displacement of goods within the canoe vary widely. Some of these later versions of observations may have been the product of poor recollection on the part of those involved. Some can only be explained as error on the part of the writers. Writers offering accounts after the 1940s clearly overlooked primary documentation that was readily available to them and that directly contradicted the version of events they advanced.

Evidence from 1917 indicates that other than its missing passenger, little was regarded as amiss when Thomson's canoe was discovered. The conclusion that Tom Thomson's death was due to drowning in a sad accident was received with grief and melancholy. It was not rejected as implausible, as not fitting with the evidence, or as having been arrived at irresponsibly. Based on testimony produced at the time, the most sensible conclusion is that Tom Thomson died accidentally, by drowning.

Epilogue

THE LAST DEATH OF TOM THOMSON

——— ——

THE TOM THOMSON mystery is a chimera. It is not what it has been made to appear. A man died in a way that we are not able to definitively establish. We can say with some confidence that he drowned. What caused him to fall into the water, however? Did he have a heart attack or a brain aneurysm? Did he simply fall out of his canoe while impaired or while trying to untangle fishing line from a deadhead? Did he slip while climbing out of his canoe? We will never know. Whether these questions merit categorization as a capital-M mystery is debatable. No amount of research is going to offer a definitive solution. In this respect, the cause of Thomson's death will remain forever a mystery.

If Thomson's cause of death is something that cannot be resolved, then why spend an entire book talking about it? The very idea seems like an exercise in frustration. Certainly, many have felt that some of the unknown elements surrounding Thomson's death are knowable; that evidence can be collected and considered, weighed against contending evidence, and that a single, most plausible answer can be established. This book was undertaken with the faith that careful, measured analysis of information related to Thomson's death would reveal that much of the "evidence" that has been called upon to support theories that Tom Thomson was murdered or committed suicide was not trustworthy. Additionally, that many of the theories incorporated fanciful speculation that could not be reliably called upon in historical argument. If the evidence could be established as shaky and the weakness of the arguments pointed out, then the theories themselves could be put in their proper perspective. Less the product of historical research and analysis, the suggestions that Tom Thomson was murdered or committed suicide are rooted in gossip, misunderstanding, and the desire to tell entertaining stories.

Much of the mystery surrounding Thomson's death was initially fed by awkward communication regarding the Thomson family's wishes for the treatment of Tom's remains. Evidence from the time indicates that his family never wanted to have him buried in Algonquin Park and tried to communicate their wishes to those at Canoe Lake. Technological problems and poorly worded telegrams from Canoe Lake produced delays that had repercussions for those living and working in the presence of their friend's decomposing body. Without word of the Thomsons' wishes, all at Canoe Lake agreed that something must be done. The exceptional challenge of having to deal with a tragic death in the small community, and perhaps some insecurity about who decision-making responsibility should fall to, resulted in decisions being made on the fly. Anxiety was no doubt compounded when the family's wishes were made known, and by the realization that the decisions made by those at Canoe Lake did not accord with the family's desires.

Conflict over such an emotional issue clearly caused consternation and frustration at the time, and the ensuing exhumation of Thomson's body further fanned the flames of hostility and suspicion among almost all involved. These difficult circumstances did not produce significant proof that Thomson committed suicide or was murdered, however. Rather, they planted seeds of gossip and resentment that found fertile ground over the decades to come.

Thomson has been characterized as a deft outdoorsman with natural skill at painting a unique, distinctively Canadian environment that he knew well. This is an image that Thomson's friends and supporters worked to advance after his death, and that was integral to the rise of his reputation. If Thomson died as a result of a canoeing accident on a calm lake in the middle of the day, this image would be significantly destabilized. It is not, however, an image that is necessary to appreciate Thomson's contribution to the development of Canadian painting. As Harold Town observed, decades of speculation regarding how Tom Thomson died have done little but cloud our understanding of Thomson's life and the importance of his art. Acceptance of what the evidence indicates, that Thomson died by accident and not suicide or murder, points to the importance of understanding his painting not through the lens of romantic myth, but as what it was, the rather more mundane, but nonetheless inspiring efforts of a skilled and hard-working artist.

That Tom Thomson's painting has become part of the national identity, one of the types of symbols that Canadians share as part of their common language, is a grand legacy for a man who had little art training, but who took the greatest pleasures in life from painting out under the open sky. That he died under that same sky, on the waters and among the trees and islands that populate his paintings is no doubt tragic, and will ever remain so. A hundred years on from his passing, however, he has not been forgotten, nor has the land he loved. Each year thousands of people flock to see his paintings and to visit Algonquin Park. As a model, as an inspiration, his influence lives on. Beyond ideas about his mental state, or his romantic life, or how he managed to get along with his peers, what Tom Thomson is remembered for is the passion that gave his life meaning.

Whether by accident or by natural causes, the fact is that death cannot be put off forever. We have no guarantee of how or when we will die, or what kind of legacy we will leave. Thomson likely cared little about the former. He would be heartily gratified, however, knowing what role he played, and continues to play over a century later, in alerting Canadians to their artistic and natural heritage.

Acknowledgements

I owe many debts of gratitude for the production of this book.

This manuscript benefited greatly from the enthusiasm and sacrifices of many writers and researchers who preceded me. I am grateful for the efforts of all of these persons, whether they are named in this work or not, and regardless of how I assess the shortcomings and strengths of their efforts.

Without the Great Unsolved Mysteries in Canadian History team — particularly, Merna Forster, John Lutz, and Ruth Sandwell — I would likely never have been inclined to pursue this topic beyond personal curiosity.

The financial support of the graduate program in Communication and Culture at York University made research for *Death on a Painted Lake* and transcription of many of the documents much easier. York University undergraduate students Caroline Verner and Karen Fernandes patiently and diligently helped with transcription and data entry for the website. These efforts made preparation of this manuscript far more efficient.

The Robarts Centre for Canadian Studies at York University provided a congenial space for research and writing as well as the able assistance of Laura Taman.

Michael Pollanen, chief forensic pathologist for Ontario, kindly provided insights into the skills required in his line of work and generously applied them to the mystery with enthusiasm.

Christl Verduyn and Kathleen Garay provided generous advice in production of the initial essay outlining my concerns with much of the historical writing regarding Thomson's death, which was published in *Archival Narratives for Canada*. Elements of that work, including the article title, echo through this manuscript.

Trina Chatelain, collections intern at the Algonquin Park Museum and Archives provided prompt and able assistance with access to interview records and photographs.

Ron Williamson and his staff at Archaeological Services, Inc. were kind in sharing their time and expertise.

Alex Parisien kindly provided her map design expertise.

This book was a joy to produce in large part due to help from the Dundurn Press team. Thanks are particularly extended to Dundurn's publisher, Kirk Howard; Margaret Bryant, Director of Sales and Marketing; my editor, Michael Melgaard; and publicist Karen McMullin.

Thanks as well to the many family members, co-workers, students, and casual acquaintances who inquired about my Thomson research, listened to my ideas, and suggested that they would buy a book on the topic of Thomson's death. I hope that you are all now reading this in your own, personalized copies.

On a personal level, just as many debts are owed.

My peers, Jen Easter and Sharon Bailey, were inspirational in helping me realize my vague idea for a book.

My sister, Melody Klages, of Owen Sound, Ontario, generously hosted me during research in the region and shared her useful contacts.

Chirag Tiwari and Tanner Mirrlees listened, supported, and helpfully provided distraction when it was needed.

My mother, Evelyn, who regularly inquired about how the manuscript was coming along and conscientiously tried to avoid "bothering me" while I was writing.

Most important, to Stephanie, my spouse — who incidentally shares Tom Thomson's birthday — and our daughter, Greta. Without the two of you all of this would simply be pointless. I hope it makes you proud. Apologies to you both for the sacrifices you were asked to make toward producing this book.

Finally, early during the writing of this manuscript my father passed away. He was instrumental in introducing me to pleasures reminiscent of those enjoyed by Tom Thomson: the allure of simple, natural things such as the smell of freshly sawn wood, and the peace of a morning spent fishing. I know he would have been excited to see this book and to actually hold in his hands the thing that I had spoken about so many times over the last decade. Writing and reading about death and memory during this period provided a welcome means through which to bring my research interests and "real life" experiences together.

A Note on the Sources

Portions of many (though not all) of the documents discussed in this book were transcribed and posted online in 2008. Some, such as selections from Mark Robinson's daily diary, were also photographed. These images are also available online. The items can be consulted digitally (in English or French) at the *Death on a Painted Lake: The Tom Thomson Tragedy* website, part of the Great Unsolved Mysteries in Canadian History project: www. canadianmysteries.ca/sites/thomson/home/indexen.html.

Source citation presented one of the more vexing challenges in production of this manuscript. A desire for accountability suggested that each piece of evidence should be clearly identified with each use. Religious footnoting would have resulted in a book that was signicantly less readable, however. The compromise reached was to strive for clear indication within the text of which document was being drawn upon at the time of use, and identification of the archival sources of documents in the Selected Bibliography. As an aid to researchers who would like to pursue the documents themselves, the author hopes the following notes will be helpful.

Much of the correspondence received by Toronto ophthalmologist Dr. James MacCallum, patron of Thomson and some of his peers, was deposited in the National Gallery of Canada archives in 1944. This collection is publicly available.

Thomson family members contributed a significant collection of 1917 materials related to Thomson's death, as well as correspondence produced in managing his estate, to Library and Archives Canada between 1981 and 2001. This collection is also publicly accessible.

Correspondence received by Blodwen Davies during the 1930s, when she was conducting research on Thomson, is also held by Library and Archives Canada. Due to their fragility, the originals of these items are not available to the public. They have been available in microfilm form, and LAC has recently made the materials available digitally.

The Ontario Centre of Forensic Sciences holds a significant collection of documents related to the remains located in Algonquin Park in 1956. The author discovered these documents as the result of a Freedom of Information request. Another collection of documents was similarly discovered in the attorney general's deposits in the Archives of Ontario.

Other items are held in less well-known collections. For instance, the Algonquin Park Museum and Archives holds a small but important collection of audio files and images related to Thomson and Canoe Lake. The diary of Mark Robinson, the park ranger who led the search for Thomson, is held in the archives of Trent University, Peterborough, Ontario.

Selected Bibliography

Addison, Ottelyn, in collaboration with Elizabeth Harwood. *Tom Thomson: The Algonquin Years*. Vancouver, BC: Ryerson Press, 1969.

Charlesworth, Hector. "Pictures That Can Be Heard." *Saturday Night* 29 (March 18, 1916).

Clemson, Gaye I. *Algonquin Voices: Selected Stories of Canoe Lake Women*. Victoria, BC: Trafford, 2002.

Davies, Blodwen. *Paddle and Palette: The Story of Tom Thomson*. Toronto, ON: Ryerson Press, 1930.

——. *A Study of Tom Thomson*. Toronto, ON: Discus Press, 1935.

Grace, Sherrill. *Inventing Tom Thomson: From Biographical Fictions to Fictional Autobiographies and Reproductions*. Kingston, ON: McGill-Queen's University Press, 2004.

Hubbard, R.H. *Tom Thomson*. Toronto, ON: McClelland and Stewart, 1962.

Irie, Kevin. *Viewing Tom Thomson: A Minority Report*. Calgary, AL: Frontenac House, 2012.

Jollimore, Troy. *Tom Thomson in Purgatory*. Margie/Intuit House Poetry Series: 2006.

Larsen, Wayne. *Tom Thomson: Artist of the North.* Toronto, ON: Dundurn Press, 2011.

Lee, Rupert. "Canadian Pictures at Wembley." *Canadian Forum* 14 (August 31, 1924): 338-9.

Lehto, Neil. *Algonquin Elegy: Tom Thomson's Last Spring.* Lincoln, NE: iUniverse, 2005.

——. *AlgonquinElegy.com*

Little, R.P. "Some Recollections of Tom Thomson and Canoe Lake." *Culture* 16 (1955): 210-22.

Little, William T. *The Tom Thomson Mystery.* Toronto, ON: McGraw-Hill Ryerson Ltd., 1970.

MacGregor, Roy. *Canoe Lake.* Toronto, ON: McClelland and Stewart, 2002.

——. "The Great Canoe Lake Mystery." *Maclean's,* Sept. 31, 1973: 30, 44, 48-50.

——. "The Legend." *The Canadian,* October 15, 1977: 2-7.

——. *Northern Light: The Enduring Mystery of Tom Thomson and the Woman who Loved Him.* Toronto, ON: Random House, 2010.

——. *Shorelines.* Toronto, ON: McClelland and Stewart, 1980.

MacLennan, Hugh. "The Ten Greatest Canadians" [Tom Thomson]. *New Liberty* 26, no. 9 (1949): 7-13.

Murray, Joan. *The Art of Tom Thomson.* Toronto, ON: The Art Gallery of Ontario, 1971.

——. *The Best of Tom Thomson.* Edmonton, AL: Hurtig Publishers, 1986.

——. *Tom Thomson: Design for a Canadian Hero.* Toronto, ON: Dundurn Press, 1998.

——. *Tom Thomson: The Last Spring.* Toronto, ON: Dundurn Press, 1994.

Plewman, Charles. "Reflections on the Passing of Tom Thomson." *Canadian Camping Magazine,* Winter 1972: 6-9.

Poling, Jim, Sr. *Tom Thomson: The Life and Mysterious Death of the Famous Canadian Painter.* Canmore, AL: Altitude Publishing, 2003.

Pollanen, Dr. Michael (Chief Forensic Pathologist, Province of Ontario). "Forensic Pathology Report, Nov. 2007." *Death on a Painted Lake: The Tom Thomson Tragedy,* 2007. Access: http://www.canadianmysteries .ca/Thomsonlinterpretations [password protected].

Reid, Dennis, ed. *Tom Thomson.* Toronto, ON: Art Gallery of Ontario, 2002.

Robson, Arthur. *Tom Thomson*. Toronto, ON: Ryerson Press, 1937.

Saunders, Audrey. *Algonquin Story*. Toronto, ON: Department of Lands and Forests, 1947; reproduced with revised maps, 1963.

Sharpe, Dr. Noble. "The Canoe Lake Mystery." *Canadian Society of Forensic Science Journal* 3 (June 31, 1970): 34–40.

Shaw, S. Bernard. *Canoe Lake, Algonquin Park: Tom Thomson and Other Mysteries*. Burnstown, ON: General Store Publishing, 1996.

Silcox, David. *Tom Thomson: An Introduction to His Life and Art*. Toronto, ON: Firefly Books, 2002.

——. *Tom Thomson: Life & Work*. Toronto, ON: Art Canada Institute, 2015.

Silcox, David and Harold Town. *Tom Thomson: The Silence and the Storm*. Toronto, ON: McClelland and Stewart, 1977.

Webb, Peter. "Martin Blecher: Tom Thomson's Murderer or Victim of Wartime Prejudice?" Heinz Antor, Sylvia Brown, John Considine, Klaus Stierstorfer, eds. Berlin, DE: Walter de Gruyter, 2003: 91–103.

Index

Other Fascinating Dundurn Books
About Tom Thomson and Canadian Art

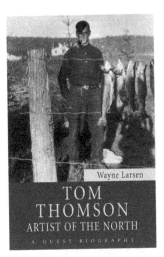

Tom Thomson: Artist of the North
Wayne Larsen

Tom Thomson (1877–1917) occupies a prominent position in Canada's national culture and has become a celebrated icon for his magnificent landscapes as well as for his brief life and mysterious death. The shy, enigmatic artist, known for his innovative painting style, produced such seminal Canadian images as *The Jack Pine* and *The West Wind*, while his untimely drowning nearly a century ago is still a popular subject of fierce debate.

Originally a commercial artist, Thomson fell in love with the forests and lakes of Ontario's Algonquin Park and devoted himself to rendering the north country's changing seasons in a series of colourful sketches and canvases. Dividing his time between his beloved wilderness and a shack behind the Studio Building near downtown Toronto, Thomson was a major inspiration to his painter friends who, not long after his death, went on to change the course of Canadian art as the influential – and equally controversial – Group of Seven.

Canadian Art in the Twentieth Century
Joan Murray

Canadian Art in the Twentieth Century is a survey of the richest, most controversial and perhaps most thoroughly confusing centuries in the whole history of the visual arts in Canada — the period from 1900 to the present. Murray shows how, beginning with Tonalism at the start of the century, new directions in art emerged — starting with our early Modernists, among them Tom Thomson and the Group of Seven. Today, Modernism has lost its dominance. Artists, critics, and the public alike are confronted by a scene of unprecedented variety and complexity. Murray discusses the social and political events of the century in combination with the cultural context; movements, ideas, attitudes, and styles; the important groups in Canadian art, and major and minor artists and their works. Fully documented, well researched, and written with clarity and over four hundred illustrations in both black-and-white and colour, Murray's book is essential for understanding Canadian art of this century. As an introduction, it is excellent in both its scope and intelligence.

Available at your favourite bookseller

 **DUNDURN**

Visit us at
Dundurn.com
@dundurnpress
Facebook.com/dundurnpress
Pinterest.com/dundurnpress